THIS
IS
PSYCHO

THERAPY

for those considering it
for those involved in it
and for the curious

Phineas Kadushin

TIP-top Press
POB 442
New York City 10025

First Printing,   1983

Published by
Tip-top Press
Box 442
New York City, New York 10025

Copyright © 1983 by Phineas Kadushin

Printed in the United States of America

Library of Congress Cataloging in Publication Data

Kadushin, Phineas, 1925-
    This is psychotherapy.

    Includes index.
    1. Psychotherapy.   I. Title.
RC480.K2   1982   616.89'14   82-61943
ISBN 0-9610000-0-7

Design and Composition by Trufont Typographers, Inc.
Printed by Book-mart Press, Inc.

THANKS

to Ghislaine Boulanger, Ph.D.
to Maria Carvainis, who led me from inchoate thoughts
to chapter headings
to Patricia Fox-Sheinwold, author of *Too Young to Die*,
who led me to strive for the writer's craft
to Evelyn Garfiel, Ph.D.
to Lynn Goldberg, who got me started seven years ago
to Carol Watson, Ph.D.
and to my clients whose actual experiences did *not*
contribute to the making of this book.

P.K.
New York City
November 8, 1982

CONTENTS

There is a solution for every human
problem—neat, simple, and wrong.
—*attributed to H. L. Mencken*

Introduction

Psychotherapy is one of the most exciting events of the twentieth century. Like space travel and relativity in the physical sciences, psychotherapy is a singular advance in the frontier of discovery in human behavior. Yet a full and understandable explanation of psychotherapy for the intelligent layperson is still lacking.

What is psychotherapy? How does it work? How does it differ from anything that went before? What, exactly, can it do for you? These are questions that must be answered. Whether you are in therapy, considering therapy, or just a curious person, you deserve a responsible reply. THIS IS PSYCHOTHERAPY proposes to provide answers.

Fifty years ago the institution of psychotherapy occupied a small specialty in medical practice and was confined to the wealthy, but now millions of Americans are in therapy at any given time. With psychotherapy so widespread, an understanding of what therapy is all about is vital to anyone living in the twentieth century. Why isn't a book available explaining the workings of psychotherapy? Why hasn't this book been written long ago?

Today a visit to any local bookstore will reveal a number of shelves devoted to "Psychology" and a few other shelves labeled, "Self-Improvement." In the first section you will see classics authored by the famous psychoanalysts. And in the second section, you will see an array of titles explaining how you can improve your personality. You may even discover one or two books containing sketchy summaries of the many types of psychotherapy presently available, or books telling you *about* psychotherapy, but not the full story of what it is or just how it works. Adding to your confusion induced by the plethora of therapies available, you will also find books written by individual clergymen, psychologists, doctors, and self-styled prophets, all claiming to have discovered the one, true, effective therapy. Salvation is all yours for less than the cost of a picnic or an evening at the movies.

If you haven't been seduced by any of the colorful book jackets and emerge from the store with your wallet intact, you pause at the curb, realizing you are no wiser or better informed than when you entered the store. You may even be in worse shape, since your mind is now addled with scores of jazzy titles. Trying to make sense out of the "Psychology" and "Self-Improvement" bazaar, you conclude, quite reasonably, there is no such thing as psychotherapy. Instead, there are dozens and dozens of psychotherap*ies*, each claiming to be the one true therapy, each demanding your faith and your money.

And so your quest for a reasonable answer to a reasonable question—what is psychotherapy?—has ended at an impasse: Like religion, psychotherapy, no doubt, takes many different forms, each possessing some advantage, each entailing some difficulty or untruth. Now you realize why a definitive, all-in-one book does not exist.

This author strongly disagrees. There *is* an entity called psychotherapy. It is a unique discovery comparable to electricity and the transistor. Its practice has brought about a distinct improvement in the lives of many. Like electricity and the transistor, it can be explained to the intelligent layperson and understood by him or her.

Your befuddlement at the bookstore arose through no fault of yours. The psychoanalytic classics were addressed to other therapists, not to a lay audience. The "Self-Improvement" titles were primarily designed to make interesting reading and lull you into believing that you can actually help yourself by reading a book. And the few books *about* psychotherapy tempt, but do not satisfy your need for detailed understanding.

This book, in its first chapter, will present what psychotherapy is and what it is not. Problems most easily helped by therapy versus problems most resistant, form the second chapter. The third chapter explains how psychotherapy actually works. The basic point of view expressed in these chapters is primarily that of the man who invented psychotherapy—Sigmund Freud.

It is only when we reach the fourth and fifth chapters that competing systems of psychotherapy are discussed. Different kinds of therapy are presented, not as the *pot pourri* found in the bookstore, but either as manifestations of clear, scientific understanding of human nature, or as expressions of befuddlement and pseudo-science. It will then be up to the reader to judge whether a reasonable case has been made for our insistence, *"This* is psychotherapy!"

The next three chapters provide a guide for the practical search for competent psychotherapy and a reasonable procedure to use when undergoing psychotherapy. The last chapter deals with the point of it all.

One caution, however: People with some knowledge of psychotherapy may find the present exposition quite elementary. It is not. It is often deceptively simple.

The story of Ellen in Chapter 2, appears so obvious at first reading that the more sophisticated reader may decide this book is not for him. Yet, in fact, a body of technical literature delineating the "schizoid character" was distilled to compose this description. Further, an attempt was made in the case of Ellen and elsewhere to scale abstract conceptions to human proportion.

While the author is primarily addressing the layperson, the last chapter and a few other sections are intended for his colleagues, too.

Thorough understanding of a complex subject can happily result in a few very simple words. "But I knew it all along," is the common response. So the knowledgeable reader is asked to test himself. Turn to the very back page. You will find a list of commonly misused and misunderstood terms. Keeping them in mind, you might care to test yourself after finishing the book to see if some of your notions of psychotherapy have changed after completing this volume.

THIS IS PSYCHOTHERAPY does not present the reader with a brand new revelation claiming to make him into a brand new person in ten easy steps. Nor does it provide him with a laundry list of all the different therapies. It is not even an introductory textbook in psychology, typically consisting of many irrelevancies and omitting the really significant aspects.

This book is rather, an attempt to present the major discoveries in understanding human behavior, discoveries of the last eighty years, and how these are applied to a discipline, an art, designed to improve the quality of your life.

CHAPTER

1

Therapy Is the Opposite
of Headshrinking

Psychotherapy is one of the most revolutionary advances of the twentieth century. And yet it remains the most misunderstood discovery of our time.

Vast amounts of misinformation are readily available to anyone who wants to know about therapy. In our age of over-information, widespread ignorance about the goals and methods of psychotherapy is appalling. Why? Why is it not a part of almost everyone's common fund of reasonably accurate knowledge?

By contrast, most Americans know that two conductors are needed to carry electricity. Even the non-technically minded are aware that airplanes are carried aloft by differences in air pressure at the top and bottom of the wings. Most high school graduates are informed about the cellular structure of living matter.

But how many people outside of the field of psychotherapy can drop an accurate phrase or two about therapy? Psychotherapy is so shrouded in misconception that even people in therapy, tend to see their therapy only

17

in the light of their particular therapist's manner, but are fuzzy about its bases.

Experts in education and medicine, the two fields most closely allied to psychotherapy, know little more. It's almost easier to find out how to make an atom bomb than to learn exactly how psychotherapy works and why.

A couple of brief thoughts might shed some light on causes for this lack of information:

1. When Freud first tried to make his discoveries public, he was greeted with horror and disdain. More often, like a belch during a crucial pause in a funeral, he was totally ignored. His followers, too, had to learn their lesson—"Keep your mouth shut and just pretend you are practicing medicine. Above all, never let people outside the field know what you're really doing."

2. It's Okay to know that everything around you, even your own body, follows certain natural laws; but no one wants to know that his head, his mind, his will, are all subject to forces beyond control. This idea is repellant to most. We need to believe we're in charge of ourselves at all times.

Because no one knows, except trained therapists, how psychotherapy works, misconceptions and plain old superstitions form a part of American folklore. Unlike Freud's time, today psychotherapy is a popular topic of novels, movies, plays, and the ubiquitous TV. With few exceptions, these are excellent sources to find out just what psychotherapy is *not*. Examples are:

Equus, a successful long run play on Broadway depicted the conflicting love-hate a teenage boy bore for his father; this was symbolized by the boy's murder of his favorite horse. The audience was then treated to psychiatric interviews of the boy which may well serve as perfect examples of "How Not To Conduct a Psychiatric Interview." This play is recommended to neophyte therapists so they can observe a "psychiatrist" in the act of making every mistake possible; both in and out of the book.

Equus's psychiatrist did everything he could to alienate the boy. He was constantly busy with his eyeglasses and his brief case. These, he used as all too effective barriers. The doctor then kept questioning the boy in such a way as to put anyone off. As a psychiatric interview, it was total disaster.

In fairness to the author of *Equus,* we might speculate that he may have been trying to portray abysmal conditions in a British state mental hospital. But regardless of the author's intent, the interview as staged on Broadway, was so convincing, that ultimately we were persuaded that psychiatrists are crazy—or at the very least, totally insensitive—and inmates are sane by comparison.

Noted British psychiatrist and family therapist, R.D. Laing suggested: those who are out, should be in; and those inside, should be busy treating the mental health personnel. *One Flew Over the Cuckoo's Nest* in its book, play, and movie versions, tells us the same thing—the nuts make more sense than their keepers.

I Never Promised You a Rose Garden, as opposed to *Equus* and "Cuckoo," is an attempt to tell the story of a therapist in action from a sympathetic point of view. The setting was a private mental hospital, a troubled youngster, and a world famous psychiatrist. Thus "Rose Garden" can, by no means, be construed as criticism of psychotherapy as practiced by fools or knaves in a primitive government facility. In its book form, the author, Hannah Green, recounted her past personal experience with a highly sensitive therapist who brought her back to sanity.

The movie, "Rose Garden" appeared quite a few years after the book was published, and in some respects seemed to bear little relationship to the novel. The film version treats us to the spectacle of a therapist plying her client with intrusive questions, badgering her, never letting up, denying her any kind of reasonable privacy or respect. Such treatment could easily drive anyone up the wall. What this sort of "therapy" would do to a withdrawn and suspicious youngster is beyond imagination.

Of course, patience and interest on the part of the therapist hardly make for dramatic scenes. Box office requirements, perhaps, demand some kind of relentless intervention by the "shrink" to show the audience the psychiatrist is busy operating on her patient and earning her keep. According to Hollywood's conventional wisdom, understanding and sensitivity will not fill up theater seats.

As it turned out, audiences were not that gullible. They stayed away from "Rose Garden" and the film flopped. But the distorted perception of the role of the psychotherapist and how he/she functions is still a stereotype of American folklore.

The heroes of "Rose Garden" and *Equus* were obviously difficult youngsters. And so the commercial media portray the kind of person who needs psychotherapy as quite "crazy." As examples of the supposed insanity of candidates for psychotherapy, the following films show protagonists who are downright weird:

Sybil, The Three Faces of Eve, and *Three Women* tell the

story of withdrawn, "proper" young women who suddenly turn into flirtatious, vivacious courtesans. Various other personality types appear and disappear with disconcerting and unpredictable frequency in the very same body of the very same woman.

One can hardly quarrel with the publishers' or movie producers' need to capitalize on this sensational aberration. Nor can one fault an actress of the stature of Sissy Spacek for exploiting "multiple personality" as a vehicle for her considerable talents. But the use of such a subject does little to contribute to our accurate knowledge of psychotherapy and its clients. It only distorts.

To further confuse the public, these extremely rare deviants serve another purpose: They are supposedly good subjects for psychotherapy. They make convenient figures for the Archie Bunkers to point at. "That broad sure gotta screw loose. She could use a good shrink." Archie, thus, retains a positive image of his own radiant "mental health." Now Mr. Bunker is *sure* that only very peculiar people go for help and he ain't one of 'em. Archie is now comfortable with his own image but remains ignorant about therapy.

But most of us are more sophisticated than the customers at "Archie's Place." We are aware that the average client, the one who seeks therapy, is quite different from the rare multiple personalities. He or she is not necessarily weird or crazy. Ordinary people (as in the film by the same name) are helped by psychotherapy, not the nuts.

Indeed, the crazier a person is, the less likely it is that he will seek help, unless forced by society to do so. One needs judgment to realize that he needs therapy.

There is another area of serious misconception which

even permeates the "mental health" profession itself. Some experts in the field still believe psychotherapy is a branch of medicine. Over twenty years ago, a great psychiatrist, Thomas Szasz, wrote a book called, *The Myth of Mental Illness*. He rightly concluded that people who need help are not "sick."

How did this myth arise? In the eighteenth and nineteenth centuries when the Western world became more humane and more civilized, the care of people who didn't fit into the social fabric passed from the hands of the religious functionaries into the province of doctors. Hence, medicine and its practitioners had to label the aberrants, "mentally ill" in order to assert their authority over the misfits. And so the term, "mental hospital," replaced the word, "asylum." We were told that a disease, not evil spirits, caused these people to behave irrationally. Instead of being exhorted or prayed over, those who couldn't conform were wrapped in wet sheets; or steel probes were thrust into their brains. Thus, medical treatment became the vogue for the "insane."

Since the medical profession was in charge, it is not surprising that the man who invented psychotherapy, Sigmund Freud, was a doctor. But unlike many of his disciples, Freud was fully aware that he was not practicing medicine. Even those of his pupils who realized they made little use of their medical knowledge in the practice of psychotherapy, believed they needed to operate under the umbrella of the medical establishment. So, as mentioned before, they kept their mouths shut and pretended they were practicing medicine.

Therefore, this book avoids the term, patient, which belongs to medicine and uses the word, client. For want of

a better word, we use this rather neutral term, client—
meaning anyone who seeks professional skill and knowledge to help solve a problem. Words such as patient, treatment, mental illness, doctor and the like are reserved for a
medical doctor whose orientation to people's adaptive
problems is physical. The M.D. and others who use primarily verbal means, as opposed to drugs or shock treatment as their major technique, are called here, psychotherapists, or the shortened version—therapists.

While psychotherapy is not medicine, we cannot dismiss the vital role played by the body. Nor can we ignore
the many ills of one's body caused by thoughts or feelings.
Psychotherapy deals with the functioning of the human
being as a whole and thus no area of a person's life is alien
to psychotherapy. One's job, friends, family, and even social class are vital to anyone's function. Surely one's very
body must also be taken into account.

To understand the role of the body, we must start
with physiology, the workings of the body: No animal
would survive if it were not able to fight or to flee. By a
process of natural selection, all animals, *homo sapiens* included, are equipped with a unique mechanism to fight
better and flee faster. The mechanism is called the auto-
nomic nervous system. It is triggered off by arousal centers deep in the brain.

For example, if you were a caveman and saw a Bron-
tosaurus fifty feet away, in order to survive, you must run
like hell. You would be aided by certain physiological
changes in your body that are designed for running in the
face of danger. Specifically, arousal centers in your brain
would cause special hormones to enter your blood stream.

Pumped hard by your heart, blood would pour into the right muscles. Breathing would be deeper and faster than normal. These changes energize your body for an emergency and are accompanied by a feeling of fear.

Now, if magically you were surrounded by a glass cage in full view of this two-story reptile, your body would still be undergoing all those changes. But instead of fear, you would be experiencing a state of "anxiety," since the monster couldn't get at you. The term, anxiety, is reserved for fear without "real" cause.

When people in the twentieth century experience anxiety, they think they are getting a heart attack or that something is seriously wrong with their bodies or their minds. In other words, when scared, people think they are suffering from a disease. Actually, they are responding to some inner "danger" which is unknown to them.

From this example it is clear that anxiety is *not* an illness: It is a normal, yet alternate, state of the body, elicited by fear or anger.

Normal? Yes, even though it is not pleasant to go about one's daily life in a state of fear; especially when no danger is actually present. Of course, constant anxiety is debilitating. Its unknown cause must be found and the unpleasant feeling alleviated. But the misperceived danger, as a cause, can hardly be placed in the same category as a virus, a cause for disease. Although anxiety is not a disease, still it is intolerable when constant and not related to the ongoing world about us.

Let's take it one step further: Since continuous and apparently irrelevant anger is so unacceptable, the body finds another way of coping. Muscles in various parts of the back, used only rarely, contract, producing painful backaches.

When certain other back muscles are knotted up by unconscious anger, the skin is stretched all the way to the head, forcing small blood vessels in the scalp to open up. And pain sensors, intimately associated with these vessels, will transmit pain to the brain. Thus people get "tension" headaches.

Some people attribute headaches to being "over tired," to eyestrain, to something they ate, or to "migraine." But the overwhelming majority of headaches endured by most people are tension headaches caused by anger; anger of which the person is totally unaware.

The person is subjected to a push-pull experience: A "push" away from anxiety because it is so unpleasant; a "pull" towards illness as a solution. A youngster who hates going to school because school evokes anxiety, finds that the only acceptable method of avoiding it, is to get sick. Being sick, the child is showered with extra measures of affection and concern. Thus, parents inadvertently teach their children to be sick when the child is experiencing anxiety.

Certain stomachaches caused by "gas" also stem from another misperceived body function. Sometimes, confronted by vague anxiety or unhappiness, people will revert to sucking: To quiet a baby, a nipple is placed in its mouth. And so we learned at a very early age to suck when we're unhappy. The salivary glands were conditioned to respond when such a need appeared. Thus we began the swallowing of substantial amounts of saliva. Since the saliva is mixed with air, bubbles distend the stomach causing discomfort and even pain.

People who experience this problem sometimes think they have appendicitis, or are suffering from food poisoning or some other digestive disease. But none of these is responsible, in fact. The cause is: air ballooning the stomach, swallowed by sucking saliva, in reaction to unperceived unhappiness or vague anxiety.

These two examples of body difficulties describe situations where there is no injury to body tissues, no disease, no trauma. The problem is called, *functional.* One part of the body doesn't work right. "Functional" falls under the general label, *psychogenic*—of psychological origin. Unaware that the problem is psychogenic, naturally a medical doctor is consulted.

After a routine examination, the doctor, depending on his or her orientation may say: "There is nothing wrong with you. Take a couple of aspirins." Or else the doctor might give the patient a hint of the cause: "People sometimes react this way to stress. Take a couple of Maalox and it will go away in the morning." Unfortunately, the reality of "medical economics" prevents doctors from spending needed time with patients to uncover the underlying cause.

Furthermore, doctors must keep in mind the Archie Bunker syndrome—people who need psychotherapy must be crazy. No one likes to be told he or she needs such help. Should the doctor recommend psychotherapy for the patient who suffers from persistent headache or stomachache, he will find himself with a dwindling practice.

It is unfortunate that some doctors, by virtue of their training in physical medicine, must dismiss functional complaints as trivial since they are not equipped, nor have the time to treat them. This is a sad situation because it is so common—over fifty percent of body "illness" brought to the attention of the general practitioner, is caused by feelings. Research published in the medical journals in the last twenty years reports this consistent finding: At least a full half of "presenting complaints" which a practitioner of general medicine is expected to cure, are of psychological origin.

People with persistent functional problems will go to half a dozen doctors until convinced that the doctors don't know how to diagnose their illness, much less treat it. Then they seek out non-medical helpers who cure psychogenic symptoms by persuasion. Other patients, incredulous or of a "scientific" turn of mind, will refuse ministrations by cult leaders, and so remain with the doctors and the pain.

Functional problems in Freud's day also were given short shrift. The doctor would tell the parent of a female child suffering from a minor but incurable ailment, "She'll get well when she first menstruates." If that didn't help, the doctor would assure the parents that the condition would improve when "she gets married," i.e. has sex. When sex didn't work, the problem was supposed to go away after the birth of the first child. And finally, the cure was to have arrived after menopause. Freud is reputed to have added, death eventually cures all problems of psychological origin. He was, of course, alluding to the fact that medical doctors are just not equipped to deal with psychogenic difficulties.

Fortunately, functional problems pose no threat to

life. They are often annoying and distressing, rather than serious. But another category of "presenting complaints," associated with feelings, can indeed be quite serious.

For example, some people with a hard, driving need to acquire possessions, money, power, and/or recognition are endangered by feelings of which they are unaware. In their unconscious, money and power provide a substitute for food. Since nothing they do can meet the impossibly high expectations demanded by their unconscious "stomach," their real stomach begins to digest its own walls. Should real food not be present, the stomach will begin to digest itself. This causes stomach ulcers. Such illness poses a threat to life and must be dealt with immediately on a physical level by a medical doctor.

Unlike the *functional* disturbances, ulcers cause injury to the body. This condition is called *psychosomatic* (mind-body), a commonly misused term. Over thirty years ago a Chicago psychiatrist, Roy Grinker, investigated stomach ulcers extensively. He and his colleagues discovered an entire category of illnesses caused by the "mind" but actually injuring the body. It was they, who first used the term, *psychosomatic.*

Thus the term, *functional,* refers to parts of the body which don't function as they are expected to, but there is no physical injury; headaches are an example of a *functional* disturbance. The term, *psychosomatic,* however, refers to actual injury to body tissues, possibly dangerous, like stomach ulcers. The third term, *psychogenic,* is the more general word. It covers both headaches and ulcers, both malfunction and actual damage.

There is hardly any part of the body which cannot be used in the service of unmet and unrecognized needs.

These needs can latch on to already existing physical problems to produce some forms of epilepsy, heart disease, and respiratory problems such as asthma; also arthritis, colitis and skin disease.

A tremendous amount of research has discovered personality types that are associated with these illnesses. The rigidity of the arthritic, both physical and emotional, is but one example. It has been estimated that 90% of dermatitis (skin disease) is psychosomatic in origin. Almost any illness has some psychological aspect to it.

But why does the body fail to function properly? Why the stomachache or why functional paralyses in *this* part of the body and *that* part? The stomach, or any other organ, refuses to function properly because it is trying to tell us something. It is using "body language". This is the original meaning of "body language", not the popular notion—expressive but inadvertent body posture.

When the cause of epilepsy is functional, the entire body is expressing a need in its own "body language". An extremely religious, completely non-sexual young woman suffered from true, organic epilepsy as a child. But after puberty, brain tests showed no further physical cause for her epileptic attacks and yet, the condition persisted. Why? She was using "body language". In the throes of an epileptic attack, her entire body was expressing a need, prompted by a lack of loving.

Although the prime cause of much of these body problems lies in feeling and attitude, the reader is cautioned against adopting an extreme "spiritualist" position. The root cause may lie in your head, but if you don't get medical help, you can, indeed, be dead—from bleeding stomach ulcers. On the other hand, medical intervention, necessary as it is, can only treat the symptoms. Psycho-therapy is needed to get at the cause.

To sum up: Suppose you were on a TV quiz show and were asked, "What's the difference between *functional* and *psychosomatic* illness?" The answer is: "Functional re-fers to the working of the body. If you're not happy with the way it's working, you have a functional complaint. You have a psychosomatic condition if there is actual damage to the body caused by an attitude."

Chances are, that even if you are a professional TV contestant, you will never be asked to distinguish between the two kinds of psychogenic illness, because of our care-fully nurtured ignorance of psychotherapy. Yet both question and answer are legitimate bits of knowledge; knowledge that should be a part of everybody's fund of information. Knowing something about the way our heads work is certainly as important as knowing how air-planes fly or electric currents are conducted.

Obesity and hypochondria are further problems of the body that are a concern of psychotherapy. While it may seem odd to place these two dissimilar conditions in the same category, often they have a common cause. A prime source of both extreme overweight and extreme concern with any one part of the body, is the fear of total disappearance.

Disappearance? What a puzzling statement! One of our most valuable assets is our sense of "self". We know that we exist; we don't even have to prove it. We can see and feel our bodies and, by extension, our homes, the possessions inside, and, with many American males, their cars. All these form a part of ourselves. We can only deal with the world if we have this sense of self, otherwise we'd be vegetables, unable to act independently.

Some few people are so frightened of total aloneness, deep down, that they, themselves, must cease to exist. People who no longer have this sense of self, an awareness of their own existence, are in "mental hospitals".

To defend against this terrible condition, others who might be prone to a dissolution of their self-hood, must affirm their existence by taking radical measures. Instead of disappearing, they march into the kitchen, and proceed to envelop enormous quantities of sugars and starches. Only when their bodies attain the grotesque shape of a huge balloon are they satisfied that their bodies, their selves do, indeed exist. Thus their very essence, their being, will not disappear.

Diets, doctors, and pills will rarely avail when one's existence is threatened. When an extremely obese person was put into a hospital and restrained from eating, a total disorganization of the personality followed—the patient went into a full-blown psychotic attack.

By contrast, support groups such as Weight Watchers have had much success in dealing with obesity because such groups are designed to affirm the existence of the individual participants. At every meeting, each member is presented before the group and rewarded for weight loss or admonished for gaining. Thus twenty or more people bear witness to the existence of the participant and his body, so that he or she need not use weight as confirmation of self.

Pain is the other means of asserting the existence of one's body. The hypochondriac, in severe cases, may be so convinced that he is going to die of cancer from this little mole on his leg, that no one can change his mind by presenting facts. Moliere, in his comedy, *La Malade Imaginaire*, presented the hypochondriac as a very funny person precisely because of the absurdity of his complaints. But it is no laughing matter if one fears obliteration and must assert his body and thus his being, through pain.

Finally: The way our bodies work cannot be understood by conventional medicine as we know it, or the way conventional medicine is generally practiced. The medical establishment has rightly been under attack in the last few years for its mechanical approach to people and its refusal to recognize that many ills cannot be cured by pills. But the medical consumer is just as much at fault for demanding pills.

Unfortunately we live in a drug culture. The fine distinction between illegal drugs sold by a "pusher" and legal drugs dispensed by a doctor is unimportant. Both the far-out addict and the conventional patient expect that all can be cured and the world made bright, round, and rosy by ingesting bright, round, and rosy capsules. And the doctor who won't prescribe these magic medicaments, will soon find himself out of business.

Psychotherapy does not offer an immediate cure. An aspirin swallowed every four hours often removes the headache or other minor pain. Therapy can be a difficult pill to swallow, but its effects are lasting. Unfortunately people today want fast, "drive-in" service, for food, for banking, and for headaches; hence they demand a pill rather than therapy.

Psychotherapy is not medicine. Indeed, even scientific insights revealed by research under the auspices of medical institutions, are all too often ignored in the actual practice of modern medicine. Psychotherapy, on the other hand, applies these insights; it is grounded on the firm awareness that the body is subject to attitude and feeling.

Psychotherapy resembles education more than it resembles medicine. Psychotherapy and education are alike in that both try to change human behavior. One aspect of their similarity was brought out in the psychotherapy of a teacher. He was in therapy for over a year. One day, when he stood up to leave, he said, "This was a very good session. But last week's session was a real bust." He was implying that the last session was a waste of time and that both the therapist and himself were responsible.

The therapist answered him, "I'm sure you've come across the parent who asks the kid, 'What did you learn in school today?' "

"It's not uncommon," he replied.

"Is it not annoying to you, because you know that education is a process, not a series of discrete lessons?"

"I get your point," the teacher nodded. He agreed that it made more sense to look over what was accomplished during the last year, rather than focus on any one individual session.

Yet, there is a fundamental difference between the two disciplines: Education's aims are to provide information and skills. Sometimes education is even concerned with broad social skills or the attempt to teach clear thinking, generally. Psychotherapy, on the other hand, tries to change even more fundamental attitudes and free the person of impediments that may stand in the way of his making good use of the benefits of education.

33

It is in the area of children who don't learn or children who are disruptive that the distinction between psychotherapy and education becomes blurred. In labor terminology, when two unions are trying to organize the same workers, there is a "jurisdictional dispute". So with children who don't conform in school, there is a jurisdictional dispute between psychotherapy and education. This is due, primarily, to a lack of clear thinking and disagreement as to the cause of the child's not learning.

"Learning disability" is a label which has become popular in the last few years. But unfortunately, labels do not explain; they only describe. If we fall into the fallacy of believing that "learning disability" explains the *cause* of a child's lack of interest in learning, we understand little. And thus we are not in a very good position to change the child's behavior.

At worst, that catch-all label has incorrect implications. An assumption is made that all children who don't learn have something wrong with their brains and special measures are needed to educate them. Quite the contrary is true for many of these children.

When a child is so anxious, fearful, or depressed that he is occupied with his own inner problems, he may have no energy left over for academic pursuits. Unfortunately, the child cannot tell the parent or the educator, "I am too nervous and unhappy to concentrate." And even if he did the adult's response would probably be, "Well, you've got to try hard to overcome it. Now go back to the classroom and learn the multiplication table."

Here is an odd situation: almost anything is possible by sheer chance—a monkey pressing number keys may add two and two and come up with four. So by chance alone, the child may be helped by special educative means without either teacher or supervisor understanding what actually happened.

Should the child be exceptionally lucky, he may be assigned to a teacher who not only has specialized skills but who really likes kids. Although he is supposed to teach the child, this teacher may be more interested in the child's welfare than in the child's spelling accomplishments. The teacher becomes a sympathetic authority figure. And the child will go through fire and water to please him/her. The child will even learn how to spell for the sake of the teacher. Thus the latest in audiovisual aids, programmed learning, or any other tricky gadgets, would have little to do with the child's new-found skills.

But does it matter how you do it, as long as the child learns what he's supposed to learn? It matters a great deal. A year after the child will have stopped seeing the caring teacher and as long as the anxiety or depression are unrelieved, the child will go back to not learning anything.

Had the child been referred for psychotherapy, an attempt would have been made to get at the root of the problem. A therapist would work with the child or, if necessary, with the entire family, to induce fundamental changes that would relieve the child's anxiety or depression.

Unfortunately, many parents do not want to hear the news that their child has emotional problems. It reflects on them and internal family events that may prove embarrassing. The Archie Bunker syndrome prevails to the detriment of the child. So even those educators who are aware that such problems may exist, stay out of the hornet's nest and prescribe further education for the child who suffers from "learning disability".

For the sake of children getting nowhere in school, it is vital that we know when to apply education and when to make use of psychotherapy. It is important to define the boundary between the two disciplines and the uses of each. Labels that explain nothing result only in confusion and then substitute the wrong kind of help.

Psychotherapy is not intrusive therapists, or weird clients. It is not medicine and it is not education. What then, is psychotherapy?

THIS IS PSYCHOTHERAPY:

By careful listening and understanding, the therapist clarifies ideas and wishes, previously ignored or unnoticed. The process dissolves inner constrictions that bar people from their goals. Repetitive, unproductive behavior then changes to a flexible, adaptive means of dealing with others. People now begin to feel better, get more control over the environment, and fulfill their inherent abilities.

To achieve full understanding of the client requires a great deal of patience and interest on the part of the therapist. Far from the "psychiatric" interrogation in "Rose Garden", the psychotherapist listens carefully with sparing comments. Just enough to let the client know that he's being understood. Or just enough to clarify when the therapist doesn't understand.

The therapist is not performing in public so he really

doesn't care if people think he's earning his fee or not. Unencumbered by box office requirements, the therapist can afford to be quiet and hear what the client is saying. Such intense concentration is rarely given its due, neither by the public nor even by the client.

A story is told about a famous "rat psychologist" (a psychologist who studies animals in a laboratory) who scoffed at psychotherapy and therapists. In his later years, he became incontinent and tried various medical treatments. When these didn't work, he was forced to try psychotherapy, much as he resisted it. The animal psychologist consulted Hans Sachs, a disciple of Freud, and undertook psychotherapy for a year. Lo and behold, therapy was effective and his problem was solved.

The psychologist, refusing to recognize the achievement in his own therapy, wrote to Dr. Sachs stating that Sachs performed no miracle—Sachs just listened to him. In fact, there was nothing that Sachs did, that could not have been accomplished just by talking to a good friend. The therapist knew he could never get the animal psychologist to realize the full value and the difficulty of listening to the other person, so Sachs had to answer him in a rather flip fashion, "It is significant that you had no good friend to listen to you."

Above all, the therapist neither judges nor advises. This is an extremely difficult task. Our culture is so permeated with "rights" and "wrongs" and we are so conditioned to "help" people by giving advice when they present a problem to us, that any other mode of responding seems almost inconceivable.

A friend of yours complains at great length and with

37

much passion that her husband occupies himself with work to the point that he spends little time with her and the children. "And then . . ." she pauses dramatically, "And then, Monday night is his night out with the boys. Heaven forbid that he should ever give that up. Just once! Four years ago when I had Aunt Mary over, whom he never sees, I got down on my hands and knees and begged him, literally begged him . . ."

After half an hour of this—if you can last that long—it's only natural to burst out, "Why don't you leave the man alone and stop trying to gobble him up? You're driving him crazy. Why can't you get some interests of your own?"

Your response is perfectly reasonable. It is clear to you that the woman is driving her husband away by her constant demands. Yet your tone of indignation, prompted by the moral imperative that even husband and wife have a right to privacy, is a whisper in the wind. Your advice that she acquire some interests of her own will be equally ineffective.

Only the patience and lack of personal judgment by a therapist will get your friend to see what she is doing to her husband. Once she, herself, understands that she is making life miserable for the man, no one will need to persuade her to stop behaving this way. Advice, born of conventional wisdom, then will be superfluous.

At this point in therapy your friend may realize that she, herself, is creating difficulties in the marriage. But no matter how hard she bites her tongue, she may not be able to stop. However, as therapy progresses, she may be able to visualize her role in life as the constant victim. She was always getting stepped on. Everyone who was ever close to her always abandoned her.

Realizing that nagging doesn't help, that martyrdom is boring and exasperating to you and everyone else, she may have no difficulty changing her behavior. The outlandish figure she presents to one and all may become so repulsive to her, that her clamorous complaining will simply evaporate. Where advice and persuasion would not avail, insight and the ability to see one's self as others see us, may cause her to exercise restraint without effort.

The therapist's ability to sit back calmly and try to understand instead of condemning, even in the face of an irritating diatribe, is no easy task. During a particularly stormy group therapy meeting, where the therapist was being assailed by three group members, another member burst out, "How in hell do you do it? If I was sitting in your chair, I'd last twenty minutes."

The case of the martyred wife was presented not only to illustrate how hard it is to listen without judging, but also to portray the lack of drama in achieving insight. It is no mean task for both client and therapist to attend the small voice of matters that are "too trivial" to bother with. Yet, it is usually done with no histrionics or fanfare.

Movies have accustomed us to expect the "patient" to rise out of her wheel chair in which she has been confined, lo, these many years, to the background of swelling chords, proclaiming, "And all along it was my father who . . . etc." But box office is box office and therapy is therapy.

It is also likely that remnants of medieval ideas play a

role in this melodrama. Exorcism is not only "box office" but still a potent thought held by many. Powers, formerly attributed to priests and rabbis, are now ascribed to therapists.

Focusing on matters that hitherto have been ignored or unnoticed, does not consist of suddenly knowing something that was totally unknown before. Upon achieving insight, people in therapy will say in prosaic fashion, "Well, of course. I've known that all along." They are quite right. Insight does not arise out of a totally mysterious "Unconscious". Ideas in the Unconscious are not guarded by a locked vault to by smashed by a therapist: They are simply unattended.

Finally, to clarify the nature of therapy, we must deal with two issues which have been a source of controversy and confusion: Analysis and synthesis; and conformity versus creativity.

What happens when you peel away all the layers? Where is the flower once you've plucked all the petals? What's left? You can't uncover all that stuff in the Unconscious and then leave the client with nothing at all. Where is the person once everything has been uncovered and analyzed? Analysis is okay, but some kind of synthesis has to take place. A therapist can't just leave his client naked. This is the argument for "synthesis": Put the pieces back together.

It is quite true that analysis without synthesis is like tearing down slums, leaving mountains of debris without rebuilding. Our only disagreement with this argument is—Who is going to rebuild? The therapist or the client?

The notion that the therapist isn't fulfilling his duty to the client unless he puts all the pieces together, assumes that the client is too weak and helpless to do it himself. Little credit is given to the recuperative and synthetic powers of the person. Unlike a flower, one need only skim off the dross, for the molten metal to shine through. Most people have immense sources of resilience that are rarely given credit.

Trying to substitute something for whatever was taken away, when the client can do it for himself, would only encourage further dependency. It hardly makes sense for the therapist to say, "Now that I've given you this and that to replace what's been discarded, you're ready to go out and face the world on your own." The client cannot face the world, if he cannot himself replace what's been cast aside. He would be forever dependent on the therapist for replacement supplies. For those who can do well in analysis, no synthesis is necessary, or even desirable.

Furthermore, if the therapist has to do it all for the client—putting him together after he's taken him apart— the therapist should not have undertaken the uncovering process to begin with.

But what about the people with few inner resources, people for whom "uncovering therapy"—analysis—is unsuitable? The solution for them is "supportive therapy". Using supportive therapy the therapist still listens with no trace of judgment and understands with no trace of condemnation. But rather than insight, the aim is support.

Interpretation of unconscious material is only done for those who can put it all together, themselves. Most people can do it very well, perhaps better than the therapist. "Supportive therapy" is for those who cannot manage confrontation with their Unconscious. Synthesis, for most, is redundant.

A second issue in understanding the goals of psychotherapy concerns the word, adaptive. It raises the issue of conformity versus creativity—headshrinking versus mind expansion.

The notion that people go into therapy to have their minds "shrunk" or diminished, suggests a most peculiar role for therapists: They are to be the guardians of public morality. "Shrinks" are believed to function like their Russian counterparts; imprisoning original thinkers and brainwashing them, lest they contaminate the rest of the population.

Unfortunately, in many cases this accusation is all too true. A national survey of therapists appeared in *The Journal of Abnormal Psychology* some years ago. Psychotherapists were asked to check off, on a long list of possible goals for therapy, those aims they strive to achieve with clients. The majority of therapists, all too frequently, listed conformity to societal requirements as an end, rather than creativity and expansion of one's abilities. Their purpose, apparently, was to squeeze their clients' rough crags and edges into a nice round hole of "adaptability"—a horrible euphemism for, "Shut up and do as you're told."

A multitude of crimes have been committed in the pseudo-scientific name of "adaptation". A child gets his first report card and is given a grade for: "Adapts to the Environment—Excellent, Good, Fair, Poor". The youngster quickly learns that the report card is an instrument used by the school authorities to apply parental pressure forcing the child to do what the school wants him or her to do.

This kind of brainwashing goes on all our lives, sometimes with rapier, sometimes with club. We would be foolish, indeed to undertake therapy with a therapist like those in the survey. Such a therapist has been so seduced by the material rewards offered by our society, that he acts as a representative of all that is repressive and dictatorial in our civilization.

Our definition of the aim of psychotherapy included the words, "adaptive" and "flexible". Such goals appear to be inconsistent with autonomy and self-realization, discouraging innovation and originality. The image of a "flexible and adaptive" person conjures up the individual who learns to follow orders, having no mind of his own. Unfortunately, the true aims of psychotherapy have been subverted under the aegis of these two words.

Regardless of their unfortunate use by the authority-minded, "adaptive" and "flexible" still have a valid and constructive use when applied to the goals of psychotherapy: Picture the fellow who insists on climbing a ten foot wall when he could just as easily have walked a few hundred yards and gone around it. He keeps climbing again and again, bruising his hands and knees. Eventually he breaks a leg. We could rightly call his behavior "rigid" and "stereotyped" rather than adaptive and flexible.

In the same way, the woman who insists on nagging her husband simply does not learn from her mistakes. She may fall down and break a leg. She may be shunned by her friends who get fed up listening to her complaints. Her husband may be ready to divorce her, but she continues in her rigid and stereotyped demands.

"But I had no choice!" she exclaims. You can show your friend ten dozen other ways in which she could gain her husband's affection other than by nagging. "I've already tried it", would be her reply. No, she can't try doing *that* because of her sick mother. No, her husband would not allow her to to *this*. She would "Yes, but . . ." you to death and end up justifying her repetitive behavior by proclaiming, "But I had no choice!"

The aim of her therapy would clearly lie in the direction of adaptive behavior. If she sees that complaints don't work, she might try to fulfill some of her own interests. Her husband would then find home a more enjoyable place to live in. People do not have to give up reasonable needs by "adapting to the environment". Quite the contrary—they can fulfill such needs by a flexible approach rather than by rigid repetition. Climbing the wall is totally unproductive.

It is not for the therapist to decide what the client should want out of life. This is the client's choice and it is the therapist's aim to provide him with sufficient flexibility so that the client may achieve his goals. Not shrink his head to fit into a cubbyhole.

The client may want to publish a book questioning the very bases of society. Or he may want to own an Olympic-sized swimming pool. These aims are not for the therapist to decide. The object of therapy is to remove constrictions and barriers so that the client will be enabled, with increasing flexibility and powers of adaptation, to achieve his own ends, whatever they are.

On both issues—putting the self together and choosing one's own goals—the therapist bases his work on respect for the person he is seeing and the person's needs.

What therapy is and what it is not, has been defined. But there is hardly any point to the enterprise unless it works. Is psychotherapy really effective? Maybe the incontinent "rat psychologist" whose condition was ameliorated by just talking to Sachs, was right. There are many articles proclaiming psychotherapy to be a hoax.

There is a special branch of psychology dealing with this very question. It is called, "psychotherapy outcome research". Much of the research is sponsored by the National Institute of Mental Health, an agency of the Federal government . "Outcome research" is concerned not only with whether or not psychotherapy works, but with how it works, and under what conditions it works best. This research makes use of elaborate statistics and then proceeds cautiously to careful conclusions. Each piece of research is subject to critical review by one's colleagues.

The scientists who are engaged in "outcome research" are hard-headed people. They don't care if a client got some wonderful insights. They only measure behavior: What was the person doing or not doing that caused him to enter therapy? What actually took place in therapy? What is he doing now, after therapy, that's different, if at all? In the great majority of studies, these scientists found that psychotherapy does, indeed, "work".

But all too often, we hear: "I know this one guy, see. He's been in therapy for twenty years and he still can't make a living." This "one guy" is only one guy, one example. It's always easy to jump to conclusions on the flimsy evidence garnered from a single instance. One swallow doth not a summer make, nor doth one client, psychotherapy negate.

Even considering this one person who was in therapy for twenty years, we may not be aware of his true condition. It is possible that he is severely disturbed. He may be in "supportive therapy". His therapist may have set the modest goal of keeping him out of a mental hospital. Were he not in therapy, he might be in an institution.

Problems of a psychological nature rarely get better. They only get worse with age. Like the world of *Alice in Wonderland*, to stay in one place, you have to keep moving forward. If you stop, you go backwards. If that client in therapy for twenty years is kept on an even keel and out of a mental hospital, his therapist is doing well.

Purely on the basis of a dollar approach, we can ask, "How much does it cost to support a person in a mental hospital? How much does it cost to keep him out?" The cost of Social Security disability benefits is minuscule, less than 1/7 to 1/30 the money that would be spent keeping this person in an institution.

But the benefit to people can't be measured by money alone. A person's freedom of action and personal choice versus incarceration in a mental hospital far outweigh dollars. As long as the man stays out of an institution, his therapy is successful. Therapy does work.

Psychotherapy is not headshrinking. It is not exorcism. It is not medicine, nor is it education. Therapists do not give clients the third degree, nor are clients all weird or crazy.

The therapist's task is to listen carefully to the client, to clarify and interpret what's being said, so the client may know himself, what he's doing and what he's feeling. The aim of therapy is to get the client out of a box—to remove barriers so that the person can gain freedom of choice and make the most out of life.

CHAPTER

2

How Long Is This Gonna Take?

"I've been analyzed!" You may have heard that statement. The speaker presents it as an absolute, implying that he's arrived at the zenith of adjustment, "mental health", and self-knowledge. An emotional super-man, he, and by contrast, we poor unanalyzed slobs are hung up in our neuroses.

But get to know him a bit and you discover that this fellow can't get along with his wife; he gets hives when he's angry; and has days when he can't get anything done at all. So you begin to think, "Maybe he really isn't cured. His doctor shouldn't have pronounced him 'analyzed' so soon."

Just whose mistake was it? The doctor's, the client's, or yours? The answer: All three. And the mistake all three may have made, is thinking of therapy as a medical procedure.

The medical model keeps sticking in our minds. The original therapists were medical psychoanalysts. They kept psychotherapy within the confines of the medical establishment for their own good reasons, as we stated in Chapter 1. But it resulted in confused thinking about psychotherapy.

When you have a disease, you visit a doctor and expect to be cured. There are no degrees. Either you're sick or you're well. So when you go for psychotherapy, you are going to expect a cure—like taking an antibotic, and 36 to 48 hours later, you're well.

The patient-doctor model seems almost like baking a loaf of bread. The bread is supposed to come out of the oven all baked and golden. "I've been analyzed!"

Actually, such oversimplication is not even true of medicine. There are many medical conditions where the patient can only be "improved" rather than "cured". But many people tend to think of medicine in black-and-white terms. And they think of psychotherapy that way, too.

"I've been analyzed" is a misleading statement because the speaker leads you to believe that everything has been fixed. Then you find out that a lot of things are still wrong. So either his therapy has been a failure, or psychotherapy itself, is a failure.

But psychotherapy is a *process*, as we said before. It is not a cure. Since therapy is a process, we can think in more appropriate terms—change and improvement, rather than treatment and cure. At this point we can ask a more sensible question, "Where was the person before therapy and where is he now?"

We learn that before therapy, the fellow couldn't hold down a job at all. Now, although he may have a few days when he can't function, by and large, he manages quite well in a responsible job. Neither psychotherapy in general, nor his specific therapy is a failure. Therapy brought him from no job to holding a job. And that is a real achievement.

But since therapy is a process, then that person claiming to have been "analyzed", has a further choice. He can stay where he is, or he could continue in therapy. There is no reason why his therapy had to stop where it did. If this fellow continues in therapy, he might get rid of his hives, get rid of "bad" days, and get rid of his wife—or, preferably, get along with her better.

Thus if we stop thinking about therapy as a cure and start thinking of therapy as a process, new vistas open up. Given enough time and if the process proceeds well, there is almost no limit in "uncovering therapy". And almost no limit to improvement.

The process of psychotherapy is like a ladder. The client is standing on the tenth rung and he wants to get to the fifteenth rung. Or he may be standing on the fifth step and wants to get to the twentieth. His particular ladder has steps that are mostly six inches high, but along comes a step that is two feet high. Then, to complicate matters, the client is blindfolded and the light is dim so that even the therapist can't see too well—the therapist can't know everything in advance.

How long does therapy take? How long *should* it take? There is no one single answer. It depends on the height of the step the client is perched on when he enters therapy; how high the rungs are in his ladder; and how high he wants to climb.

True, these answers are hardly satisfying. Therefore this chapter is devoted to filling out more detailed answers to two of the factors: On which step of the ladder is this particular kind of client standing now? How difficult will it be for such a person to climb up? Various kinds of problems will be sketched together with an estimate of the factors making it relatively easy or difficult to progress up the ladder.

The last element, how high the person wants to climb, is clearly up to him. So this question can only be answered by the individual entering therapy. But before we take up the different kinds of problems with which a person may enter therapy—his height on the ladder—we will describe two people with widely differing goals. Bill and Ellen can thus serve as models of people who made contrasting choices as to how far they wanted to go in therapy.

Bill, a certified public accountant in his mid-thirties, came for therapy with a rather odd complaint: When he would reach out for anything concrete, be it a cup of coffee or a pack of cigarettes, his hand would shake. He feared an interview for possible job promotion because his hand might tremble. The boss, noting this, would surely disqualify him.

There was nothing physically wrong with Bill, nor anything emotionally disturbing in his life. His wife, his children, his present job, his friends were all in good working order. He just wanted the shaking to go away. The therapist believed that reaching out for anything was accompanied by anxiety even though Bill was not aware of it. He didn't actually *feel* anxious. The trembling hand was the only cue that suggested anxiety.

After nine sessions, Bill stood up, shook the therapist's hand, and thanked him for his help. "The shaking has completely disappeared, thanks to you. I'm sure it may be just the tip of the iceberg, as you said. But this is as far as I want to go. Life is just fine for me now."

The therapist had done very little for him. He simply listened sympathetically to Bill. Bill "reached out" for help and the therapist didn't disappoint him. The shaking was probably due to Bill's fear that he would be refused whatever his request might be, even the morning paper. That is why it shook no longer when he realized that someone, in this case a therapist, would not reject his reaching out for help.

In contrast to Bill, Ellen's choice was entirely different. She had been in therapy for fifteen years, not merely nine sessions. Ellen originally came for help because she was regarded as the constant wallflower, the person whom no fellow would ever ask out on a date. So she wanted the "key".

The golden key she dreamed of, would open up the magic door to social success. Like the TV ads for jeans, mouthwash, or perfume, Ellen wanted the therapist to provide her with the hypnotic honey attracting swarms of sexy swains.

After two or three years of therapy she began to get the "knack" and found that it was not too difficult to attract men. The "key" didn't work every single time. But it worked enough of the time so that her original objective in therapy had been accomplished.

But along the way, Ellen began to realize that life had more to offer than dates. Something was lacking. In her original loneliness, she believed that if only she had lots of boyfriends, the loneliness would dissipate. As it turned out, the quantity of boyfriends didn't help. She began to realize the need for one person, not many. However, it had been necessary to start on the bottom rung first: she believed that a lot of men would be the answer. Having accomplished this, another step could be mounted.

But the process of getting closer to one person was a more difficult task than she had ever imagined. Ellen now understood that only by creating a close relationship with one person, would the loneliness vanish. More than that, she needed to become a whole person herself.

Ellen is still in therapy; climbing her own ladder whose top rungs have only recently come into view, as she shifted her goals. People, she realized, are not "dates". They are people. To get close to another person, she would have to become a person herself, not a robot.

Obviously, Ellen and Bill differed widely in their goals. Bill wanted a change in only one small aspect of his life, Ellen aimed for a complete restructuring of her existence. The role of the therapist is to help each as far as he/she wants to climb; not to insist or push a client beyond his/her desires. So, ultimately, it is the client who must decide how long therapy will take. It just depends on what he or she wants out of life.

The other two elements—where the person stands on the ladder upon entering therapy and how high the person's ladder is and the separation of its rungs—these are not a matter for personal choice. Neither Bill nor Ellen had any say about where they stood on their ladders when they entered therapy. Bill, at least, was married, while marriage for Ellen was not in sight. Secondly, they had no choice as to the height of each step. Ellen had no friends and was, at the time, incapable of making them. Bill, on the other hand, had many friends and acquaintances. Their individual ladders differed as did their positions on them when they entered therapy.

People not only vary in the kinds of problems they present, clients vary in age, background, and a multiplicity of other factors affecting their positions on the ladder of therapy. This chapter is devoted to a consideration of some of the various elements promoting or retarding progress in therapy.

Age is the most obvious and clear-cut factor determining movement in therapy. The younger person tends to be more flexible and more prone to change. The older person with crystallized behavior patterns, will find change more difficult. However, the old maxim, "you can't teach an old dog new tricks" is not true. It just takes longer, and the new tricks are less dramatic.

The age factor is most clearly illustrated in the case of a four-year-old boy. He saw a neighbor whose clothes were on fire, run from a burning building. The mother of the child, a registered nurse, put out the flames and administered first aid to the victim. The child then developed nightmares, wet his bed, and became so fearful that he could hardly play or do anything at all.

After only four months of therapy, the child returned to his normal state. He stopped having nightmares, wetting the bed, and began to enjoy playing again. While four months of therapy is a very brief segment of time, it is not unusually short for youngsters. At age four, four months was fully one-twelfth of the child's entire lifetime.

Thus length of time in therapy may be considered as a proportion of one's years, rather than as an absolute figure.

A second factor contributing to the duration of therapy is the ostensible reason a person gives himself for entering therapy. What moves the person to decide to seek help?

A person who enters therapy under duress, is not going to make as much progress as the person who decides to go under his own steam. If the judge tells a man, "You have two choices: Get some therapy or go to jail," the man hardly has much choice. He will enter therapy and fight the therapist at every step. On the other hand, if a person is feeling anxious and unhappy for no apparent reason and sees therapy as a solution, he is in a favorable position to move right up the ladder. In current jargon, the person is "highly motivated".

Sometimes even a person who enters therapy under duress, has some hope of stepping up the ladder. His original notion of enforced therapy may change in the course of his sessions. For example, a young man fearing the draft during the Vietnam War came to the therapist's office. He decided that should the draft board present him with "Greetings from the President," he would be able to tell them, "I am in psychotherapy and thus not psychiatrically fit for duty."

It was three months before the therapist discovered the real reason this client entered therapy. The therapist knew that as long as the young man believed that he really didn't need therapy and was simply going through the motions in order to escape the draft, progress would be difficult.

The therapist suggested to him that there were any number of other ways to avoid the draft. Some of these ways would not even label him with a stigma of "psychiatrically unfit." Why did the client choose psychotherapy as a way out? Could it be possible that he was trying to reach not one, but two goals simultaneously by seeking help? Was there a part of him that realized having no job and no girlfriend was an unsatisfactory way to live? Was he satisfied accepting financial support from his mother?

Perhaps the fellow realized in some small corner of his mind that he did, indeed need help. Draft avoidance, although it was a very real problem, served as a convenient pretext, giving the young man false reassurance that he didn't need therapy; that he was merely going for help to look good to his draft board.

With the therapist's help, the client reconsidered his motives for seeking therapy. Awareness of the need for a fundamental change in his life, positioned him to begin stepping up the ladder. Thus is is possible for a client to change his apparent reason for seeking help. Equipped with valid grounds, he can make progress.

A third factor, crucial to one's position on the ladder and the height of the rungs, is the original age during which a client has undergone a difficult situation. A very young infant is most impressionable. Should a baby undergo a series of traumatic and continuous incidents without corrective experiences, the child may well be marred for life. But a school-age child with positive early experiences can more readily manage unpleasant incidents. The older child can emerge unscathed, where an infant would be harmed. The age when one experiences psychological trauma is such an important factor, that it deserves further attention:

During World War II, the southern part of England was taking a terrible beating from constant German bombing. To escape death, many British children, and infants especially, were sheltered in the northern part of England. Since England was engaged in a life or death struggle, the number and quality of the people assigned to care for these babies, was most limited. Many of the infants received little or no attention and were fed merely for survival.

At the end of the war, it became apparent that a large number of British children were very peculiar. They did not play or study or behave like "normal" children. Their condition seemed to resemble "mental retardation."

John M. Bowlby, a British psychiatric investigator, traced their condition to routine lack of affection in the northern shelters during the war.

Leo Kanner, an American psychiatrist, noticed the very same peculiarities observed by Bowlby, in his own young clients, children of the wealthy. Seeking the cause of the child's difficulty, Kanner found repeatedly that the parents appeared cold and unfeeling: They reacted to their children with an antiseptic lack of warmth. The oddity of both British and American children was thus traced back to an early absence of care.

Final confirmation of this fundamental need for parental love and attention, beyond mere food and shelter, comes from animal psychology. Harry F. Harlow, a noted scientist at the University of Wisconsin, reared newborn chimpanzees without their mothers. The chimps were fed with an eye dropper and given a "mother substitute"—a towel draped over a chicken wire form. When these apes grew up, they were totally unable to mate: Proof that even chimpanzees need personal attention while growing up. Deprived at an early age of the company of parents or peers, they cannot relate in a normal fashion to other apes.

Bowlby, Kanner and Harlow dealt with extremes. But how about the ordinary person? Can their findings apply to people whom we consider normal, who didn't seem peculiar? Indeed they can. Just as a boulder is easier to identify than a grain of sand, so knowledge about the cause of severe disturbance may shed light on a mild disturbance. Extreme parental deprivation gives rise to extreme disturbance. Comparatively mild parental deprivation gives rise to relatively mild disturbance.

Although we have used the term, mild, we must not forget that such deprivation took place at an early age. When uncorrected by subsequent child rearing, this deficit is hard to make up. A loner called Ellen, whose therapy took so long, is just such an example.

When she first entered therapy, Ellen wanted the magic key to social success, suspecting that men regarded her as a creep, a "lemon," wanting nothing to do with her. Like Harlow's apes, she was unable to "mate."

But also like children investigated by Bowlby and Kanner, the roots of Ellen's social isolation lay deeper than appeared on the surface. So Ellen's therapy did not consist of teaching her tricks of social intercourse. It was the effects of her early childhood that needed correction.

Ellen's parents were childish, self-centered people, unable to give her sufficient care or attention. As a second, unwanted child, she suffered even more indifference from them. Ellen grew up with an odd quality of unrelatedness to people. She tended to see others, not as real persons, but as cardboard figures—things, objects. No wonder she was rejected by men. And by women, too.

As she grew up, Ellen learned for reasons she could not fathom, she herself, seemed inherently rejectable. She was not aware that by her manner and her dress she was declaring to the world, " I am an unloved and an unlovable person." The few and fleeting friendships she did have were with people who had the very same deficiency. No wonder she was unable to establish a close or firm relationship with people of either sex.

Underneath Ellen's oddly unfeeling exterior there was an unrequited hunger for closeness. But the need for affection, previously denied her, was too urgent to expose to the world.

Now an understanding of Ellen's isolation emerges: Some people, although unable to articulate it, could sense Ellen's underlying demand for love. And they were repelled by its intensity. They did not want to be used as cutouts, paper dolls from whom Ellen would try to extract endless supplies of love. Others noted in passing her unfeeling exterior and regarded her with a corresponding lack of interest. Still others were put off by her dress and posture proclaiming her unlovability.

Unlike Bowlby's deprived, war scarred children, people like Ellen are not visibly crippled by early misrearing. They manage to get by in our society. They are simply regarded as social undesirables. Ellen's style of behavior was one mode of adjustment to life. Other people with this same deficit in their early childhood react to the world in different ways:

The first way some try to cope with life, is by maintaining an impenetrable exterior. A cold, mechanical surface of acceptable performance covers a maelstrom of unmet needs. One gets an impression of a robot talking to a computer.

If such a person is an accountant, who deals primarily with numbers and works in a large organization, no one will notice his lack of warmth and feeling. The accountant, so damaged, can create the illusion of a full-fledged personality by issuing the expected and conventional responses to any given situation:

The accountant can even get excited at the prospect of his favored baseball team winning the pennant. He can make the usual passes at his secretary, and is regarded as a "good Joe" by his peers. He can even be married and have children and still keep his mask on.

But the man is devoid of humanity. He escapes unnoticed by others and unaware of his own deficit, until his hand begins to tremble. Others, very much like Bill, the accountant, may go through their entire lives with no apparent problems. Unfortunately, they savor very little of life. They merely exist.

Another path to acceptance by society, is carefully disguised fury at all who would deny the person his needed supply of love. Such hatred can be so all-encompassing that the entire universe is regarded as his enemy. He must be crafty enough and clever enough to frustrate the conspiracy against him. He often is highly intelligent, creating universal systems and theories. When not too removed from the real world, his theories even have intrinsic value.

He can also appear to be a person of apparent warmth and understanding. And yet his insight-laden understanding of people is brought about by his need to guard against unexpected attack. People, to him, are *still* cardboard figures, dangerous, if not craftily understood.

A third method of coping with the world in an attempt to meet an overwhelming need for affection, is that of the "con artist." His charm, his ability to sell igloos to Zulus, is too well known to detail here. Since our society glorifies and rewards the consummate "salesman," such a person rarely enters therapy. When this manipulator of other people does slip up, he usually breaks the law and is put in jail. It is almost superfluous to add that the con artist, with all his shrewdness and ability to get along with others, is incapable of any real humanity, any real feeling for others. He simply tries to push his cut-out figures on the chess board he perceives life to be.

Can these three personalities, these hollow people, be persuaded to give up their distorted approaches to others and become part of the human race? Maybe. If their systems are not too crystallized; if they begin therapy at an early age; and above all, if their drive to change their approach to others is powerful, then improvement is possible. But because their needs were left unmet so early in life, psychotherapy is a long and difficult process. By contrast, people who were deprived at a later age, can progress more rapidly.

Can early parental deprivation be detected by the therapist so much later in the person's life? There is a fine

line of difference which a sensitized person, be he therapist or not, can pick up. The therapist asks himself, "How
does this person make me feel? Am I fully human to him
or am I just an object?" Often it may take a few meetings
for "company manners" to be discarded. The difference
between a human and an apparent robot, can then be
discerned, and the early deprivation be inferred in the
case of the automaton.

The final factor contributing to the length of time
therapy will take, is the degree of pleasure or displeasure
afforded by the complaint. Two extreme opposites are:
addiction versus anxiety.

Propelled by the threat of jail and the fear of total
disintegration, an addict might present himself for
therapy. But the immediate pleasure offered him by a
"fix" is far more powerful than the far-off hope of becoming a useful member of society. Nothing the therapist
could possibly offer at the moment, could begin to compete with the sublime sense of peace offered by a drug.

Moreover, the addict may sense in a small part of
himself, that should he truly give up any notion of ever
taking the drug, he will enter a deep depression. The
onset of depression following withdrawal from impulse-
ridden behavior makes therapy difficult, if not impossible,
with such people.

The addiction, whether it be drugs, gambling, alcohol, food or even "love," is governed by impulsive behavior and serves as a defense against depression. "If only
I bet on this one last horse . . ." or "This man, truly, will be
my one last love . . .". Giving up these false hopes, seeing
them as false, will result in deep unhappiness.

Perhaps the only method of ensuring that the addict stop his or her destructive behavior in pursuit of an empty grail, is the quasi-religious group. Daytop Village and its imitators or Alcoholics Anonymous offer belief in a charismatic leader, or a deity, plus group pressure and support. These substitute for the destructive magic so craved by the addict. Such pressure groups succeed where conventional psychotherapy is useless.

At the very opposite pole to addiction, is anxiety. Addiction offers an immediate and intense pleasure when the craving is satisfied. Anxiety, on the other hand, offers nothing but unpleasant feelings. Heart palpitating, palms moist, butterflies in one's stomach—these manifestations of fear are all to be avoided. Their removal is cause for celebration.

The only fundamental relief is the path of psychotherapy. Thus there is every motive for the person suffering anxiety to crave a change. There is no reward for remaining anxiety-ridden.

The "phobias"—specialized anxieties—are almost as unpleasant as general anxiety. These irrational fears of height, closed spaces, or being stared at, limit one's activities and afford no pleasure. Of course it is possible to avoid going on airplane flights, if one is afraid of heights; it is possible to avoid elevators if one fears closed spaces; and it is possible to avoid public speaking if appearing before an audience sends one into a panic. But there are many times when it is inconvenient to do so. Thus the phobia provides no pleasure at all and the problem, itself, serves to commit one to change.

Depression, too, offers nothing but misery for the

sufferer. The unhappy person has much to gain and nothing to lose by change. Hence the prospect for improvement is fairly high.

Depression, itself, varies more in intensity than almost any other malfunction. Deep depression can totally incapacitate; moderate depression debilitates; mild depression is rarely identified. It is noted as "lack of energy."

Judging from the prevalence of advertising offering immediate relief for that "down in the dumps" feeling, mild depression must be a common condition. The purveyors of nostrums can "put zest in your life," "throw the blues out the window" and offer you happiness in a brown bottle with a "new, improved" label. Others ascribe a lack of vitamins as the cause, so they persuade you to buy vitamins or adhere to the latest fashion in diet. But these conditions over which people have no control, all indicate mild depression.

Shortly after the first World War, the Federal government began to take action against the slick sellers of snake oil and other dangerous remedies that were supposed to make people happier. Some soft drinks were named after the leaves of the coca plant, since cocaine was the prime ingredient of these cola drinks. These "soft" drinks containing a "hard" drug did, indeed, make people feel happier. When the Federal government finally forced the manufacturers to stop infusing these beverages with cocaine, it had been estimated that over half the population of the United States was addicted.

While the addiction to cocaine has roots in the physical adaptation of the human body, the original ingestion of "coke" need not have occurred unless one is depressed to begin with. Such widespread addiction to cocaine, half the population of the United States, could not possibly have happened unless a great many people felt depressed at the outset.

Mild depression, common 60 years ago in the days of cocaine in "coke," is still common now. Although the drug has since been removed from the cola drinks, the makers are still permitted to suffuse it with caffeine, a stimulant. TV advertising for these drinks is now directed at this same vast, unhappy population. Commercials picture youngsters cavorting around beaches, engaged in sports, and engorging themselves with the brown, bubbly stuff. The implication is—"Drink our caffeine-laden elixir, and you, too, can be as happy as these muscular, sexy, carefree youngsters."

The more honest person, however, instead of quaffing that brown stuff, will first admit to himself that he is unhappy. He is then in a position to become convinced that neither vitamins, cola drinks, nor tonics will make him happy. By virtue of such honesty, such a person will find himself at least three steps higher on the ladder. He or she is now ready to begin psychotherapy.

Psychogenic body problems—like depression, anxiety, and the phobias—are unpleasant, sometimes even dangerous. Thus they are amenable to therapy. But unlike depression and anxiety, malfunction of the body can offer a special reward.

A Puerto Rican woman was referred for psychotherapy because of a partial functional paralysis of her left arm and left leg. After an initial difficulty in communication due to the language problem, the following classic story emerged:

Mr. Gonzales, the husband, flew to Puerto Rico to nurse his aged mother who was suffering from a stroke. Mrs. Gonzales, waiting months for her husband's return, finally became impatient and flew down to the island to see what was keeping him. She found him living with another woman. Mrs. Gonzales then dragged her husband back to New York. Upon returning, she developed the paralysis.

After these events were related, the therapist asked Mrs. Gonzales, "Could you tell me what exactly was wrong with your husband's mother?"

"She was paralyzed on her left side," the wife replied.

"So if the same thing happened to you, your husband would rush to your side and give you all kinds of care and attention." As if by magic, the paralysis disappeared.

However, not all psychogenic problems are solved so easily. Mr. and Mrs. Gonzales were essentially a firmly united couple. Mr. Gonzales had no intention of leaving his wife and regarded the affair as a mere adventure, a boost to his masculinity.

Hence Mrs. Gonzales was prepared to give up her paralysis. If the ailment were the only glue keeping the couple together, it is likely that nothing could have persuaded her to drop it. People are often loath to give up their functional and psychosomatic problems because these often serve a deep-felt need, even though the ailment may cause them considerable pain.

Another difficulty in the therapy of psychogenic problems is that often they are associated with actual physical disturbances and it becomes difficult to separate the two. The client insists that psychotherapy won't help him because the pain is "real."

Of course the pain is real. Psychogenic difficulties differ vastly from malingering, pretending to be sick. The suffering experienced by people with these problems is no less distressing than diseases with a physical cause. But it is far easier to demand a pill for pain than to deal with one's psychic pain. Hence the insistence that the malfunction is physical.

The therapist must take into account a balance between two forces—a push versus a pull: The client's wish to push away from the misery of the pain, versus the client's pull towards his need for the illness. The therapist's task is to tip the balance in favor of relief. Unlike anxiety, there are times when the client can only be persuaded with great difficulty to give up his need to be sick.

Martyrdom is a problem more difficult to solve than anxiety, phobias, depression, or even psychogenic problems. On the surface, the martyr's life seems most unhappy. One would think that the martyr would be glad to change his outlook. Unfortunately, this is not so.

The martyr actually enjoys being a martyr. He receives a kind of bittersweet pleasure from his stance. Unappreciated by those close to him, ignored and even reviled, the martyr emerges as holy, noble and pure. Any possible sin he may have committed is more than atoned for, by all his suffering. Thus he stands free of guilt, righteous.

Due to the fact that women in our society are often in a powerless position, dependent on their husband's earnings and brainwashed into subservience, martyrdom is one of the few outlets permitted them. The complaining housewife mentioned in Chapter 1 is a good example.

"I work and slave over a hot stove all day long . . ." and fantasies of being present at one's own funeral: "And then you'll be sorry for everything you did to me . . ." are stereotyped examples of martyrdom. The martyr says, "See what you did to me." He is thus pointing the finger of guilt at the *other* person and simultaneously he is indulging himself both in pleasure and this permissible outlet for hostility.

Psychotherapy for martyrdom consists of showing the martyr precisely these two aspects of his stance: 1. The pleasure he or she gets out of such a position, and 2. The hostility he or she spews forth on the other person. However, the martyr's contention is exactly the opposite: He gets no pleasure out of life and he is never aggressive. Getting such a person to see that such a stance provides him with both pleasure and an aggressive outlet, can be most difficult.

There is one final factor which increases the height of the steps or even causes a rung to be missing: The very setting of psychotherapy is seen through the distorted glass of the person's own problem. Since the person comes into therapy with a problem making life unpleasant for him, he will see psychotherapy, too, as an unpleasant process.

Thus a martyr will perceive the therapist as one of his tormentors. The therapist is not helping him or alleviating his problems. He is helping to cause them. The therapist doesn't understand him and is critical of him. The therapist doesn't even regard him as a person worthy of respect. Should the client regard the therapist as his main persecutor, the client may well leave therapy.

The depressed person regards the world as a terrible place. Everything in life is awful. Nothing is any good. Why should psychotherapy be different? Thus psychotherapy, too, is ineffective and the client is doomed to eternal misery.

A client suffering from anxiety will generally be very critical of himself and everything surrounding him. Thus, the closer the therapist gets to him, the more the therapist gets to be *his* therapist. But naturally, *his* therapist can be no better than the client. So his therapist must be completely incompetent, a bungling fool. The client may not realize that he is really making a statement about himself, not the therapist.

To help pull the client up the ladder, beyond this missing rung, is a difficult task. The therapist must rely on the client's own objectivity, his ability to look at himself and at least wonder if it could not be true that the client's own problem may be causing him to regard the setting of therapy, itself, in a jaundiced light.

How long will therapy take? There is an old rabbinic tale that suggests an answer: A man was traveling by foot to a distant village. On the way, he saw an old man sitting under a tree. He approached the old man and asked him, "How long will it take me to reach the village of X?" The old man said to him, "Get away from me." The traveler couldn't understand why the old man was angry, but since he realized that he could get no help from him he continued on his way.

A moment later, the old man called out and asked the traveler to come back. When he returned, the traveler asked the old man, "Why were you angry at me?" The old man replied, "I wasn't angry at you. I merely wanted to see your stride."

During the course of this chapter various problems clients bring to therapy were described. It is possible you may have recognized elements of people you know in some of these sketches. Your ability to apply these character descriptions to others suggests an awareness and concern about the human condition. This insight may well lengthen your stride and shorten the height of the ladder for you, should you decide to undertake psychotherapy.

It is even possible that you may have recognized aspects of yourself in one or more of these personality descriptions. If this was the case, then, should you decide to go into therapy, the task will be lightened even further. A therapist must rely on the client's ability to stand outside himself and examine himself, even if the image is not very pretty. If you were able to see yourself in this chapter, the rungs of the ladder will be even closer together and your ascent will be less halting.

3

How Do People Change? Transference, Resistance, and the Defenses

If you want to improve your life, why can't you do it yourself? Why do you need a therapist? Just make up your mind to do it, exercise determination and discipline—and the course of your life will change.

But does this method work? Let's take a common situation: New Year's Day is always a good time to institute change. So come January 1st, you, plus millions of others, resolve to stop smoking, drink only two beers, be more concerned with your spouse and less with yourself, put in less time at work and more at home. But if you are like many of us, subject to human frailty, by January 15th the good resolution has been swept away with the New Year's confetti.

So maybe Easter is a better time. That is the time when Nature starts her new year. But again, chances are that your good intentions roll down the hill with the Easter eggs.

There is another way. A friend told you about a marvelous new book called, *How To Get Rid Of Your Neuroses.* You find it every bit as marvelous as your friend did. It has you pegged to a "T." The author must have had you in mind when she wrote the book. And she has some good advice telling people how to stop smoking, drinking too much, and spending too much time away from home. So you make up your mind that once and for all, come New Year's Day, you're going to make a resolution . . .

The upshot is, that even with the aid of a "How to . . ." book, you are not able to accomplish anything permanent. Unfortunately, experience with such books can be damaging, because people are not able to live up to promises made. They think of themselves as weak-willed and indulgent; thinking less of themselves makes them worse off than before.

A word about the "How to . . ." books: Books designed for self-improvement mentioned in the *Introduction,* are known in the publishing world as "self-helps." Often these books sell in the millions, making a lot of money for the authors and publishers. Unfortunately, the reader is not helped, only the people who get the proceeds are—they are "self-helped."

Dale Carnegie was one author who helped himself very well, but now his book is obsolete. *How To Win Friends And Influence People* has been replaced by the "psychology self-helps." The "psychology" books, sometimes with remarkable insight, point out why people act in ways that promote discord and make for unhappiness. But even after a careful reading, these books leave people with the fruitless assignment of making resolutions.

Why are people prone to accept the "self-helps" as a method of improvement? And why after one fails, does one buy another book? And another? The American tradition of boundless optimism espousing the infinite capacity of the human will, backed by an unparalleled technological achievement since the birth of our nation, led us to believe there is nothing we can't accomplish. We just need the will to do it, so there is no reason why we can't change ourselves if only we buckle down to the task.

However, in the last few years, a note of realism has begun to seep through American consciousness and to sober its "high." Due to some recent conspicuous failures of the American Dream, many of us are discarding the naive optimism of the Fifties. Are we becoming more savvy and less trusting? The Age of the "Self-helps" may soon be at an end.

We cannot analyze ourselves. The only person in the history of mankind who succeeded to some extent, was Sigmund Freud. But instead of trying to change himself, he was only interested in finding out about himself. There is a big difference. Finding out about yourself is only the first step in changing yourself. Freud took this first step by setting aside a regular time for analyzing his own dreams. And he discovered elements of the human psyche that no one ever knew.

The spirit of scientific curiosity led Freud to penetrate a jungle with no trace of a trail. Even though Freud made amazing discoveries, he, himself, changed little:

Stomach problems troubled him, which disappeared only when he began to suffer from a physical disease: terminal cancer of the jaw. Thus his stomach ailments were clearly *psychogenic*.

Freud could not change himself because he did not have the benefit of *transference* to his own therapist. So— what is transference and how did it begin?

In the early 1880s, Freud worked with a senior partner, Dr. Joseph Breuer. Dr. Breuer had a patient who was later given the pseudonym, "Anna O." In the course of therapy, "Anna O." fell in love with the doctor. Dr. Breuer regarded this state of affairs as messy and unethical, so he referred her to Freud. And Freud found that "Anna O." fell in love with him, too.

Such repetitious behavior, Freud realized, deserved investigation rather than repudiation. In trying to understand "Anna O.'s" feelings, Freud discovered *transference,* the greatest instrument for effecting fundamental change in human behavior that ever existed.

As Freud and his disciples found out later, transference is not a simple "falling-in-love" process. It is an incredibly complex state with many convolutions and permutations. To fathom something of its flavor, a present-day example of transference is presented—the story of Burt and Jean.

Before relating the saga of these individuals in a marriage, a few words of caution: Psychotherapy, to many, is a totally unknown wilderness. This is due, in part, to the secretiveness of Freud's disciples. At the time, they had sound reason to keep the mysteries of psychoanalysis locked in their professional journals.

When Freud first delivered a lecture on infantile sexuality to the general medical profession, he was greeted with hoots and howls, "Do you mean to say that innocent children have sexual urges? You have a dirty mind!" Freud didn't care if the whole world thought he was a dirty old man. He just went on doing his research.

But most of his disciples had thinner skins. They didn't want people to think psychotherapists were crazy or perverted. So they made a mystery of what went on during the fifty-minute hour behind the double doors.

There is much in the deepest recesses of our minds that we would prefer not to know. Unfortunately, material which is not easily accessible can cause us to act irrationally. Now let's examine the case of Burt and Jean. Perfectly reasonable people as these two can behave like veritable maniacs with each other. Friends and do-gooders, anxious to help, tried to apply reason or use common sense to quell combat. But rational thinking and good intentions for this nice couple was as effective as a flea in a flash-flood; reason could not prevail in the face of needs stemming from the dark of the psyche.

America, 1983 is not Victorian Vienna. The time has come to breach the wall of secrecy by the early psychotherapists. The story of Burt and Jean is told with nothing censored. Thoughts elicited by transference, that would strike the Archie Bunkers as perverse, will be fully exposed.

Burt and Jean, a married couple, were in therapy for over a year, each with his/her own therapists. Although Burt was progressing in this therapy, he informed his therapist that because the relationship between him and Jean was deteriorating, they reluctantly decided to give up their individual therapists and see a marriage counsellor. Burt's therapist suggested that first they try a few joint sessions with him, because of his training and interest in couple therapy.

Jean and Burt arrived at the office under a great deal of tension. Jean had given up her female therapist. Much later in her individual therapy, she revealed strong reservations about seeing *any* male therapist. She feared manipulation by him. She had been indoctrinated with the women's liberation contention that male therapists "brain wash" their female clients or worse.

Burt also brought anxiety to this first joint session. In the course of explaining the problem, Burt began to raise his voice. As he proceeded, his anxiety turned to anger at Jean. Before long, he was in a state of absolute fury.

The therapist was puzzled at all this anger, since Jean didn't seem to be doing anything except looking at Burt submissively. When questioned, Burt repeated a long list of accusations which had a hollow ring.

"To be so angry," the therapist contended, "something must be taking place right now that's making you so infuriated." Burt didn't know what it was and kept insisting that it was recent events at home that so enraged him. But the therapist wasn't convinced. The anger was now.

Finally, the therapist noticed that during Burt's diatribe, Jean was sending the therapist covert glances. These looks had a soft, childish, flirtatious quality. When the therapist called attention to this behavior, Jean reacted like a child who was caught with its hand in the cookie jar. Burt was noticeably relieved.

"I guess you were quite anxious when you came here, Burt, because somehow you knew that Jean would try to flirt with me. You must have believed that no man could withstand Jean's seductiveness. And Jean, you too, have good reason to be nervous. It's not easy to see Burt's therapist who is likely to side with him. I imagine that when you feel threatened by a male, you resort to flirting automatically without even realizing that you're doing it."

Burt was greatly relieved, since his jealousy, which seemed to be the main problem between the two of them, now appeared to have a basis in reality. Jean realized that the therapist didn't condemn her for being provocative, since most of the time she wasn't aware of what she was doing.

In addition to joint sessions, both Burt and Jean were also seen individually. She couldn't help but repeat the seductive act with the therapist. Each time it was pointed out to her, she would become infuriated with herself because this was contrary to everything she believed in.

Jean had the conviction that women are people. They ought not resort to "feminine" wiles. Unfortunately, the way she actually behaved was diametrically opposed to her values.

By dint of our labeling seductive behavior often enough, her relationships with male superiors and her husband underwent a marked improvement: situations that previously had been fraught with difficulties seemed to disappear; she no longer had to take a subservient and seductive role with men. When something displeased her, she was able to assert her point of view, clearly and forcefully. No longer did she provoke Burt into fits of anger.

Unfortunately, there was one man with whom she was still unable to converse without hints and promises—

the therapist. Jean directed a flood of sexuality, dammed by a rising wall of guilt towards the therapist. Long silences during the sessions were a product of this dam, guilt holding back the rush of sexuality. A clearly established *transference* had taken place.

An obvious remedy is apparent. Jean could simply stop therapy. Yet Jean knew that if the therapist disappeared as a major figure in her life, others would soon take his place; and improvements in other areas of her life, would come to naught. Her pattern would repeat.

Now what did the therapist achieve? Suppose Jean's irrational feelings were, indeed, confined to the therapist alone? Was not the therapist playing with fire? Where does he get off amusing himself with people's deepest feelings? Why did he have to do this?

The therapist helped to foster Jean's transference so that her feelings to males could be interpreted to her in the here and now. Jean could talk all day long about her unhappy situation, what her impossible husband did yesterday, or the nasty trip the boss was laying on her—nothing would change. The therapist would nod his head and sympathize and Jean would continue to feel threatened by all male authority figures and continue to try to seduce her way out.

The immediacy of seeing one's behavior in the therapist's office at the very moment it happens, can exert a powerful force for change. By contrast, talking *about* events of yesterday or yesteryear has little effect. Moreover, the benevolent neutrality of the therapist who is genuinely fond of his client, violates the client's unreal perception of him as threatening. Jean was caught in a situation known to comic performers as the "double take:" "This is how it is. Yes, indeed . . . Hey, no! It's just the opposite!"

Such a corrective experience is not "playing around" with Jean's deepest feelings. A therapist does not encourage transference frivolously. He does it with full understanding of its grave responsibility. True, transference is a messy, perhaps "dirty" experience, but so is bringing up an infant. It entails changing dirty diapers.

As Jean's therapy continued, her guilt and sexual feelings towards the therapist changed to anger. She became enraged at his withholding sexual interest in her. She believed that he must regard her as a mere "patient," unworthy of any attention beyond the allotted time of the session.

This made her even more angry.

In an attempt to bring Jean face to face with reality, the therapist tried to correct a misconception. He does not regard her as unworthy. He does not despise her. He finds her a very attractive woman. If she were not his client he would very much have liked to date her.

Hearing that the therapist finds her attractive, Jean experienced a rapid reversal in feelings. Instead of the Great Authority, the therapist now became a "creep", a "nerd" who held no further interest for her.

Jean, like many American women (and the obverse for American men), had divided males into two distinct categories: The unattainable Captain of the High School Football Team, a Burt Reynolds or whomever currently

reigned in Hollywood, the Doctor, any man with Power—
versus obtainable others, the drips and the creeps, all totally lacking in sex appeal.

The moment Jean would meet a man for the first
time, she would automatically make this classification. The
Man with Power would tug at her heart. He must be
placated and seduced. All others were to be despised.

When the therapist told Jean that he found her attractive, she confided to him a rapid turnabout from worship and attraction, to complete negation of him as a man.
The therapist, in her eyes, immediately became the creep.
The therapist said softly, "I don't think I've changed that
much." By this quiet confidence, the therapist suddenly
metamorphosed back again to the "macho" figure.

From that moment on, Jean underwent rapid improvement in many areas of life. The uncanny alterations
in Jean's perception of the therapist wrought a profound
change. She began to see men realistically. And she saw
herself, too, as she actually was. Not only the world of men
opened up but every aspect of life seemed to change.
Without interpretation of transference, this could never
have happened.

To further her progress and increase areas of insight,
Jean joined group therapy. There, she encountered a
man whom she despised as the ultimate "creep". Setting
up the final criterion of her own success in therapy, Jean
decided that when she could regard this man as another
human being with flaws and virtues, that would be the day
she no longer needed therapy. Jean could hardly imagine
that this could ever happen.

Yet it did. To her great surprise, she became rather

fond of the man. And to her even greater surprise, the therapist changed in her eyes from being the repository of all goodness and power, to being just a man, like all other men: all worship and awe were gone. And the therapist knew that by "resolving the transference" her therapy was over. Whatever rungs on the ladder remained, she could climb by herself.

The course of Burt's therapy was less dramatic than Jean's. But transference, attitude to the therapist, was intense. Burt's problem centered around competition: He was strongly combatant with other men, yet ineffective; his earnings, by which our culture judges male effectiveness, were hardly above poverty level. What was going on in Burt's psyche to cause the malaise?

Possessing many of the abilities that make for monetary success, Burt was weighted down with underlying conflicts. These conflicts, which at first may sound *outré*, will be illustrated by comments on American life so that Burt's unconscious motives may not seem so peculiar to the reader. Indeed, Burt's conflicts, although more pronounced than usual, may serve as a prototype for many of the difficulties faced by American males today.

One difficulty faced by Burt and many American males is labeled by some therapists as "latent homosexuality"—the fear of repressed homosexual interests. The conventional psychological explanation for "latent homosexuality" points to the strong prohibition in our society against male homosexuality. Female homosexuality is either ignored or regarded as unimportant. Thus women are permitted to kiss or embrace one another, while men are not. Unless a man opts for out-and-out identification as a "gay", he must rigidly refuse to acknowledge any possible mild sexual feelings to another man.

At first glance this explanation for Burt's behavior sounds wildly implausible. However, it is correct as far as it goes, yet it glosses over a matter of genuine importance: It is not homosexuality *per se* which is so proscribed for men. It is *femininity and passivity* which is regarded with contempt and loathing, even though these are basically human characteristics but are apportioned to the female sex only, by our cultural consensus.

Using a method employed in the last chapter—the greater visibility of a boulder contrasted to a grain of sand—we shall take an extreme situation: The ultimate act of degradation in prisons, forced by the stronger male against the wishes of the weaker, is to compel him to submit his mouth or anus as a receptacle. The male who acts as a female in this sexual connection is regarded as less than human. A man who would actually enjoy such congress is unspeakable. No wonder passivity and "femininity" in men is so forbidden!

Thus even writers are looked upon with some doubts as to their masculinity. Witness the naiveté of such authors as Hemingway and Mailer who seem obliged to prove their masculinity constantly, no doubt to offset their passive needs. Methinks not only the lady, but the man, even of Hemingway's stature, doth protest himself too much. Nowadays, fortunately, most of us find excessive displays of masculinity suspect.

Yet rigid repression of male passive and receptive needs still causes difficulty for many men. And so, the "macho" pose: The victor.

84

With this rather extensive introduction to the touchy subject of male passive needs in our culture, Burt's transference is better understood. Although Burt was sitting on a volcano, the fiery lava underneath him differed only in degree, not in its nature, from most American males.

The therapist became Burt's primary need object. On one level he yearned for the therapist, much as a female might yearn for her lover. But on a level of greater awareness, he would hate the therapist. Added to all this, was his jealousy of the therapist caused by Jean's feelings for the therapist. Thus, interpretation of transference was the one means of resolving these conflicts.

Whence Burt's irrational jealousy? Outside of prisons, the ultimate degradation for a man is to permit another man to take "his" woman away from him. If another man puts his penis in the place reserved for the first man's penis, the latter is symbolically allowing his own body orifices to be used as a receptacle. The woman is a mere substitute for his own body openings.

Burt's barely controlled rage against an imagined opponent, believing some man was out to get "his" woman, becomes more understandable in the light of his passive needs. A part of him denied, even as some small part of him welcomed, the other man's penis in his own body or that of "his" woman, Jean. In this case, the "other man" was the therapist. Needing to go the other way, one can imagine the intensity of Burt's rage.

Burt's anger during the first joint session now becomes clearer: In the American culture, the size of a man's penis is often measured by the amount of money he makes and by the position he holds. The therapist was seen by Burt as wealthier and holding a position of greater authority than he—hence, more powerful. As a result, Burt was trapped between his jealousy of the therapist versus his affection and passive need for the therapist. These opposing needs were centered about Jean as the go-between. Hence his misunderstood rage was first vented on her.

Even with our illustrations from the current American scene, the reader may still find this material bizarre. Perhaps the therapist is gifted with an all-too-fertile imagination. However, we must keep in mind that space does not permit a full account of every therapy session. Burt's underlying impulses, revealed in therapy, were sketched only briefly. Supporting matter from Burt's day-to-day life was necessarily left out.

Just as proof of the pudding lies in the tasting thereof, so these notions about Burt's make-up were validated by the rapid rise in his income. Burt did not choose poverty. Yet his intense need to compete with men all his life in a totally ineffective fashion, were resolved when his irrational feelings to the therapist, his *transference*, was clarified. The understanding of Burt's transference involved a calculated risk of bodily harm to the therapist.

Taking such a risk, however, was vindicated by a remarkable change. Burt, who so feared physical contact, was able, finally, to clasp the therapist's shoulder and to permit the therapist to do the same to him. He no longer needed to compete irrationally with the therapist or other men, nor did he fear competition.

The *resolution* of his sexual transference to the therapist and thus his inner conflicts about his own sexual identification—masculinity versus feminity, became clear in his work and leisure: He took over a failing plumbing business and began to prosper as a plumbing contractor. Yet he retained his interests in poetry and ballet. He was a complete man with few hangups about his masculinity. As a result, his relationship with Jean greatly improved.

However, questions about Jean and Burt's attitude to the therapist still remain: Why did Jean feel such intense guilt about her sexual feelings to the therapist when nothing actually happened? We can understand this irrational guilt only in the light of her wish to violate a universal taboo—it could not have been the therapist she wanted. Why was Burt so afraid of any physical contact with the therapist, but not with other men?

Jean and Burt transferred feelings: Old feelings and modes of behavior once felt towards their parents; now transferred to the therapist. Without transference, and without understanding its nature, these feelings could not be altered.

In the last chapter, the point was made that even apes need the company of parents or peers to function fully. So humans need adult care and attention to become "human". Of course we must have the biological equipment to become human. But without adult care, we would be more animal than human. Cases have been studied of children who managed to survive when their parents abandoned them in the woods shortly after birth. These children, although biologically human, acted more like animals than human beings.

"Socialization" is the name behavioral scientists give to the process of bringing up infants to become human. Deficiencies in socialization show up as problems later in life. It follows logically, then, that such defects may be corrected the same way the flaws were originally formed—by a relationship with another human being.

However, if a relationship with another human is all that's needed to correct defects, people would be greatly improved simply by getting married. And some people are improved that way.

Unfortunately we often pick a mate whose flaws fit into our own problems as neatly as two parts of a jigsaw puzzle. Even friends and people at work are often chosen that way. Martyrs, who need to suffer, will pick sadistic mates and associates to feed their addiction to suffering. If the associate doesn't respond the way the martyr expects, the martyr will then provoke him into sadistic behavior, to assuage his need.

"Creeps" force people to regard them as they see themselves—as creeps. Thus relationships contracted during the ordinary course of one's life, tend to feed into one's defects, rather than correcting them.

But with a therapist, who is trained not to respond to a client's quirks, the relationship can be helpful. However, even seeing a therapist five times a week, will take forever to cause change if only a relationship exists. Another instrument is needed.

Fortunately, psychotherapists are able to use another human trait as a powerful instrument for change: We tend to relate to people who are close to us or who hold power over us, in many of the same ways we once related to our parents.

A child may learn that when mother says, "No", he can turn to father. Father can always be swayed by whining and tears. The child, now an adult, manipulates supervisors at work the same way he beguiled his family. Conversely, the child who was shamed by his parents into proper performance at school, now becomes the conscientious over-performer at work. Merely by raising his eyebrow, the boss can evoke shame in him.

The closer people are to us or the more authority they wield, the more we distort our perception of them: We try to force them to fit the mold of our parents. In the ordinary course of life, these distortions make for problems, which are rarely resolved.

In psychotherapy, these *transference* distortions, these misperceptions of the therapist, are pointed out to the client, enabling a corrective process to take place, as in the case of Burt and Jean. Thus transference is the greatest tool for correcting a person's upbringing, yet to be discovered.

In the course of Jean's and Burt's therapy, the therapist "fostered" their transference. This was accomplished by keeping himself unknown.

An unknown situation, one that is unclear or ambiguous, permits us to read into it more of our own needs than a sharply defined situation. If, for example, we fear the dark, it is because we can't see what's there, so our fears take over. Taking it one more step, the vague, ill-defined ink-blots, used by psychologists, permit us to perceive the shapes as our wishes dictate. And the forthcoming job interview with an unknown boss makes us fearful, because we never met him and don't know what he is like. He can be made into an ogre if that's what our unconscious suggests. The therapist is trained like the dark, the ink-blot, or the unknown boss, to be ambiguous. Thus the client will project his needs on the therapist.

An expert therapist remains relatively unknown by not sharing with the client his own hopes or fears, or any details of his day-to-day life. This is how the therapist fosters transference. True, many people find it difficult to tolerate a silent therapist. The task of the therapist is to evaluate how much of himself to reveal and how much to withhold with each client.

When a client can take a great deal of frustration, the therapist is able to remain blank in the interest of promoting transference. For a client whose tolerance of frustration is low, who tends to need much from the therapist, the therapist must reveal more of himself, lest the client's fears take over to the point where little can be understood or accomplished. Thus by varying the amount of self-revelation, the therapist has a means of pressing the accelerator or stepping on the brakes.

Serving as the object of the client's hopes, fears, needs, and rage, is difficult, but not impossible. Some people find it difficult to believe that male therapists are not easily seduced by attractive female clients. Seduction occurs far less frequently than many would like to believe. The therapist is aware that his female client does not really know him. She sees an ink-blot, not a person. Her admiration is thus placed in proper perspective.

During the first few sessions, some female clients will try to seduce their therapist. If he is alert, the therapist will realize that the woman is saying, in effect, "All this therapy stuff is nonsense. I'm going to show you that I am a woman and you are a man. I've always managed to get what I want and I'm going to get you, too."

Awareness of the woman's hostile and infantile approach—I want, therefore I take—is usually enough to act like a bucket of cold water. Seeing people as objects, toys to be grabbed, this woman beguiled her parents successfully. And, no doubt, bulldozed her way by artifice through the rest of her life. But the buck must stop here. That is why she is in therapy.

Very different is the woman who, after many sessions, indicates she would like the therapist to be her lover. It is readily apparent that she wants the therapist to be her parent, not her lover. This insight, too, is usually sufficient to discourage the therapist from a romantic adventure.

Contrary to the opinion of many, sexual or romantic temptations for most therapists, are not the primary difficulty in serving as a parent substitute. The most difficult task for the therapist is—being the object of the client's anger. It is unpleasant to be shouted at, to be despised, or to be called dreadful names. But then, if the therapist couldn't stand blizzards, he never would have become an explorer. Realization that the client is not raging at him, but at a parent substitute, keeps the therapist on the path of psychotherapy.

Most therapists are aware of the importance of serving as objects for the clients' anger. They do not mind being subjected to really nasty epithets: Pure expletive can be useful. Language such as "asshole" indicates the client is exposing deep and early childhood rage, possibly associated with toilet training. The therapist seizes on profanity to help the client obtain insight.

But the more subtle, focussed criticism is sometimes

difficult to bear. Being called "a bungling fool" or "you don't know what you're doing," are accusations that can play on a therapist's fears. Fear that he is not doing the job.

Yet the therapist need not be daunted even by these remarks. He or she must remember that deep in the throes of transference, the client has little means of judging the therapist's performance. The therapist may, indeed, be a bungling fool or he may be a genius, or neither; the client is too involved in his own problems to make a reasoned judgment. So instead of taking the criticism at face value, the therapist puts name-calling to good use.

The male therapist may now have a clearer notion about the position of the father in the client's family. He might ask himself these pertinent questions: Was the father, indeed, a bungling fool? Did it make the client unhappy? Does the client therefore demand that the therapist be superman lest he seem foolish and weak like the client's father? Is that why the client is so furious because he caught the therapist in a minor error?

On the other hand, a client absorbed in name-calling need not be altogether helpless. It is still possible to assess the therapist. One way a client has of judging the therapist's performance, is by the therapist's ability to absorb abuse. If the therapist is not intimidated or drawn into reacting to the client's anger, the therapist is doing an essential part of his job.

By contrast, any self-proclaimed therapist-Savior will never permit attacks or abuse from his followers. He cannot tolerate any expression of mild annoyance. One does not get angry at a god; nor even at his prophet. It would be blasphemy.

Difficult as transference may be for the therapist, it is even more difficult for the client. The client is asked to express his deepest feelings whether they be need, affection, or rage. But at some point, the therapist will bring the client up short, saying, "Okay, enough. Now let's pause a moment and take a look at what you've been saying."

The client is being asked to examine the product of his own fury. Even more, the client is asked to shed his anger and side with the very same person at whom he was just raging—the therapist. As rewarding as it may ultimately be, it is not an easy task for the client.

His task is called, a "working alliance." No matter how abusive the client may become, he is still expected at some point, to use his reason and intelligence to inspect what he just spewed forth.

The client, at times, may be so vituperative that the therapist may doubt if he still has a "working alliance." Is the client aware in some part of himself, that he is still in therapy? Or is he conducting a personal vendetta against the therapist?

The therapist is assured if the client, for instance, shakes his finger in the therapist's face and shouts, "What's the matter, can't you take it?" No matter how angry this client is, he still alludes to one function of a therapist—to serve as an object for rage without reacting.

There are very few exceptions when the client insists session after session that his anger at the therapist is "real" and therefore must *not* be examined. Or that the client's wish to go to bed with the therapist is "real" and therefore must be acted upon and not understood.

In such cases, the therapist, in spite of his best efforts, realizes that the intensity of the client's transference to him precludes understanding. He no longer has a working alliance with the client. And the client must be referred to another therapist perhaps of a different sex or one who differs in some way from the present therapist.

Two questions are posed. First—what is the value of releasing such feelings?

Over the course of years, ideas, not feelings, are often beclouded and disguised. The client's verbal account of his childhood has value; but we don't know what the child believed at the time or what he thought was going on years ago in his family. By contrast, feelings are rarely disguised. They linger on in much the same form they took during childhood. Thus, using the client's feelings, we can return to the scene of the accident and apply a corrective experience.

The second question: Is not the release of feelings sufficient by itself to make a person feel better?

In his early investigations, Freud concluded that release of strong emotions, in itself, had a beneficial effect. He called such release, catharsis. In those days, since medicine had so few tools at its disposal, emphasis was placed on the few available means. Two of the most popular treatments were emetics and enemas which caused catharsis. If the patient got rid of the "poisons" within, he would be cured. The same process was carried over into psychotherapy by way of analogy. If you get rid of poisonous feelings, you'll feel better.

Later, Freud found that analogies belong to rhetoric, not to science. Catharsis did no good at all. The value of releasing feelings lies in understanding them not merely in vomiting—spitting them out.

This was Freud's conclusion over half a century ago. Today's in-vogue catharsis is called, "Primal Scream." This "new" therapy differs little from the catharsis of Freud as the release is only temporary. Since the leaders of the Primal Scream movement have ignored the history of psychoanalysis, they and their clients are doomed to repeat it.

The desired permanent relief, remarkable and miraculous, occurs only when a client recognizes early feelings as purely transference, unconnected with reality. Such relief must be experienced, and even then, it's hard to believe.

Occasionally an odd condition can occur where transference does not seem to exist: A female client in her twenties led a confused and unhappy life. She was, at the time, married to an older man who dominated and pulled at her, dictated her every move, and seemed to suck the very marrow out of her bones. Previously, in her early teens, she had been pregnant and was abandoned by the man responsible. Since abortions at that time were illegal and dangerous, she bore the child and then gave it away.

Besides this, there were many other unhappy incidents in her past life. But perhaps the most traumatic concerned another older man—her stepfather who initiated her in sexual activity for four years. When she was thirteen, feeling so guilty for her own role in this activity, she told her mother. The stepfather was put in jail, but not until the client had undergone a lot of terrible court scenes. It is likely that her guilt was augmented by the legal procedures, since our society often maintains the fiction that children are "innocent" and do not have sexual feelings. It was her stepfather alone who was supposed to be guilty.

The young woman regarded the therapist as a kindly, fatherly type of person to whom she could talk freely. Transference was not evident, until one day when she walked into the office, white-faced and shaken. When finally she was able to speak she said, "Just as I came into the waiting room I suddenly felt the most horrible feeling like I wanted to vomit. But it wasn't so much physical; it was more of a feeling."

The therapist told her that this was a feeling of intense guilt. "You told me of your stepfather's activity and the pleasure it afforded you. I think you have forgotten these guilt feelings, which must have occurred after the experience."

She replied, "Yes, and I had that same feeling toward you. I guess I must have wanted you to do that to me."

Transference was so intense, that it had to be delayed until sufficient trust in the therapist was established. Yet when it finally made an appearance, the effects were profound. The client's entire life changed for the better. She separated from the man who dominated her so strongly, remarried most happily, and had a wanted baby. She wrote briefly two or three times telling the therapist how different life was for her, and how much satisfaction and happiness she was feeling.

Transference can be a very powerful instrument for change. A radical and permanent removal of difficulties, inner difficulties, reflected in behavior towards the outside world, can be effected by insight into transference and the manner in which it works.

A client once put it another way: "I am about to embark on a lengthy and difficult journey. There is no direct route. I see you as a series of buses. I transfer from one to the other in an attempt to reach my destination. But once there, I disembark alone."

Resistance

Arriving at the stage in therapy where transference is recognized by the client, can be a slow and sometimes painful experience. Since undergoing transference is unpleasant, it is often preceded by the client's attempt to escape or block out such understanding by impeding the process of therapy. This is called, "resistance." Not all resistance is caused by transference feelings, but much of it is.

The young woman who was the victim of her stepfather's attentions did not transfer to the therapist until she had been in therapy for many months. This delay, or resistance, was caused by her intuition that living through the old guilt once again with the therapist, would be most unpleasant.

She was not unique. Many of us have at least a few unpleasant memories. If we have none, it is likely that we prefer not to know about them. We may even be aware of those early events, but the memory is drained of unpleasant emotion.

With the best intentions in the world—trying to speed up therapy—we shy away from enduring such passions ever again. Often, no specific memories are ever recovered as in the case of Burt and Jean. It does not matter. Jean's and Burt's explosive feelings were brought to the fore. And it is these feelings that the client resists by impeding his or her therapy.

Resistance is another very good reason why you can't be your own therapist. Like transference, resistance is unknown to the client. And so the client needs someone outside of himself to point out his resistance.

Walled off by resistance, the most intelligent and clear-headed person can rationalize in a way that the disinterested observer may find both amusing and irrelevant. The resisting client discovers very good reasons why he couldn't come to the therapy session on time: "After all, I don't own a helicopter, so I couldn't fly up in the air over the traffic!"

"But you could have allotted more time."

"I did. I even started out early."

"But you knew that traffic would be especially heavy."

"Sure, and that's why I allowed myself more time. But how was I to know that this truck would turn over?"

It is a waste of time to tackle with rational arguments a person who has such a strong need to reduce her therapy hour. The client who resists therapy will swear by all that's holy that he was compelled to be late by outside circumstances beyond his control.

Aside from lateness, there are many ways of resisting therapy: Talking about details of day-to-day life that carry no real significance; responding to the therapist's interpretations with an automatic "no"; silence, followed by, "No one can talk for 45 minutes straight;" developing a psychogenic ailment like a stomachache two hours before the session, forcing the client to stay home; and finally, quitting therapy altogether—ending therapy under the guise of claiming to have made no progress at all, or because so much progress has been made that the "cure" is complete.

Often, perfectly legitimate needs can be used in the service of resistance. The wish to know about psychotherapy is an example of such a need. Psychotherapy differs radically from other relationships so that people are frequently puzzled by what the therapist is doing. They are curious why he's not giving advice, why he's repeating what they're saying. They want to know how this will help them. They justly believe that consumers of psychotherapy have a right to know what they are buying.

But sometimes the need for an explanation of psychotherapy can take place at a crucial juncture in therapy. Just as the therapist is about to tie up all the loose ends so the client may gain a full appreciation of vital material, the client may pull the emergency "off" switch by demanding to know how psychotherapy works.

Thus a perfectly legitimate need for information can be used to resist the process of psychotherapy. Should the therapist ignore the client's request, the client may rightly feel that the therapist is arbitrary and authoritarian. Should the therapist interpret the request as resistance, the client may strongly disagree. He believes that his request is reasonable and not at all motivated by resistance. Should the therapist say, "Not just now . . . later . . . ," the client may feel this to be a parental strategem. His transference carries him back to the time when he was told, "Can't you see I'm busy? When you get old enough to know . . ."

Psychotherapy then comes to a dead halt. The therapist knows the client is resisting and the client knows the therapist is ignoring a legitimate request.

How can we break up this log jam? The impasse could be breached if a book were available giving the client the information he needs. Thus a person's right to know what he's buying can be satisfied and therapy can proceed unhindered.

The need for such a book to resolve this problem was one of the reasons for the publication of THIS IS PSYCHOTHERAPY. Therapists can now tell their clients, "Your interest in how psychotherapy works is legitimate. But because both your time and mine are valuable, you can get the information you need by reading THIS IS PSYCHOTHERAPY. Now let's go back to the thought you just raised about getting a divorce."

Resistance may set in even before therapy begins. Some people may spend many months considering various therapists: They find Dr. X too expensive. They disliked Miss Y at first sight. Mr. Z is too young so he must be inexperienced. They finally abandon their search for a therapist and cop out, because they just couldn't find the right one.

Others, fearful of stirring up dark forces beyond their control, just never enter therapy. Whatever their excuse, it is called, resistance.

There is another way to resist therapy before it ever begins. It is exemplified by a friend who, in preparation for becoming a psychotherapist herself, studied the functioning of therapy, psychotherapists, and mental health clinics. She thus knew the field well. She managed invariably to select a therapist for herself whom she intuitively realized, would not do anything except provide support. She instinctively shied away from a therapist who might insist that transference be worked through.

Human beings differ; no two people will resist in the same fashion. So a textbook exposition has limitations. Instead, a presentation of resistance in story form can convey more of its sense and essence:

> *The door to the waiting room flew open just as the therapist began to wonder if she was going to show up at all. As she struggled out of wraps and scarf and galoshes, the therapist closed the office door and sat down, prepared to listen.*
>
> *"It was just impossible. The traffic, I mean. They closed off the South Side highway and I had to go through the local mess. And then at the last minute, Wendy put up such a howl . . . You can see I didn't mean to be late. I know half the session is gone and I almost decided it wasn't worth coming. I mean, I really am sorry to be late. I hate to be late going places and I certainly didn't plan on being this late, although I knew I was going to be late."*

The therapist nodded in acknowledgment. There was no need for apologies since the client could make whatever use she wished of her allotted time. The therapist, unlike a friend, could not be diminished nor injured by her lateness. Neither would the therapist display appreciation for her struggle to see him in the face of great difficulty. It was her choice to arrive or not to arrive.

That she was distraught was evident, so the therapist simply asked her, "How did the vacation go?"

"Oh, it was all right. Candy got totally out of hand one time when we were walking on the beach. She threw sand at her sister and wouldn't stop when I told her to. Wendy kept calling her names and the two of them were disgusting. I'm afraid I went to pieces. I got really hysterical with the two of them."

"I'm sorry to hear that," the therapist sympathized. Yet he knew the children were acting up as a result of a more fundamental problem: "What's been happening with your husband?"

"Well, we haven't had sex in a month. I'm beginning to wonder if he cares at all. We got into an awful row on the last day. It started when he criticized Wendy's table manners and I told him there is no reason to pick on her. And Candy simply throws food all over and I don't think she should sit at the table with adults until she learns to behave herself."

The therapist noticed that the focus shifted away from the conflict between the two adults and resumed its usual pattern of discussing the children's misbehavior, a safer topic. "You mentioned you haven't had sex in a month," he said.

"It just didn't happen. But you don't seem to understand; now that Wendy is in pre-adolescence, she's beginning to get completely out of hand."

The therapist realized he'd have little chance of getting through on the subject of husband-wife conflict so he decided to shift to the client's own feelings: "When you felt you lost control on the beach and got into hysterics . . ."

"No, Wendy got out of control. I just can't seem to make an impression on her."

It was obvious that even the client's overt feelings were not amenable to examination at this point. The therapist had little choice but to permit the client to talk about her children: a distraction from her own problems.

"So Wendy is really giving you a hard time."

"No. No. You don't understand. It's not Wendy. She can be very good at times. It's Candy. She's totally impossible."

The therapist began to realize that she would not agree with anything he said. He decided to test out this notion. She had just said that Candy was worse than Wendy. So the therapist stated, "Candy seems to be more of a problem than Wendy."

She shook her head impatiently. "No. Candy can be reasoned with most times. But like I told you before, Wendy is entering a difficult period and she's the one with the real problem."

"I imagine each of them presents their own special problem."

"No, no. It was the beach. When they start in on each other, it's always at the beach."

"Yes, the beach does present difficulties. Unfortunately, we'll have to stop now."

As she began to gather galoshes and scarf and handbag, she mentioned casually, "Oh, I won't be coming back anymore. I think I'll just have to solve my problems by myself."

The therapist was not surprised. Yet he decided to give it

one more try, "This is an important decision. I don't think it should be dismissed so briefly. I think we should have one more session to discuss it."

He really did not want her to leave when she was so unhappy. By showing his feelings he conveyed concern, even though his overt message confined itself to the objective decision whether or not she should continue in therapy.

The reader may doubt that anyone could be so contrary. Yet it happens to be a composite of many different sessions with different clients, when resistance reaches its peak.

Can any intelligent person be so obtuse as this client? Was she aware of saying "no" to her own words? The therapist, avoiding interpretation, could only summarize and rephrase. But when a client is moved by powerful forces to resist the process of therapy, he or she can be totally unaware of the compulsion to declare the sky is green when the therapist suggests it is blue.

This "client," composed of many individuals, all intelligent and competent in their own fields, was facing a difficult dilemma. Is she an adult, capable of standing on her own feet? Is she nurturing her family while helping to support it financially? Or is she a child so dependent on the therapist that she can't go away on a vacation without missing him and secretly blaming him for not being there with her?

She is both. She is both adult and child. The relationship with the therapist permitted archaic feelings of need plus the fear of being left all alone to come forth. Her adult self cannot allow such unacceptable feelings to emerge and so she must run hard and run fast from the therapist—the object of such babyish needs.

Lest this explanation for the client's behavior appear too fanciful, a story from American folklore may be more fitting:

A salesman with a flat tire found himself on a little traveled road. Lifting the lid of the trunk, he saw to his chagrin that the car jack was missing. He had no choice but to hike to the nearest farmhouse a mile back.

On his way, he began musing, "I'm going to interrupt the farmer at his work and he'll be peeved because it's the haying season. I'll ask him for a jack and he's going to ask me what I need it for. After I explain, he's going to question why I didn't check the car tools before I started out. I'll have to say that I had no reason to suspect that anyone would have taken the jack. Then he's going to shrug his shoulders, tell me he's busy, and I'll have to wait. By then it will be nightfall. I'll never make my appointment, my sales figures will drop and . . ."

By the time the salesman reached the farmhouse and knocked on the door, he had worked himself into a fury. The farmer's wife opened the door and before she could say a word, he shouted, "Keep your godamned jack! Who the hell needs it anyhow?"

Pressed by the insistent need of help and nurturance throughout her adult life, knowing that others are too busy to respond to babyish needs, believing that an adult should not have such unworthy motives, the client was sure that the therapist would not offer her the indispensable car jack.

The client is angry at being refused, even though neither she nor the therapist ever mentioned the jack. The therapist is then confronted by the client's insistence, "The hell with your jack. I don't need it. Even if you had the last jack on earth, I'd never ask you for it. So keep your jack and your words of wisdom and your interpretations. I'd rather walk back to my car and sit and wait. Even if another car never comes."

The therapist responded to her unasked demand at the end of the session by saying, "I really do think we should have one more session."

He meant, "I do understand that you had a miserable vacation. I further understand you needed me then and when I wasn't there for you, you became furious. I understand that things at home are worse than ever. I am sorry that you don't want my jack but I will offer it to you anyhow, since I know you would find it hard to proceed without it."

What happens finally? Does the client accept the jack? Does she return for another session?

Since this client was only a composite, the following answer is hardly satisfying: Some do, some don't. But those who do return for another session, in spite of resistance in acknowledging dependency needs, these clients stand a good chance of a breakthrough in their therapy. They are the clients who possess enough willpower to try to resolve childhood needs. And it is they who emerge more truly adult.

Acting Out As Resistance

There are times when psychotherapy, far from helping people, seems to worsen their problems. The woman in psychotherapy, who once existed only for her children, now won't speak to them. The affable colleague at the office suddenly keeps his door closed and refuses to engage in a friendly chat. Some people in therapy seem to change their entire behavior—for the worse.

Friends of the client then become divided into two camps: The pro- and the anti-psychotherapy partisans. The "pro's," helped by psychotherapy themselves, decide that John has an incompetent therapist. It's just a matter of persuading him to get a new one—theirs. Or some may be more passive and say, "Well, you know how the old saying goes: You have to get worse before you get *worse.*"

The "anti's," suspicious of psycho-anything, point their finger and say, "I told you so. There was nothing wrong with John to begin with. Shrinks are all crazy anyhow, and it just rubbed off on John."

But there is a reason for John's behavior. His annoying antics may be caused by a resistance called, "acting out": Unconsciously wishing to be treated in a certain manner by the therapist, the client will provoke those closest to him. They, in turn, will behave toward the client in the way he would like his therapist to treat him.

John, the affable colleague, closets himself in his office because then everyone will come knocking on his door and say, "John! What's the matter? Aren't you feeling well? Is anything wrong?" John really wants his therapist to show such concern.

Using another way of acting out more directly, the client behaves towards those closest to him in the same way he would like to behave to his therapist. People outside the therapist's office, in real life, provide more reasonable targets for the client, since the therapist will not respond to provocation. The client thus "acts" his transference "out" or outside the office, rather than voicing his wishes directly to the therapist.

Allied to "acting out" is the client who throws an ashtray at the therapist's desk. Some therapists call this behavior "acting in," that is, inside the office. The principle is the same. The client engages in an action rather than putting his feeling into words.

Acting out is one form of resistance. Shameful or unworthy attitudes towards the therapist are expressed by behavior outside of the office. This is a camouflage against putting them into words in the therapist's presence. Thus awareness of transference is avoided by acting out.

You may note that the term, acting out, is narrowly defined. People who use "psychology" jargon often employ this term incorrectly. Any kind of behavior, by anyone at all which they consider obnoxious, is labeled "acting out." Teachers and parents employ the term, acting out, to describe a child's misbehavior.

In correct usage, a misbehaving child "acts up," not "out." Properly used—"Johnny *acts up* whenever we have guests." Acting out correctly used: "As an attractive therapist, Janet must have a lot of trouble with male clients *acting out*. The clients probably turn to promiscuity outside of the office."

The distinction between "acting up" and "acting out" can also be utilized as a sensitive detector for ferreting out the well-trained therapist versus the ill-trained. The well-trained therapist will rarely use the term, acting out, incorrectly.

Unrecognized acting out can be the rock upon which many a course of therapy will crash. It is the kind of resistance clients are most loath to acknowledge. Furthermore, it can cause much grief for the people close to the client as well as for the client, himself. It is to be understood and thus avoided.

Considering therapy or in therapy, you are better equipped if you are forewarned of the peril of acting out. Aware that the problem may occur, you are in a better position to understand the therapist's interpretation should he or she consider you to be acting out. Thus your therapy may proceed unhindered.

The Defenses

When a client comes twenty minutes late for his session, chances are resistance is in operation. But exactly how did the lateness happen?

"I just don't understand it," he shakes his head in bewilderment. "I've been seeing you for three months and I completely forgot about our session today till I looked at my watch and suddenly remembered the appointment. When I got here I was sure your office was on North Tenth Street. But of course it's on North Ninth. I'm usually a pretty well organized person . . . I just don't understand myself."

Harry Stack Sullivan, noted psychiatrist and founder of the "Interpersonal" school of psychotherapy, suggested that we not only have a memory, we have a "forgettery" as well. Our forgettery operates when need conflicts with reason—as in avoiding the therapist when he or she becomes too threatening a figure.

Sullivan's apt term, *forgettery,* is a different way of expressing Sigmund Freud's original notion of *repression.* Freud implied that people don't just forget an idea and lose it entirely: they stuff it down somewhere unreachable. In the example of the tardy client, when the need to see the therapist overcame the fear of seeing him, the client suddenly looked at his watch and remembered the appointment. The hypothesis, repression, suggests more properly, that he *recovered* the repressed memory from its hiding place.

Repression is used not only in the service of resistance: It is a common phenomenon used to eliminate any unpleasant material; all people at some time employ repression. The notion of repression suggests that at the outset, everyone of us has a phenomenal memory. We never lose a single thought throughout our lives except by physical deterioration of the brain.

But if you know there is nothing physically wrong with your brain, how could you possibly forget the name of your best friend, Luther? It's right on the tip of your tongue, but you can't get it out. Later in the day, you are busy trying to balance your checkbook and your mind drifts off. You recall the last time you went to lunch with Luther, he kept you waiting for half an hour. When he showed up, he had a perfectly good excuse so you couldn't possibly get angry with him.

Now **LUTHER** is illuminated in bright neon red. How could you ever forget his name? Here is how: Your annoyance at him may have connected with old rage directed at an early figure. That figure deserted you, left you all alone; Luther and that figure became one. Instead of mere annoyance, your Unconscious wanted him out of the way completely. Since murderous thoughts in general, and towards Luther in particular, are not acceptable, you did the next best thing—you eliminated him by repressing his name.

Repression is only one of the five major defenses. They are listed in developmental stages—in the order they were originally formed: *denial, projection, repression, undoing* and *reaction formation,* and finally, *isolation.* The earliest, most primitive defense, *denial,* is formed in infancy. The latest, most sophisticated defense, *isolation,* is shaped at the age when children learn to speak with some fluency.

Denial is a method of looking at something without seeing it at all. Those given to superstition will gaze at 13 North Main Street and insist they are looking at number 15.

With his gift for the elegant turn of phrase, Harry Stack Sullivan suggested the term, *selective inattention.* Our unconscious carefully selects what we don't want to see and then tunes it out of awareness—we focus upon this unpleasant stimulus with the full weight of inattention. (Did you just read "attention" for "inattention"?)

A person suffering from headaches will remark, "I'm so glad I haven't had a headache for days." What triggered this statement? He began to feel a headache coming on and preferred to deny it rather than acknowledge it.

Or, "I have no idea whom this person in the dream represents. Certainly not my mother." The phrase, "certainly not," alerts us to the forthcoming use of *denial.*

Projection is a defense used by people who blame others for motives they find unacceptable in themselves. Preceding Freud, the Talmud enjoined: "Whatever is wrong with you, don't ascribe to your fellow man." Unfortunately this injunction doesn't work too well with the person who is prone to projection. He will exclaim, "Who? Me? It's the other fellow who is doing all the projecting. I honestly admit to my tiny peccadillos. It's the other fellow who refuses to admit his crimes."

Projection is most often used as a defense against overwhelming hostility. We may experience rage for a minute or even an hour. But when rage is constant and consuming, people can no longer bear it. It must find an outlet. The fury then becomes projected onto others.

When the underlying rage and the consequent need for projection increase, the person so afflicted may hear the radio telling him that "they" are out to destroy him. The FBI is monitoring his telephone. His wife is plotting with his enemies to poison him.

His rage is thus ascribed to others. Since "they" are out to eliminate him, he must be clever and shrewd enough to foil their plot and bring their scheme to naught. Projection is the prime defense of the paranoid.

In common misuse, the term, paranoid, implies fearfulness: "I get paranoid about walking down the street at night."

But the correct understanding of the paranoid suggests total lack of fear: The paranoid person is so enraged, he has no room for fear. The people endowed with his projected rage can never harm him. Because the paranoid is so furious, he is protected by his greater cleverness and thus knows how to frustrate their schemes. So he need not fear his enemies.

However, projection as a defense is not confined to

the paranoid or to other candidates for a mental hospital. Most of us have made use of projection at one time or another. A friend whose major flaw was stinginess once complained, "If Bob really cared about me as he claims he does, he would have given me the five bucks instead of making a point of lending it to me. He's so stingy!"

In criticizing others, we zero in on just those flaws we, ourselves, possess. Mark and Luke in the New Testament, with great insight, warned people to examine first the beam in one's own eye before pointing to the mote in the other fellow's.

Undoing and *reaction formation* are twin defenses, both aspects of the need to do or feel the very opposite of an unworthy impulse. *Undoing* denotes action while *reaction formation* denotes attitude.

Sally must check and recheck the gas jets a dozen times before leaving the house to make sure they're off. A block away from her house, Sally wonders if the last time she checked the stove she may not have turned the gas on instead of off. So she returns to make absolutely sure it's off.

Why on earth must Sally keep checking the gas? She must *undo* her unconscious impulse to destroy her house, a symbol and reality of her marriage to Paul. Each time this destructive wish is on the brink of popping up, she undoes it by checking the gas. The angrier she becomes towards Paul, the more often she must check the gas to save him and the house from her wrath.

Undoing is the classic defense of the "compulsive personality." The term, compulsive, in common use often is a label for any annoying behavior. But correctly used, the behavior must be a way of *undoing* unwanted impulses like

113

"compulsive" ashtray dumping by a guest. Somewhere, somehow your guest wants to dump on you or your house. So she cleans instead of dirties.

Reaction formation, too, consists of countering an unacceptable wish by proceeding north when the impulse directs one south. But reaction formation refers to an attitude rather than an action.

The traditional American male's attitude to homosexuality is a prime example: "If any queer came near me, I'd beat him up so bad he'd never try it again." If the man were truly indifferent to homosexuality, he'd shrug his shoulders and say, "Different strokes for different folks."

The saintly liberal with the uncritical knee-jerk response to every humanitarian cause is another example of reaction formation. He marches at the head of every demonstration for civil rights. He stridently espouses equality of the sexes. He is first to decry the fate of starving refugees.

But the underlying attitude shows its face in his behavior at home. His wife will tell you that his brave attempts at the kitchen in the name of equality between the sexes, only result in more work for her. She is the one who knows that he is really not such a saintly person. In fact, she may inform you that under his kindly exterior he can get quite sadistic.

Isolation is the final and most sophisticated defense. It originates with the child who cannot understand why his good and loving mother gets angry with him at times. So he invents the tale of the wicked witch and the fairy godmother. Thus the angry mother and the loving mother become two different people isolated from each other.

The literal-minded and "scientific" personality, devoid of warmth and feeling, is an example of the defense of isolation. His coldness and aloofness in dealing with others are no proof that feelings do not exist. Instead, passion has been driven underground while the visible person stands isolated from human emotion.

The walls erected by the person whose prime defense is isolation are seen most vividly in Harry's case. He would appear in the waiting room at exactly four o'clock. Never early, never late. Harry enters, sits down and begins talking. He launches into a forty-five-minute paragraph unmarred by human kindliness or malice—a doctoral thesis of unrelenting facts down to the last penny and crumb. After the final word has been articulated and the therapist indicates time is up, he rises and invites the therapist to his wedding. The therapist did not know he was getting married.

Rising marks the session is at an end, that is, a wall has been raised signifying that now he need not speak "therapy." At this point his words do not "count" as part of the psychotherapy process and therefore should be ignored by the therapist as mere conventional pleasantry. Yet his post-session remarks are more significant than anything told in the formal session. The therapist now has an opportunity to point out a vital aspect of his functioning.

The description of the five major defenses would seem to imply that defenses are superfluous structures interfering with efficient behavior. Not so at all! Defenses are essential to human existence. If they were to be dissolved suddenly without proper preparation, the individual would find himself in a mental hospital. Often defenses even promote effective action.

Charley, a computer specialist, was able to summon the defense of isolation at will. One time he was driving along the highway at a reasonable speed of 50 m.p.h. when suddenly he felt that something drastic had happened.

The steering mechanism of the car fractured. A lower knee joint crumpled, the front wheel was on its side, and the body of the car slid on the concrete paving, issuing showers of sparks. Charley turned off the ignition and brought the car to a halt slowly and carefully. The police were called and arrangements were made to tow the car away.

Making these arrangements took over an hour. The policeman could not help but admire Charley, "I've never seen anyone so calm about an accident. I'd be shaking if it happened to me."

Charley replied, "Fact is, I don't feel anything at all and I'm just doing what has to be done. When I get home I'm going to buy a bottle and go to sleep because I know it's going to hit me then."

It was fortunate that Charley was able to isolate the experience and drain it of all feeling. Had he not, he might have jammed on the brakes and the car would have turned over.

But isn't the function of psychotherapy to remove defenses? And then what happens to the client when all defenses are penetrated and the person stands denuded of his barriers? Would he not be unable to cope?

The trained therapist is aware of a person's need for defenses. He makes a telling interpretation only when he is certain the client is ready to receive it and not before. Should the therapist err and try to remove a defense before the client is ready, the insight will be deflected and have no effect. The client gazes blankly at the therapist and says, "I don't think I understand you."

Fortunately for us all, defenses are remarkably effective barriers. Even irresponsible therapists who strive for "real feelings" and "reliving your childhood" are usually unable to achieve such dangerous ends. The "experiences" are often spurious and contrived. The barriers remain intact and do their work.

However, there have been rare cases when a poorly trained therapist has been able to strip away defenses prematurely. Such cases existed seventy years ago when Freud warned of the dangers of "wild analysis" conducted by untrained therapists. Deaf to Freud's warning, "est" therapists and others have stripped away needed defenses and have sent their victims to mental hospitals.

Yet it is reasonable to assume that such persons were so fragile to begin with, that their disintegration would have happened anyhow during the normal course of life. People are commonly subjected to turmoil and trauma since no one can be stuffed in styro-foam eternally.

There is a world of difference between the untrained therapist and the expert. The well-trained therapist is uniquely equipped to gauge the client's strengths and weaknesses. He or she will proceed with caution so that removing defenses, rather than harming the person, will be of benefit.

How do you get people to change? It's not easy. The theme of this book was suggested by H.L. Mencken, who was quoted at the beginning: "For every human problem there is a solution—neat, simple, and wrong."

Conventional solutions and the conventional wisdom, "self-help" books and therapist-Saviors are as ineffective as snake oil and magic charms. The long and complex way as distinct from Mencken's neat, simple solution, lies in expert therapy making use of our knowledge of transference, resistance, and the defenses.

CHAPTER

4

The Marketplace of Psychotherapy and Ideas About Human Nature

Few of us would care to admit we decided to buy a car purely because of its luxurious upholstery or the engaging manner of the salesman. Fewer still, would admit to buying a house merely gazing at its baroque shutters and the red and gold leaves dropping gently from the maple framing its entrance.

Unfortunately, caprice tends to rule some people. Only later do they discover the car has a reputation for spending more time in the repair shop than on the road. And the lovely facade of the sun speckled Colonial served to conceal a wet basement which can only be remedied by changing the entire topography of the land surrounding it. So the more rational consumer lifts the hood of the car and examines the basement of the house.

Buying psychotherapy is a decision of more consequence than buying a car or even a house—results of therapy may determine who is sitting next to you in the car or who is living with you in the house, or even whether you will own a car or a house at all.

Unfortunately, in buying psychotherapy even the more reasonable of us don't bother to lift the hood or examine the basement. Some choose a therapist because of his or her "empathy", meaning: the therapist sympathizes with the prospective client and offers a warm shoulder. Others, more tough minded, not admitting to the need for sympathy, will choose a therapist who inspires confidence and holds promise of presenting an ultimate solution. And still others, the more conformist or establishment minded, choose a therapist on the basis of his or her "credentials", signed and framed papers issued by the ordained authorities.

But is it not reasonable to choose a therapist because he seems to care about you or because the therapist appears to know what he's doing and can offer a firm solution? Certainly it makes sense to choose a therapist who is properly credentialed!

This author begs to differ. It does not make sense at all because you have not lifted the hood or examined the basement. Even properly papered therapists with many years of training have been known for their defective valves and wet basements. Their notions of human nature, their theories about what makes people tick may lack valves entirely or conceal a swimming pool, rather than a basement.

Psychotherapy, like any other effective discipline, is based on scientific principles, in this case theories of human nature—just as medicine is based on anatomy and physiology; and engineering is based on physics. Lifting the hood or examining the basement of psychotherapy leads us inevitably to an examination of principles of human behavior and to the exciting discoveries of the last eighty years in the field of psychology.

One of the most intriguing discoveries—but certainly not the only one—has been psychoanalysis. The more knowledgeable reader has probably noted that the first three chapters presented psychotherapy based on psycho-analysis, one valid theory of human nature. But again, not the only one. Why psychoanalysis?

Simply because psychoanalysis, as a theory of human nature, has stood the test of time and has been widely accepted as a useful theory in the practice of psycho-therapy. Thus, if you were to make an appointment with a typical, well qualified therapist or if you were to enter therapy through a reputable clinic, it is likely that your therapist would employ at least two or three ideas or theo-ries derived from psychoanalysis. Thus we have presented psychotherapy of the normative or main-line variety.

At one time, the main-line therapist was a psychia-trist, an M.D. But today therapists come to psychotherapy through different professions or disciplines. Therapists may be social workers, psychologists or psychiatrists. Psy-chotherapists also differ in age, sex, political orientation, and life-style.

Is all this confusing? It need not be. The first step in selecting a therapist and a school of therapy is lifting the hood, examining the basement. What are the underlying theories of human nature forming the basement of psy-chotherapy? What makes people behave as they do?

This chapter begins the exploration of available therapy and therapists with an attempt to make sense out of the different theories of psychotherapy and theories of human nature. In succeeding chapters various techniques applying the theories will be evaluated; the original discipline or profession of the therapist will be considered, be he social worker, psychologist, or psychiatrist; and other attributes of the therapist will be weighed.

But the present chapter serves to lift the hood and examine the engine. What are the basic theories of psychology and human nature?

Furthermore, this chapter will attempt to answer a question that may have occurred to some while reading the previous chapters: "Why did you use psychoanalysis to explain how psychotherapy works? Are there not other well-known therapies of the main-line varieties?"

Indeed there are. The most widespread therapies, those in most common use in clinics and private offices throughout the country are: psychoanalysis, behavior modification, and types of group therapy. But the theories underneath these therapies were selected for serious consideration here not only for their common acceptance, but for reasons we will discuss below.

Other theories are mentioned and then dismissed, some briefly, some irreverently. Is there justification for this approach? The reader must decide at the end of this chapter if a reasoned and reasonable approach has been made.

Let us consider the different schools of therapy. They glut the market like goods at an oriental bazaar, with each shopkeeper hawking his wares. How is it possible to make sense and order out of these endless competing stalls and booths, each flying its own sales banner emblazoned with claims and counter-claims?

Surveys have been made to judge these claims. However, an evaluation of the different schools of psychotherapy is too serious a matter to be left to an observer's personal whim and arbitrary preference. The layperson who may be looking for a suitable therapist—with the course of his life depending on such a choice—cannot rely on the bias, personal prejudice, or unrevealed criteria in the present surveys.

Summaries of the current psychotherapy scene imply notions like, "I just don't like the way the 'behavior mod' people operate, so I won't even call it therapy." Or, "Psychoanalysis is so full of gobble-de-gook that you are advised to stay away from it." Or, "Group therapy is only for clinics."

Even if you are not seeking therapy, but would like to have a clear understanding of the field, you have the right to know what the criteria are in any survey, upon which the observer is basing his evaluation. How objective are these criteria? Where did the surveyor derive them from?

A shopping list of the different therapies with the evaluator's personal opinion appended to each, simply will not do. The reader is entitled to clearly stated criteria, the derivation of the criteria, and their application to the different schools of therapy.

Let's start at the beginning with a description of psychotherapy few would dispute: *Psychotherapy is the practical application of a body of scientific principles concerning human behavior, to an individual case.*

A body of scientific principles refers to a theory of human nature. *Practical application* suggests the use of specified techniques. Thus two elements of psychotherapy emerge: *Theory and technique*.

Trying to evaluate the different therapies, trying to make sense out of them, is impossible unless we distinguish between theory and technique. This distinction is vital to a systematic understanding of the different therapies.

Often the terms used by innovators in psychotherapy and their followers serve only to compound the confusion between theory and technique. An excellent example is the word, psychoanalysis. It refers to two completely disparate events:

1. Psychoanalysis is a theory about human nature.

2. Psychoanalysis is a specialized technique of psychotherapy.

Although this distinction may be clear to experts, the use of a single term, psychoanalysis, meaning both theory and technique—two totally different modes—can be highly misleading to the layperson.

Now a foundation is laid for an inquiry on two different levels—theory and technique. These form a basis for two criteria:

1. Is this school of therapy based on a useful theory of human nature?

2. Does it have a technique adequate to fulfill its stated purpose?

Theory is the subject of this chapter; techniques will be weighed in the next.

"But why does one need a theory? Theories are fine for bartender-therapists, but I want my therapist to *know* what he's doing. I don't want him spinning theoretical yarns. I want help, not theory!"

Not so. It is the amateur psychologist with his foot on the bar rail, the fortune teller and astrologist who operate *sans* theory. They use common sense and platitudes that are broad enough to include everybody and are of use to no one, because they lack a cohesive theory of human nature.

A prospector for uranium can't get away without theory and science. He must have a clear idea about the origin of the earth and the formation of geological strata. Otherwise he'll have only a vague notion where to dig. He could starve and freeze on the tundra.

While the green countryside may be full of diviners with water sticks, they are not to be found in the frozen North. The icy wastelands will tolerate only geologists equipped with science. The water diviners know better than to risk the tundra. Unfortunately, psychotherapy presents a green and luscious field for practitioners without science or theory. Like the water prophets, they feed on people's lack of knowledge and their vulnerability. We need a therapist-geologist, not a therapist with a forked stick and a forked tongue.

Since science is required for both prospecting and psychotherapy, it might be well to clarify what science is about. **SCIENCE** conjures up test tubes, unearthly electronic sounds, blinking lights of red and green, and culminates in a violent explosion. No. That's not science. That's juvenile science fiction.

Aside from bad science fiction, there is another misconception: People believe science is a collection of facts and labels, like bird watching. The object is to see how many birds in the bushes are like those in the bird picture book. Bird watching with this aim in mind, is no more science than space opera replete with bug-eyed monsters.

Real science is quite different. It starts with a problem and a hunch, continues with an experiment, and concludes with a theory.

Let's start with a problem: What makes water evaporate? You and I know what makes it disappear but a cave dweller, called Gethel, did not know.

Gethel was also the only person in his tribe who did not know what makes water evaporate. The other tribesmen didn't stop to think about why water gradually vanishes from a cup. And if Gethel's troglodytes did ask themselves why, they knew the answer immediately—the great god Wodin caused it to happen, as he causes everything.

But Gethel was known to be a little crazy. So, like Socrates, he didn't know why water evaporates. One day, unlike Socrates, he decided to find out.

From previous observation and a wild hunch, Gethel decided he would try something out. He didn't know at the time that he was conducting the first scientific experiment on the face of the earth. So with no fanfare, he set out a pan containing one Urd of water on the floor of his cave. Then he took a jar and filled it up to its narrow neck with one Urd of water. And he left the cave to repair an animal skin down by the river.

When he finally finished working on the skin, he returned to his cave. Gethel looked at the pan and the jar. Measuring the amount of water left in the pan with his crude Urd-cup, he saw that about half the water was gone from the pan. But the jar was almost as full as when he had left.

Gethel sat down cross-legged on the floor of the cave and remained motionless for the rest of the day. The tribesmen knew the Spirit was upon him, so they didn't intrude. But Gethel was not in a trance; he was thinking.

Pondering the problem of the disappearing water, Gethel came up with two theories:

1. Evaporation of water is caused by the great god Wodin. The god cupped his paws in the pan, took out the water, and made it disappear. But when Wodin tried to reach into the jar, he found its neck too small for his paws, so he had to leave it alone and could not remove any water.

2. Water disappears by contact with air. Since the surface of the water in the pan was exposed to lots of air, half an Urd was gone. The jar, by contrast, offered very little water-air surface in its narrow neck, so little water was gone. To test these two theories, Gethel devised two experiments.

First he poured an Urd of Water into one pan and another Urd into another pan. He then prayed to the god Wodin to remove water from just one pan; this would substantiate his first theory. But no matter how much ritualistic bidding Gethel employed, when he measured the water in the two pans, identical amounts of water remained in each.

To perform his second experiment, he went to the local smith and borrowed a bellows. Gethel again set out his two pans with an Urd of water in each. To increase contact with air on the left pan, he blew on it with the bellows. He then measured the remaining amounts of water in the two pans and found, as his hypothesis suggested, more water had disappeared from the pan he blew on, the one with more air contact.

Gethel returned the bellows and went back to his cave. Once more, cross-legged on the floor, he was absorbed in thought. It's not easy to abandon a firmly held belief, yet the evidence against the Wodin theory was overwhelming.

Wodin had not responded to his entreaties or to ritual. Was Wodin deaf? Was he blind? Was he away somewhere? Or maybe he didn't even exist. No, that's unthinkable. Maybe Wodin was peeved about something. But Gethel realized that he could speculate about the Wodin theory till his beard grew white and his teeth fell out and nothing useful would come of it. The Wodin theory was a blind alley. It was neither useful nor fruitful.

But the Contact With Air theory had produced results. It was substantiated by an experiment and could be further tested by at least two additional experiments that Gethel would devise. These could generate further ideas and tests, producing more theory. So Contact With Air was to be preferred over the blind alley Wodin theory.

Unfortunately, the tribe of Geth was wiped out by an unknown disease. Millenia passed while mankind wasted time with the mindless tinkering of the alchemists and the pointless word juggling of the philosophers. Finally science was rediscovered by Copernicus, Galileo, and other intellectual descendants of Gethel.

The fable of Gethel serves to illustrate one method of

science. But the most important lesson is still hidden in the story: For every hour Gethel spent in pouring water, measuring, praying, and blowing, Gethel spent ten hours in thought. Only a minor part of science consists of laboratory work. The major part of science consists of thought. Science is not a collection of facts assembled by experimentation like matching birds to pictures. The aim of science is to produce fruitful and productive theories which can be tested by experiment.

Fruitful? Productive? Gethel's first experiment led to the next two, thus his theories and thought were productive: They led to further theory and experimentation, expanding human knowledge in the process.

Gethel's revolutionary discovery—the discovery of science, itself, its aims and methods—suggests these ideas:

I. **The aim of science is useful, productive theory.**

   A. **Valid theory is based on experiment and measurement.**

   B. **A theory should include all known facts.**

   C. **A useful theory limits itself to accounting for the facts. It avoids useless embroidery.**

A. *Experiment and Measurement.* Gethel was not content with a couple of hunches. He had to experiment in order to test out his ideas. To conduct a careful experiment, Gethel found it necessary to measure water with his Urd-cup. If Gethel had built up an elaborate theory on the basis of what he believed he saw and not what he measured, he wouldn't be a very good scientist. But Gethel realized that a hunch, prompted by what he believed he saw, was fine to start with. However, a formal experiment requiring as careful measurement as he was

129

capable of, was necessary for concluding that water evaporated by contact with air.

But accurate measurement was beyond Gethel's instruments. Gethel knew how crude a tool his Urd-cup was. So he didn't publish results claiming that 0.52789 Urds of water had evaporated. He didn't go beyond the level of measurement his Urd-cup provided. He could only say for sure, *"More* water evaporated in the left pan than the right pan."

In measuring human behavior, our tests or instruments are as crude as Gethel's Urd-cup. We can properly say that Ted's I.Q. is higher than Bob's I.Q. but we can't correctly say that Ted's I.Q. is five inches greater than Bob's. Inches measure height, not intelligence. Points on the I.Q. scale are not absolute like inches. I.Q. points are only a convenient way of saying, "Greater than . . . less than."

A useful theory is based on experiment and measurement. Even if the measurement is crude as it must be, in measuring human behavior, it is still valid if extravagant claims are avoided.

B. *A theory should include all known facts.* Gethel was a careful experimenter but he wasn't careful enough. When he returned from the river to examine the first experiment, he barely noticed that a tiny bit of water was gone from the jar. Gethel was too concerned about the major difference between the disappearance of the water in the pan compared with the water in the jar, to consider the small amount of water lost in the jar.

In a further experiment, if Gethel wanted to verify possible water lost in the jar, he could have filled the jar up to a point in the neck where a tiny bump jutted out. This technique would have enabled him to see if a tiny amount of water was lost; and if so, he could have spared himself hours of useless speculation about the Wodin theory.

By inference, an agent other than Wodin's paw would have been responsible: either Wodin could get his paw in the jar or he couldn't. If he could, more water would have been missing; if he couldn't none would have escaped.

This kind of detective work would have been sufficient to exclude the Wodin theory and save much head work. As it turned out, Contact With Air explains the small amount of water gone from the jar. It includes this little fact, too.

Poor scientific thinking resulting in faulty theory is caused by ignoring facts—pretending that data do not exist. Theories which do not include all the known facts should be regarded with suspicion or thrown out entirely.

In evaluating theories of human behavior, we must keep this "inclusion" criterion in mind. Does a specific theory of human nature take in the many nuances of behavior people are capable of? Or does it arbitrarily lop off facts as unimportant just because they don't fit the theory?

Behavior modification—a school of therapy meriting serious consideration—is flawed because it excludes not only little facts, but large areas of human behavior: dreams and fantasies are regarded as of no account; responses to Rorschach ink-blots are ignored; nuances and subtleties are glossed over. All these are hard facts ignored by most therapists of the "behavior mod" school. A useful theory is *inclusive* of all available facts.

C. The last criterion by which a theory may be evaluated is whether or not *the theory limits itself to accounting for the facts and avoids useless embroidery.* Theory should be lean, stringent, or parsimonious in its construction. Had Gethel known that theory should be lean, he would have suspected the "fat" and fancy Wodin theory at the outset.

Contact With Air is a stringent, parsimonious idea. It avoids needless complexity. By contrast, the Wodin theory is "fat," complex without cause. It assumes that Wodin can be everywhere at once, that he has a paw, that his paw is five Dins long and three Dins wide so it could fit into the pan but not the jar, that his paw can be cupped, that Wodin understands the language of the Geths, that he will or must comply with the prescribed ritual, and on and on. The Wodin theory is needlessly complicated, embroidered, for the explanation of evaporation, contrasted with the lean, elegant Contact With Air theory.

With the profusion of facts thrust upon theorists of human behavior, it is a difficult task to account for all the minutiae that people are capable of. Some founders of psychotherapy schools have fallen into the trap of constructing "fat" elaborate theories. They get carried away with the pleasure of coining new terms, confusing the act of creating neologisms with the act of creating valid theory.

For example: Carl G. Jung (1875–1961), Swiss psychiatrist and former disciple of Freud, produced a multitude of theories—products of a brilliant mind accounting for facts in the most uneconomical way possible. Jung's notions, like a Rube Goldberg machine designed to scratch your back, will have twenty succeeding gadgets, one pushing the next, and the next, and so forth.

A number of myths, held by tribes all over the world, are similar. Jung explains their similarity by a "fat," embroidered theory: a "racial Unconscious" presumably transmitted by heredity.

The universality of these myths can be explained in a more simple fashion: Just the world wide existence of the human family consisting of a mother, father, and children, all expanded into fantasy figures, is sufficient to account for the same myths found in many cultures all over the world. Simpler, isn't it?

Criteria for useful scientific theory must be applied to ideas not only about the physical world, such as evaporation of water, but also to theories accounting for human behavior, as well.

Theories: Psychoanalysis and Stimulus-Response: Originators, Developers, Negators, Complicators, Elaborators

What basic theories of human behavior have been most useful and productive for psychotherapy? Who originated these theories?

It is an old truism when a timely thought becomes widespread and institutionalized, the original notion soon changes beyond recognition. Some have even suggested that were Jesus to return to the Twentieth Century, no one in any established church would listen to Him; today's money lenders might even place Him in an institution. In the field of science, Gethel and Galileo might escape imprisonment; but at the very least, they would be bewildered at the sight of the atomic particle accelerator at Brookhaven National Laboratory.

Any unique and original idea with relevance to its age will be changed by other investigators. The theory will be seized by a host of thinkers and scientists and developed, elaborated, applied, complicated, tinkered with, plagiarized, criticized, negated, and popularized beyond all recognition. The originator, were he to be confronted with his brain children, might shake his head in confusion, sit down on the curb, and cry.

Fortunately, the evolution and devolution of human behavior theory has not been as radical as theory in the physical sciences. Three basic theories of human behavior are still useful, fruitful, and recognizable:

Freud's psychoanalytic theory, Thorndike and Pavlov's stimulus-response theory, and group interaction theory still form the necessary skeleton upon which further theory and useful technique are fleshed out. The three theories have their developers and elaborators, but the original theories are still useful, productive, and faithful to their primary form.

By now it has become apparent that just listening to the shopkeepers extoll the virtue of their goods, is hardly the way to buy an effective piece of merchandise. So does it not follow that a potential buyer of psychotherapy be not swayed by clever public relations? We need to lift the hood and examine the engine. We need to know the theory behind the method.

Understanding the three basic theories in human behavior, psychoanalytic, stimulus-response, interaction, is not terribly difficult. Once fully grasped, the reader's orientation to psychotherapy may undergo a radical transformation. The whole field can now make sense and the hucksters' hawkings become irrelevant.

134

Because they have stood the test of time, psycho-analysis, stimulus-response, and interaction theory have been singled out as the most productive and useful theories in the field of human behavior. Much experimentation and further theoretical thinking have resulted since the publication of the original statements of these three theories.

By contrast, other theories that once were in vogue, have been dropped as useless and non-productive. Theories based on the bumps of your skull or how fat or skinny you are, have lost credibility because they didn't prove out experimentally or generate further theory.

Thus Freud, Pavlov and Thorndike, and the group interaction theorists have proved to be the Gethels and Galileos of the science of human behavior. As we examined Gethel's Urds of water, let us now examine the experiments and theories of the pioneers of the science of human behavior.

Originators of Psychoanalytic and Stimulus-Response Theories

The explosion of knowledge and theory of human behavior happened at the turn of the century. A twenty-four-year-old American instructor of psychology at Columbia University published his dissertation in 1898. It was called, *Animal Intelligence: An Experimental Study of the Associative Processes in Animals.* His name was Edward Lee Thorndike.

Thrown out of his room for harboring too many cats and baby chicks, Thorndike found refuge for himself and his animals in the cellar of the Boston home of William James, the famous philosopher. Eventually New York's Columbia University offered Mr. Thorndike a permanent home for his chicks, his cats, his dogs, his stop-watch, and his twenty-four puzzle boxes.

Thorndike's cats could escape from inside the boxes either by pulling down a rope or by pushing up a bobbin. The first time a cat was put in the box, it made many different movements all over the cage. When the animal finally pulled the right rope or pushed the correct bobbin, the door opened. The second time the cat was put in the box, using a stop-watch, Thorndike noted that less time elapsed before the door opened. Placed in the box again and again, it took no time at all for the cat to rush to the rope or bobbin and open the door.

Thorndike called this process trial-and-error learning. Each time the cat was put in the box and tried to get out, was called a "trial." Thorndike took a sheet of graph paper and plotted the results. On the bottom horizontal line he marked the "trials" and on the left vertical line he marked the time each trial took by minutes and seconds. The graph showed a decrease in time upon each succeeding trial.

When Thorndike looked at the graph he had plotted, he was overjoyed. He rushed to his fellow scientists to show them the slope of the line. It looked like a perfect ski jump. The ski jump slope is called, a "logarithmically decelerating curve."

Thorndike had demonstrated that the process of learning, in its simplest form, followed a mathematical formula. The slope of the line was then called, a "learning curve." Not a hit or miss notion, this logarithmic line is close to being a scientific law.

Elsewhere in the world, men and women of science were conducting experiments on animal behavior. About a year or two after Thorndike published his results, a former student for the Russian Orthodox priesthood revealed the results of his experiments on "psychic secretions": they were part of his study on the process of digestion.

Nobel Prize winner, Ivan Petrovitch Pavlov was a fifty-year-old professor of physiology and a skilled ambidextrous surgeon, at the Military Medical Academy of Petrograd, when his work on the "conditioned reflex" became known. Generations of psychologists held Dr. Pavlov in awe, but he would have nothing to do with them, regarding psychology as mere philosophy. He was a scientist, a physiologist (Personal communication, Robert S. Woodworth, 1944).

Many know that Pavlov's dogs salivated at the sound of an electric bell before food was offered. But not many know that the amount of saliva was measured carefully by drops. Pavlov's graph of the "conditioned reflex" depicted time, trials, and drops of saliva. Another graph showed "extinction" of the response when no food was offered. Both graphs bore a close and amazing resemblance to Thorndike's ski jump learning curve.

Both Pavlov's and Thorndike's almost simultaneous experiments uncovered conditions under which animals learn better, forget less easily, learn to distinguish between highly complicated stimuli, and follow mathematically regular laws: laws almost as clear-cut as those in the physical universe.

Thorndike and his cats, Pavlov and his dogs innovated a basic theory—the learned or conditioned response to a given stimulus. It is called, stimulus-response theory.

The two theories differed, however, in the way they obtained a response. Pavlov *elicited* a response from his dogs by putting meat paste on their tongues. Thorndike *waited* until the desired response occurred. His cat learned by means of his cage—the instrument used. Thus Pavlovian learning is called, "conditioned reflex," and the Thorndike type of learning is called, "instrumental conditioning." Both theories use the term, reinforcement (reward), when the dogs were given the meat paste and when the cat escaped from the cage.

Now on to the second basic theory of human behavior: *The Interpretation of Dreams* burst on the Viennese medical scene in 1900, about the same time Thorndike discovered the learning curve in New York City and Pavlov discovered the conditioned reflex in Petrograd.

But instead of the Nobel Prize awarded Pavlov and the accolades given to Thorndike, forty-four-year-old Sigmund Freud was refused appointment to the university: Freud spent his life in medical research, but he was a Jew who declined conversion to Christianity, so the university passed him by. Fortunately, he didn't need the laboratory facilities found only in a university. Instead of animals, cages, timing equipment, and operating rooms, he needed human beings. There was no dearth of patients since he was an established, even famous neurologist with a specialty in child neurological problems.

Concluding that fancy medical procedures to cure neuroses did not work, Freud decided to listen carefully to what his patients had to say. He watched, rather than performed; he used scientific and detached observation, rather than frantic and unknowledgeable effort. His theories resulted from putting together what he heard and saw into a meaningful form. But it was almost half a century later before *experimental* evidence for psychoanalysis appeared.

The theory of psychoanalysis tries to account for the trials, travels, and tribulations that the life force (libido) of a person encounters, when blocked by the social environment. The libido is permitted a partial flow into one area and is dammed up—confined—only to flow in another direction.

The theory becomes complicated because of the very complexity of family and social prohibitions fencing us in as growing infants. Attempts by scientists to "lean out" the theory—make it more stringent—for the purpose of making hypotheses that could be tested out in the laboratory, are valid insofar as the hypotheses warrant. But of necessity, the laboratory hypotheses must encompass far less of human function than Freud, in his original theory, took into account. Thus psychoanalytic theory retains its complexity in order not to ignore known facts of human behavior.

Early in a child's development, three theoretical structures emerge: The Id, Ego, and Super-Ego. At birth the infant is all Id. "It" wants, so "it" takes.

The Ego mediates between the demands of the Id and the child's environment. Partly conscious and civilized, the Ego functions using the unconscious defenses outlined in the last chapter. The Ego copes with the environment, and uses intelligence to transform vague urges into ideas and speech. An important part of the Ego is a sense of one's self and an awarenes of one's body. The self and the body, exaggerated by the obese, were sketched in Chapter 1.

The Super-Ego is unconscious. It metaphorically stands *over* the Ego, prohibiting thoughts and actions, engendering guilt and nightmares, and lowering the person's sense of self-worth.

The object of therapy is to replace unconscious Id and Super-Ego with the conscious, reasoning Ego. Useful as the Super-Ego may have been during early childhood and in the early life of mankind, preserving society from disintegration, the Super-Ego is no longer necessary to civilized man. The Ego is sufficient to prevent murder, for example, by encouraging conscious moral choice rather than solving the problem by spurring the Super-Ego on to do battle with the Id.

Remember your friend, Luther? You repressed his name because he made you wait lunch for half an hour. Such repression is not efficient. Your Id wanted to do away with him while your Super-Ego said, "No." Your Ego, then, had to repress the entire battle. If your Ego were fully in charge, you'd merely be annoyed with him and wouldn't have to waste time trying to remember his name.

In common use, the term, ego, means self-esteem: "He's a very bright, capable person. But he hasn't accomplished much. He doesn't have enough confidence, enough *ego*." But in psychoanalytic context, ego refers to the mediator: "He gets a lot of things done without fretting. He doesn't have to keep fighting his impulses. His *Ego* is unhindered."

As previously mentioned, "conditioning," both Pavlov's and Thorndike's, gained almost immediate acceptance, while psychoanalysis found the going very rough. Even today it is not fully accepted. Lack of knowledge and education does not account for this fact. The acceptance or its lack, lies in the difference between the subjects of the experiments: Conditioning was first verified with animals; psychoanalysis was discovered by working with human beings.

It's perfectly Okay to teach animals new tricks. After all, they are only animals who don't know what they are doing. But when it comes to human beings—"What do you mean I don't know what I am doing?" We flatter ourselves with the misconception that we are in control all the time. As "captains of our souls" we are perforce responsible. Any evidence to the contrary, such as the uselessness of making New Year's resolutions or the ineffectiveness of the "self-help" books, is met with a massive use of defense—denial. We refuse to see evidence no matter how apparent, of our own helplessness in the face of our impulses.

Both stimulus-response theory and psychoanalytic theory posit, assume areas of function beyond control. Psychoanalytic theory labels such areas, "unconscious;" stimulus-response theory is not concerned with either awareness or unawareness, so this area is simply not labeled. But a startling demonstration of the power of the Unconscious can be presented by transforming a small area of human function from the Unconscious to the Conscious. Moreover, this demonstration is indicative of the basic unity between stimulus-response theory and psychoanalytic theory.

When you go outside in the bright sunlight after being indoors in a dim light, the pupil in your eye will contract. This reflex of the iris, known as the "iridic reflex," helps the eye adapt rapidly to changing light conditions. It happens willy-nilly, whether you like it or not.

Conditioning the iridic reflex is an experiment you can do at home. Find a subject who doesn't blink too often, a light with a silent switch (you don't want to condition the subject to a "click!"), a notebook and a pencil. Ask the subject to look at the unlit light bulb, say, "Contract," and immediately switch the light on.

After 200 or 250 trials, say, "Contract" without turning the light on. If you observe carefully, you will find a slight contraction of the pupil just after saying the word. Do not be distracted by the contraction following an eyeblink. Reinforce this conditioned reflex a few more times by saying, "Contract" and turning on the light. Now ask the subject to contract his own pupil. You will again notice a slight contraction.

If you ask the subject how he did it, he will probably say, "I don't know. I just did it," or "I just willed it." Your results can be explained either by psychoanalytic theory—making the unconscious conscious—or by Pavlovian conditioning theory. Whichever theory you use, the two theories are close, almost identical.

Now who developed these theories? How were they enlarged?

Developers

Developers of psychoanalytic and stimulus-response theories managed to bring together much of these two basic theories of human behavior in the attempt to create one single theory. In addition, the Developers provided experimental evidence in the laboratory for verifying aspects of psychoanalytic theory.

These two tasks were pioneered by two people who later rose to prominence. The American Psychological Association, with affiliates throughout the world and scores of thousands of scientists and practitioners as members, is *the* organization of psychologists. The American Psychological Association was established to promote psychology as a science and, to a lesser extent, as a profession.

Robert R. Sears and Neal Miller were each elected, at different times, to serve as presidents of the American Psychological Association. Their research in the Thirties and early Forties brought psychoanalytic theory and stimulus-response theory together and provided a host of experimental results verifying analytic theory in the laboratory. Further ingenious methods to substantiate psychoanalytic theory were used at New York University in New York City in the Fifties. More recently, studies of the two hemispheres of the brain itself yielded evidence in agreement with Freud's theory of the way the Unconscious works.

Entire libraries are chock-full of scientific articles verifying psychoanalytic theory. The bias in favor of psychoanalytic theory in this book is thus based on decades of intensive thought and experiment with a theory which is

143

both stringent and inclusive. That is why it was chosen as one of three theories adhering the closest to our criteria, outlining a scientific approach to human behavior.

But what about the other therapy in widespread use today? Behavior modification in various forms is becoming increasingly popular in clinics and private offices throughout the country. Is anything wrong with it? Is not "behavior mod" an application of stimulus-response theory?

Yes, it is. And it is a therapy worthy of thoughtful evaluation. Behavior mod is another application of theory based on science. But—we previously mentioned, behavior modification in the effort to operate with the most stringent possible theory, ignored important aspects of human behavior: Not only are dreams and fantasy regarded as of no account, but even the entire past life of the individual is "stonewalled."

Conversely, stimulus-response theory would suggest that one's early childhood, in which vital conditioning took place, would be of supreme importance. Early learning, the infant's first reinforcement to its cries—the reward of milk to suck—are very important in psychoanalytic theory, but denied a place in the thinking of the behavior mod therapists.

Such an obvious contradiction seems incomprehensible. But this is how it happened: Two developers of stimulus-response theory, Clark L. Hull and B. Frederic Skinner, branched out in two directions.

Clark Hull was born in 1884, about the time when Freud was puzzling over why "Anna O." fell in love with her doctors. A professor of psychology at Yale University in New Haven, Connecticut, Hull gathered about him many disciples to form the Institute for Human Relations at Yale. The research associates included Sears and Miller, the two future presidents of the American Psychological Association.

Hull possessed one of the most powerful, theoretical minds in the history of psychology. A developer of stimulus-response theory, his interests lay more in scientific method, logic, and mathematics than in understanding how the cat got out of the box.

One of Hull's ideas was the "hypothetical construct"—making a theory about possible structures that may exist somewhere between a stimulus and a response. Because there was room in his theories for such structures, Freud's Id, Ego, and Super-ego could find a home with Hull.

Thus Hull's disciples, Sears and Miller, were encouraged to investigate psychoanalytic theory extensively under Hull's aegis, trying to find roots for Freud's theory in the stimulus-response model.

B.F. Skinner is better known to the public at large than Hull. Also in New England, he presided at Harvard University. The puzzle box he used for his animals became known as the "Skinner Box." Skinner was born twenty years after Hull, in 1904.

Skinner was less theoretical and more pragmatic than Hull. Although he lived in New England, he was not of New England's rarified ivy. Born in Susquehanna, Pennsylvania and undergoing his formative years in psychology at the University of Minnesota, Skinner remained the Missouri skeptic who says, "Show me." He rejected most

145

theoretical constructs and implied that animals and people go direct from stimulus to response without anything in between. Or else they go directly to response if there is no stimulus. Hull's "in between" structures were unacceptable to him.

Turning to the philosophical implications of his work in later years, Skinner began to have second thoughts. If you push a button, you can get people to salivate. Push another button and you can get them to do anything. That could be dangerous in the hands of an unscrupulous dictator.

Skinner had no room in his theory for the psychoanalytic idea of Ego. He did not believe, as Freud did, that therapy can free people of their impulses (Id) so that their willing, self-propelled wishes (Ego) could take over. Skinner's theory provided little room for the humanity of humans.

So Professor Skinner was in a quandary. How could he reconcile his theory with democracy rather than "Big Brother?" His two books, *Walden Two* and *Beyond Freedom and Dignity* were an attempt to find a way out of the implications of his theory—man as a machine. It was the opinion of many, that Skinner never found a way out of his own puzzle box. Unlike his pigeons and white mice, Professor Skinner walled himself into a Skinner Box with no food lever and no exit. The human debris, the results of applied Skinnerism, are doomed to perish as the conditioned criminal in *A Clockwork Orange*.

Applications of Stimulus-Response Theory

Skinner's limited use of theory gave birth to behavior

modification. His disciples negated psychoanalysis and claimed that Freud's intervening structures like the Ego and the Id are a myth. Caring little what happened to the person in the past, they merely ask the client, "What's wrong? What do you want changed?" They then proceed to "desensitize" the person to the stimulus that triggers the undesired response.

In the interest of proceeding with the leanest possible theory, their stance is close to a know-nothing position. Please note that behavior mod is not the only possible application of stimulus-response theory, but only of Skinner's variety—not of Hull's.

Suppose you go to a behavior mod therapist with a headache. The therapist will have little difficulty in removing the headache: immediate treatment of your complaint, like swallowing an aspirin. Suppose you then get a backache; you go back to the behavior therapist—you take another aspirin. When your backache is cured, you get an unbearable stiffness in some other part of your anatomy. Do you return to the behavior therapist? Do you take yet a third aspirin?

Because of his theoretical position, the behavior mod therapist cannot acknowledge that all your aches are due to a single theoretical construct called, unconscious anger, repressed because of pressure from the Super-Ego. "Pure mythology," says the behaviorist.

The psychoanalyst replies, "Is trigonometry mythology just because you can't see it? You can't bring a ship from New York to London without 'sine' and 'cosine.' And you can't free a client from all his psychogenic aches and pains without a structure called, 'repressed anger'—even if you can't *see* the repressed anger."

147

The therapist with a psychoanalytic point of view could have added, "Can't you see your client is constricted not only in his body, but in his entire life? His tight body is only one problem. How about his tight pocketbook, his tight prejudices, and his tight mind?"

Skinner's limited version of stimulus-response theory gave birth not only to behavior mod, but also to another kind of therapy limited to one small segment of a client's life—a single response. "Bio-feedback" is a specialized therapy for people with certain psychosomatic problems; problems that could be dangerous to their health. Like the experiment you performed on the iridic reflex when your subject learned to contract his pupil at will, bio-feedback conditions other reflexes to respond to the patient's will. This can be helpful when time is short. For example:

A person may respond to unconscious anger with a dangerous rise in blood pressure. But until psychoanalysis could effect a fundamental change in the patient, he could well be dead. Bio-feedback comes to the rescue by teaching the patient to lower his own blood pressure.

A blood pressure indicator giving continuous readings is hooked up to the patient. He then watches his own blood pressure go up and down at random—like Thorndike's cat when first put in the cage. When the patient sees his blood pressure go down or hears a tone, he is reinforced by this glad tiding. Like Thorndike's cat the patient, by trial-error-and-success, learns how to keep his blood pressure down. He does not know how it happened; it just happened, and that is sufficient.

Bio-feedback may be regarded as emergency psychotherapy. After the patient's survival is assured, he may then become a *client* in psychotherapy. He may now be concerned about the whys of his life-style that brought about the high blood pressure. Many people with this problem have high expectations and are then disappointed by life—by their work, by their relationships. Enough concern about where they've been, where they're going, and why life offers them so little, may lead such people to consider psychoanalytic therapy.

Unlike bio-feedback, behavior modification often eradicates problems that are merely annoying rather than dangerous. But problems like the phobias, the specialized anxieties mentioned in Chapter 2, may be only the tip of the iceberg. Behavior mod can inhibit rather than extinguish a phobia, thus doing nothing for the condition underlying it. Behavior mod therapy often sticks a band-aid on a fracture. But, as we said, who wants to swallow aspirin forever?

If you are troubled by a persistent headache, it may make sense to visit a behavior therapist. Should he or she get rid of the headache and you find that all else is well, you've saved much time and effort. You may congratulate the therapist and yourself. But should you find other problems appearing, as they probably will, you might as well make up your mind to enter psychoanalytic therapy. A quick solution is not for you.

Negators of Psychoanalytic Theory

Having discussed the originator and developers of psychoanalytic theory, it is now time to return to our friend, Gethel. As with all original and timely ideas, Contact With Air Theory was negated and complicated.

In his later years, Gethel acquired fame that spread beyond the borders of his tribe. Applying his Contact With Air Theory to practical use, Gethel directed his tribesmen to lead sea water into large, *shallow* flats. The tribe of Geth thus obtained much valuable salt and became rich by trading with other tribes.

The tribe of Teth, living a few miles away, became envious and decided to compete with the Geths in the production of salt. So they sent their leader, Tethel, to the tribe of Geth to learn how it was done.

Having learned the secret, Tethel returned to his tribe and told them, "Gethel digs only shallow flats to make salt. But I am wiser. We will dig *deep* ditches and produce more salt than the Geths."

This "improvement" resulted in no salt at all. The deep ditches did not have enough surface exposed to air. The "improvement" resulted from a lack of understanding of Gethel's theory. So when a week passed and little water evaporated, Tethel told his tribe there was a grave omission in their procedures—they had forgotten to pray to Wodin (obviously, a useless complication). After another week passed and the water still did not evaporate, the tribe made a sacrifice to Wodin, a further complication.

Finally, Tethel told his tribesmen to collect the salt that forms on the rocks at low tide—this proved to be a negation of the Contact With Air Theory. "Anyone can see salt forming on the rocks," Tethel pontificated. "This is a common-sense approach. Evaporation of water by Contact With Air is nonsense."

Thus Tethel negated the theory and his tribesmen

were happy with such a reasonable, common-sense approach. But because so much time was required to collect the small salt deposits, no one hunted or fished and the tribe died of starvation.

Returning now to the Twentieth Century, Alfred Adler (1870–1937), a modern-day Tethel, was the first disciple of Freud to negate psychoanalysis and propound his own theory of human behavior. Believing psychoanalysis was too complex and mystical, he proceeded to collect the salt that forms on the rocks at low tide. Anyone can see salt on the rocks, but has anyone seen evaporation? Has anyone seen the Super-Ego? Of course not. Let's just use some common sense and deny salt when made by evaporation, and claim it is not salt at all but a kind of magic snow.

So Adler's theory is easily understood. Like salt on the rocks, it can be seen by everyone. It is based on common sense: Nobody likes to have a weak arm or a weak head. So instead, people *compensate* for imagined inferiority. Like Demosthenes, the Greek orator who shouted above the roar of the waves to overcome his speech impediment, people strive loudly for superiority and mastery to overcome their "inferiority complexes." This notion makes sense; but Freud already had a more inclusive idea called, *reaction formation*. However, reaction formation is only one of the defenses and explains only a small corner of the human function.

Like Adler, Harry Stack Sullivan was another "common sense" negator of Freud. Dr. Sullivan studied the seriously disturbed people in St. Elizabeth's Hospital in

Washington, D.C. Never committing anything to writing, Sullivan's "Inter-personal" theory is available in edited versions of his recorded lectures.

Sullivan's excellence lay in his command of the English language. Freud's "defense mechanism" became "dynamism"; "denial" was changed to "selective inattention"; "repression" to "forgettery." Unfortunately, psychoanalytic theory was ignored in favor of a "common sense" approach: Paranoia, for instance, he attributed to a "malevolent transformation," which labels, but does not explain.

Sullivan ignores the mechanism of projection and claims that the child learns distrust by his own parents' suspicion of the child's motives. Proposing imitation of the parent is common sense, but it limits one to collecting salt on the rocks.

Fritz Perls, of German origin, a trained psychoanalyst originally, was another negator of almost all of psychoanalytic theory. Almost—but not all. He retained one essential part: His therapy consisted of the attempt to make the client aware of aspects of himself of which the client was previously unaware. In the language of "Gestalt" therapy, Perls claimed to unite "split-off parts" in order to make the individual into a whole and unique configuration. "Configuration" is the English translation of the German *Gestalt*.

"Gestalt" psychotherapy derives its name, but not its substance, from academic *Gestalt* psychology. The German academic *Gestalt* psychologists noted that we never see a triangle as three separate sticks. A triangle is seen as a whole, unique configuration (*Gestalt*) possessing a quality of "triangleness." The same is true of the learning process. An ape given a meaningful task like standing on a box *and* using a stick to reach a banana, unreachable by stick or box alone, gains sudden, whole, and complete insight into the problem. He sees the solution as a *Gestalt*. This notion is applied legitimately to perception, learning, and even group behavior.

Dr. Perls lifted the term, *Gestalt*, from academic psychology and applied it to his form of psychotherapy. Making unconscious "parts" of the individual, conscious—one aspect of psychoanalysis—Perls renamed, "getting split-off parts together." The person then becomes his own whole, unique configuration or "Gestalt."

It is evident that Perls' aim is identical to that of psychoanalysis: He discovers aspects of the person, previously unknown, and brings these to the fore. But what use is made of these hitherto unknown "parts"? Are they hoarded or are they dropped? Academic *Gestalt* theory would hold that these "parts" are essential and, like a triangle missing its third side, upon recovery, should be meticulously pasted back on to the person. Then the client would become "whole" again; he cannot be a full configuration without these valuable "parts".

Yet in practice, Perls allows these valuable pieces to be sloughed off. He treats them as impediments, like the childhood distortions of psychoanalytic theory. Thus Perls' practice belies his word—*Gestalt* theory is ignored and psychoanalytic goals are pursued. Perls has yet to demonstrate the relevance of *Gestalt* to psychotherapy.

Total negation of psychoanalysis is associated with the "human potential movement." Discarding the person's past, notions about the structure of his or her personality, or any formal theory, the protagonists of this movement stand for "self-actualization."

The term was coined by a little-known medical scientist, Kurt Goldstein. Born in Upper Silesia in 1878, he studied in Germany where he rose to prominence as Professor of Neurology and Psychiatry at the Universities of Frankfurt and Berlin. His "organismic" theory suggests that the prime motive of the *organism* is to fulfill its own potential or capacity for being whatever it is capable of being. As interpreted by Goldstein's followers, self-actualization has become an admonition to people rather than scientific theory, a value rather than a hypothesis: "You must fulfill yourself."

In the latter part of Chapter 1, we suggested that once constricting elements of the person are eliminated, the individual will fulfill himself without further help from a therapist. Unless problems are removed, no amount of urging will help.

People have been told from the time they went to school, to shape up. Their report cards carried an implicit admonition to improve when the teacher wrote, "Not learning up to capacity". Clothed in scientific garb, the human potential movement still strives in vain, urging people to "self-actualize".

Carl Rogers and Rollo May, former Protestant clergymen and Negators of psychoanalytic theory, have been leaders in the human potential movement. As kindly Christian men, they would like to see people happy and making the most of their lives. To that end, Rogers adopted the notion of limited usefulness suggested in

Chapter 3, that mere association with a therapist of good-will is enough to create positive change. We suggested that such association without interpretation of transference will take forever.

Human potential therapists do not subscribe to transference or to a systematic removal of childhood hangups. Instead, a mystical "I-Thou" meeting of two people—therapist and client—plus faith in the human spirit, is substituted for theory based on observation. Thus the therapist, in Rogers' "non-directive" counseling simply reflects what the client says and feels—neither client nor therapist having any notion where they are headed.

Credit must, however, be given to Dr. Rogers for careful measurement and reports of the apparent success of his method. But faith healing, too, has been known to achieve results. The refusal of non-directive counseling to acknowledge many known facts of human behavior, precludes its consideration as a scientific theory of psychotherapy.

The human potential movement, under the leadership of other therapists, spawned weekend resorts, such as Arica and Esalen, to celebrate the human spirit; to encourage people to actualize themselves; and to believe they were being uplifted. Under the banner of self-actualization and encounter ("encounter" means that people meet one another) they frolic in the sun and only a Scrooge would quarrel with their pleasure. But if the stated goal of these "retreats" is change, their antics bear little relation to their aims.

The common denominator of behavior modification, "Gestalt" and the human potential movement, is the sole and exclusive primacy of the present. Only what is happening now is of any importance; one's childhood is trivial and irrelevant.

While psychoanalysis emphasizes the present in the use of transference—what happens between client and therapist in the office—the present is underlined only as the result of the person's past. "As the twig is bent. . .". To ignore the individual's past, as do the Negators of psychoanalytic theory, is to deny facts. The result: defective theory and quick, but short-lived therapeutic results. "One swallow of aspirin doth not summarily a cure make."

Complicators of Psychoanalytic Theory

We may remember Tethel, who needlessly complicated Gethel's Contact With Air theory. Tethel added unnecessary "improvements" such as praying to Wodin and making sacrifices to him. C. G. Jung was cited as just such an example in psychotherapy. He embroidered psychoanalytic theory with a "racial Unconscious" and other "fat" structures, explaining facts the hard way.

Wilhelm Reich and his former disciple, Alexander Lowen, also continued in Tethel's footsteps: digging deep ditches and praying to Wodin. Reich's "orgonomy" posited units of sexual orgasm impinging on us from the heavenly bodies. Properly concentrated in special closets called, "orgone boxes", these "orgones" can make us feel better. Lowen's "bio-energetics" suggests units of biological energy that could be released to energize people. Observed phenomena of human behavior hardly need such complex and "fat" theories, unsupported by experiment. These are best left to science fiction writers.

Elaborators of Psychoanalytic Theory

The last category of theorists and therapists who followed Freud, are the Elaborators. Freud's genius in discovering psychoanalysis is indisputable, but he was not the last word. Further elaboration of the theory was inevitable and necessary.

So Sears and Miller, who became presidents of the American Psychological Association *developed* the experimental and more theoretical work. But it was left to Doctors Klein, Horney, and Berne (among many others) to carry on the *elaboration* of psychoanalytic theory along more practical lines relating to clients and their therapy. In other words, Isaac Singer invented the first practical sewing machine, one that could do continuous stitching. But developers were needed to apply advances in metallurgy and electricity. Elaborators then proceeded to make the machine capable of the zig-zag stitch and button-holing.

Klein, Horney and Berne are cited here as Elaborators of psychoanalytic theory not necessarily because their work is more innovative than others, but to suggest to the reader how elaboration of the theory may be furthered in different directions. Klein probed deeper into the human psyche, Horney explored some of the upper levels of the defenses and the Ego, while Berne investigated how human defenses are marshalled when people relate to each other.

Melanie Klein was a German psychoanalyst who fled from Hitlerism and found refuge in England. Dr. Klein was encouraged to specialize in the therapy of pre-kindergarten children, possibly because men believe that women and children have a natural affinity for each other. Relegated to block building in the playtherapy room, Dr. Klein emerged into the lecture halls of adult science, building with theory, rather than with wooden blocks; thus disproving the male treasured belief.

Since her clients were so young, Klein discovered motives that were buried in early infancy. Her conceptions may sound incomprehensible if not downright absurd, yet they are based on valid observation. To observe rather than to impose cultural values, is a therapist's prime occupation.

Klein advanced the notion that the child is envious of the mother, her ability to procreate, and her capacity to nurse. In a jealous rage, the child may try symbolically to scoop out the contents of her breasts and symbolically destroy her unborn children. Klein also suggested that even an infant may alternate between depression and concern with an imagined "persecutor".

Such conclusions are so far removed from adult concerns that Melanie Klein's work has been ignored in most surveys of the different therapies. Lack of attention to her work is regrettable. It is hoped that this will be rectified.

Karen Horney was also a German psychoanalyst who fled from Nazism. She found refuge in the United States and established a clinic. There she taught and supervised a new generation of psychotherapists. The clinic is located in Manhattan at the foot of a bridge leading to Long

Island. Perhaps the location of Horney's clinic at the entrance to a bridge between two islands, is symbolic of the bridge needed between laypeople and therapists. Horney was the first to write a book for laypeople, inviting them to enter therapy and telling them what it is all about.

Horney dealt with some of the upper levels of people's defenses and thus her work is more understandable than Klein's. This does not imply a judgment of the value of either therapist's contribution.

Horney labeled one aspect of the Super-Ego as "the tyranny of the Should". Some of us are completely dominated by our beliefs of right and wrong, what we and others ought or ought not to be doing. She described the seductive appeal of martyrdom and love; the "search for glory"; and how the neurotic makes special claims and believes that he or she deserves better treatment than others. Some of her ideas are incorporated in descriptions of persons entering psychotherapy found in the latter part of Chapter 2.

Horney also proposed that people tend to fall into one of three categories by the way they behave towards others: 1. Moving towards others, 2. Moving against them, and 3. Moving away from people.

Fortunately for the layperson, Horney's books were written for a wide audience. Not addressed solely to therapists, her writings avoided the use of technical language. Her terminology imparted to psychoanalysis immediacy and relevance, thus making the description of psychoanalytic theory more human and to the point.

The third Elaborator in our trio is Eric Berne. Nineteen sixty-four was a landmark year in the publishing industry when the book, *Games People Play* by this San Francisco psychoanalyst and group therapist, burst on the "self-help" scene. It totally changed the face of this multi-million-dollar genre of perennial best-sellers. *Games People Play* became the grandfather of the "psychology self-helps".

The book launched a "new" therapy with all the apparent trappings of a brand new fad; a secular religion that held promise of a total life change for its parishioners. It was called, TA (Transactional Analysis) and its lay adherents spread the good word far and wide with all the zeal of the "est" or "Primal Scream" converts.

However, under the hoopla and chromium plating, Eric Berne, unlike others, came up with a solid silver contribution to the elaboration of psychoanalytic theory. His group technique will be presented in the next chapter; his theory of the individual will be presented now:

Using a typical everyday conversation, Berne quotes a husband asking his wife, "Where are my cuff-links?" An important part of Berne's theory lies in these possible answers:

1. THE CHILD-WIFE: You always expect me to keep track of your things.
2. THE PARENT-WIFE: Why can't you keep track of your own things?
3. THE ADULT-WIFE: They are on the desk,
   or
   I don't know.

Berne regards "Child" and "Parent", examples one and two, as altered Ego-states. Another understanding suggests that the Child-Wife projects her own Super-Ego

160

onto her husband, placing him in the role of Mother—
"Your demands that I keep track of your things are overwhelming. As a small child, I can't be expected to work so
hard."

The Parent-Wife adopts the role of the conventional
Super-Ego in the form of the Harried Mother—"You
keep me busy from morning to night keeping your things
in order. You are a bad child for making me work so
hard."

The Adult-Wife, example three, responds to the
question projecting nothing and assuming no role. She
simply answers the query with fact. Thus Eric Berne
added to our knowledge of human behavior by depicting
the way adults revert to roles learned in their childhood.
His elaboration of psychoanalytic theory furthered the
connection between the person's past and his present
functioning.

What directions will further Elaborators of psychoanalytic theory take next? The answer is in the future. Psychoanalytic theory, productive in the past, will continue as
a framework for the understanding of human nature and
for the improvement of our lives.

Group Behavior

And now to the third area of theory, basic to psychotherapy, concerning the behavior of people in groups. Up
to this point discussion has been centered around the individual. But since people function in a society, theory about
the role of the group is required for full understanding.

Two theories dominate our understanding of group behavior:

1. Group Pressure:
   The group forces its opinion on the helpless in-
dividual—a one-way street. The theory may be
named "Follow the Leader" or "Don't be Different".
The first to verify this theory, in his laboratory, was
Dr. Solomon Asch.

2. Group Interaction:
   All individuals in a group, influence each other
back and forth—a two-way street. The group is affected by the individuals in it; and the individuals are
affected by the group. The theory may be named,
Group Interaction. An originator of this theory was
Dr. Kurt Lewin.

The Group Pressure Theory is really not new to us.
Freud, and the other theorists following him, showed how
the child is molded by the pressure of the group—in this
case, his parents and the forces of society surrounding
him. Even Sullivan, who named his theory, "Interpersonal", conceived a theory which was not back and forth,
not very "Inter". Sullivan, Freud, and all theorists we have
discussed up to this point, considered the individual alone,
and how others impinged on him. They thought only in
terms of a one-way street—the child at the center with
parents and society influencing, prodding, controlling,
and directing this helpless blob of humanity.

The effects of Group Pressure on the individual were
demonstrated by Dr. Solomon E. Asch, an American professor of psychology. He designed an experiment to verify
this one-way theory in his laboratory.

Dr. Asch stood in a classroom in front of eight male college students and drew a four-inch line on the blackboard. Under the four-inch line, he drew a five-inch line. Seven of the students, coached ahead of time, proclaimed the two lines identical in size. The eighth student, who didn't know he was set up as a "patsy", followed the other seven and agreed that the lines were the same size. After the experiment, the eighth student was "debriefed" and told that he was "set up". He exclaimed, "If I'd been first, I would of called it different."

This experiment, giving rise to many more by other investigators using Asch's premise of Group Pressure, marked one trend in a brand new field of human knowledge called, social psychology. While many theorists before Asch, including Freud, suggested that we often play "follow the leader", Asch was the first to measure the effects of group pressure experimentally.

Asch repeated the Group Pressure experiment many times with scores of individuals "set-up" beforehand. He found that the theory did not always work. Group Pressure, in fact, influenced only one out of three "patsies". Typical of the uninfluenced two-thirds was a student who stuck to his guns and said with embarassment, "I always disgree, damn it!" But he did disagree and so did most of the "patsies", suggesting that this one-way Group Pressure theory has limitations.

The limitations of the theory, however, are due more to the situation inherent in a laboratory demonstration. The psychology laboratory, removed from life, where group members are new to each other, is only a one-time event. Asch's experiment, thus, is not a true test of the full possible effectiveness of Group Pressure.

Real-life groups of long duration show the tremendous amount of pressure that can be generated by the group and the group leader. The effects of a long-standing group, encompassing the entire environment, can sometimes be devastating. This country learned of these effects to its shock and horror when body after body was flown out of Guyana in witness to the power of a vicious leader named Jones, on his helpless followeres.

Based on the same principle, yet helpful rather than pernicious, are the many and varied pressure groups for addicts mentioned in Chapter 2. Weight Watchers, AA, or groups for drug addiction are effective in stopping people from their unrelenting cravings. So far, only the theory: "Follow the Leader" and "Don't be Different" has worked with addicts of all kinds.

Unfortunately, there are groups for ordinary people, non-addicts, employing group pressure, an unnecessary dimension. "Gestalt", "Bio-energetic" groups, and certain psychoanalytic groups, led by uninformed therapists lacking knowledge of group interaction theory, use group pressure. They select one member to be "worked on" while other members encourage the "chosen one" to behave according to the group's standards and chastise him when he doesn't. So the one-way group pressure theory is used to stifle individual initiative and growth.

Another example of this type of group pressure, by an uninformed, untrained leader used the theory with frightening effect. In this group of suburban couples, one or two men were continually selected as scapegoats, while a couple of the more hostile women in the group were encouraged to lead the persecution of the victims.The effect on the unfortunate husbands was devastating. *Lord of the Flies* was recreated in the name of "therapy".

The Group Pressure theory—the one-way influence of the group on the individual—when misused, leads to abuses in the name of "therapy", to cult horror stories, and forms the basis of fascist societies. The Group Pressure theory, in addition to serving such evil ends, is also scientifically misleading. It presents an incomplete picture of many real-life groups, thus failing to meet one criterion of a useful theory: Group Pressure is not fully "inclusive".

The family is a typical example of a real-life group whose workings cannot be fully explained by this limited one-way theory. Let us return to the peculiar children studied by Bowlby in England and Kanner in the United States (Chapter 2). These odd children were regarded as the products of unfeeling, uncaring parents.

Psychotherapists even tagged the mothers of such children with the scientific sounding epithet of "schizophrenogenic mother". This jawbreaker was a pseudo-objective way of saying, "That bad mother caused the child to be so crazy."

But what of the child? Does the child do nothing in the family except sit like a lump of clay? The mother, labeled with that nasty medical-sounding term, has the right to say, "This kid is ruining my life. I don't know what to do anymore. He's driving our entire family crazy."

In answer to the unfortunate, guilt-ridden mother's complaint, the Interaction theorists come to the rescue with a two-way theory. They say to her, "Your cry for help is legitimate. Your child is not a lump of clay. He is, indeed, acting on family life. But what of your husband? Does he not have a role? And your other children? And the grandmother sitting in the corner, pursing her lips in understated disapproval? Could she be the real power in this family unit?"

Interaction theorists correctly underline the fact that a child is not simply the product of parental pressure. The child has a role, too, as does everyone else in the family group. In a group of two or more people, each element in the "system" has an influence on every other element. The second unit, in turn, can influence the third—or the first. Thus group behavior is understood as a two-way street.

We recall that Asch's groups managed to influence only one out of three "patsies". Can people in a one-time laboratory type of group be induced to change using a more effective route? Can their opinions and consequent behavior be altered in a different fashion? The answer to this question was discovered by a refugee from Hitlerism, himself a victim of group pressure and oppression. His name was Kurt Lewin, a professor at the University of Iowa and later, at M.I.T.

But even Dr. Lewin had to give in to group pressure. The correct German pronunciation of his name was Levine, but since everyone called him Dr. Loo-in, he became subject to the Group Pressure theory and agreed to be called, Loo-in. As a life-long Zionist, Lewin could not be accused of pretending to a non-Jewish name—but just went along with the American pronunciation.

Kurt Lewin was a brilliant innovator. More than any other investigator, he is responsible for the two-way street—the interaction theory of group behavior. Parts of

Lewin's theory are taught in every school of business administration in the country.

If Asch's "Follow the Leader" or "Don't be Different" theory worked only one out of three times, what works better? Lewin discovered a better method when he addressed himself to a serious problem: Housewives were spending a limited family budget on junk food. How can we get them to buy the right food?

One group of housewives was given individual instruction privately in effective nutrition; twenty to fifty percent changed their food buying habits. "Follow the Leader" was tried in the form of a lecture to the second group. The result: Only a ten to thirty percent change. The third group engaging in a back-and-forth discussion, resulted in a group decision to buy more nutritive foods. This group decision, stemming from the interactions of its members, resulted in a fifty to one hundred percent change.

Kurt Lewin's Interaction theory, properly understood by trained group therapists, is used in a highly effective fashion to promote self-understanding and growth, rather than conformity and obedience.

The role of the trained therapist is not to charm, to seduce, to force, or to bludgeon. The therapist observes what group members say and do to each other; and the effect one member has on the other. Then the therapist's observations and interpretations of the group interaction promote insight for the individuals and expand areas of awareness and control of their lives. Obviously, the selection of the group therapist is as important as the selection of one's individual therapist.

During World War II, Alexander Wolf, M.D., an American psychoanalyst, treated soldiers with psychiatric problems. Faced with an overwhelming number of servicemen who required help, Dr. Wolf realized that individual therapy for a few people in the Army was like trying to ladle out the ocean with a teaspoon. So he gathered a group of eight soldiers, sat them down in a circle, and attempted psychotherapy . . . group therapy.

Since Interaction theory was just in the process of development, Dr. Wolf may not have had the perspective of Lewin and other Interaction theorists. So he adopted Freud's approach to clients: Since the therapist doesn't know what is happening, he keeps quiet, listens, and tries to understand. Rather than "leading" his group, Dr. Wolf sat back and observed.

As the members interacted, Dr. Wolf noted that the servicemen *transferred* to the therapist the father image, just as in individual therapy. But some of the soldiers also transferred to one another: perhaps an older member became a big brother to a younger soldier. The "big brother", in turn, regarded the youngest group member as his own younger brother or even his own son.

With such varied possibilities for transference, Wolf realized that the interaction type of group therapy had values of its own, not simply as a wartime expedient. By expanding the range of transferences, interaction group therapy offered clients the possibility of exploring facets of their personalities that could not be reached by individual therapy.

The application of psychoanalytic theory to groups using Interaction theory, marked a unique advance in modes of therapy available to people seeking help. Fur-

ther application of Interaction theory to families and to
other group modalities will be discussed in the next
chapter.

Now that you've read to the end of the chapter, an
essential idea is in your grasp, one that even many therapists may not have considered. What is psychotherapy all
about?

It is first of all an attempt to understand human nature and then, to construct theories about the nature of
humans. Following our criteria for the evaluation of productive, useful theory, we set forth three theories, functioning in three areas of human behavior:

1. Stimulus-Response, concerned with the basic
building blocks of the human experience,

2. Psychoanalysis, an attempt to cover the wide and
complex range of individual human experience, and

3. Interaction, an understanding of group behavior
founded on the two-way street illustrating the effect
people have on each other.

Since the roots of the two prominent therapies, psychoanalysis and behavior modification, have often been
misunderstood and misconstrued, let us take a second
look at Stimulus-Response, the elemental theory of
human behavior:

Hull and Skinner cut two diverging paths between
stimulus and response. Hull paved a wide road over the
mountains, providing a view of the entire scenery of
human behavior. Traveling along Hull's road from stimulus to response, the psychotherapist finds guard rails and

wide shoulders to park to set up his camera and focus his binoculars. Hull's highway leveled acreage for structures like Id, Ego, and Super-Ego.

"Skinner blazed a straight-and-narrow path between stimulus and response," cries the behavior therapist. "If you take Hull's road, it will take all day. Take the Skinner trail that cuts straight through the jungle of theory, and you'll get there in a few minutes."

This author finds the seductive simplicity of Skinner's behavior modification leads to traps and pitfalls. Human behavior is complex and requires a theory intricate enough to encompass its byways and nuances. Hull's and Freud's survey of the geography of the human landscape opens a new territory for the road builders. How the roads are graded and paved, will be the topic of the next chapter, Techniques of Psychotherapy.

5

Techniques of Psychotherapy

Method, technique is what the client sees when seated before the therapist. The therapist may be as silent as the Sphinx, as many psychoanalysts are, or as active and talkative as most "Gestalt" therapists appear. The therapist may even interrogate the client in minute detail as Harry Stack Sullivan, founder of the "Interpersonal" school of psychiatry, encouraged his disciples to do.

The therapist may be highly trained, aware of every movement of his body, every nuance of his voice. Or the therapist may be totally unconcerned about his manner, preferring to "act naturally".

Psychotherapy today exhibits a range of methods unknown thirty years ago. Some of the methods are unusual: One family therapist visits the home and insists that every person in the house, even every neighbor, be persuaded to join the session. This same therapist whose designated client was an obese 16 year old girl, reported his first action upon entering the home: He zeroed in on the

freezer and threw three gallons of ice-cream into the gar-
bage. Such radical intervention, although seemingly un-
warranted, may be valid if supported by a clear theoretical
mandate.

So the prospective client has a wide array of techniques to choose from in selecting a therapist. We shall
begin a discussion of the many and varied techniques
available with an example of a method which has achieved
a formidable degree of public recognition in the last ten
years.

Mr. and Mrs. Brown lived in a suburb of the capitol
city of the Silo State. They owned two cars and a house
where they lived with their two children and a dog. They
were known to their neighbors as pleasant, charming people whom everyone liked. They rarely argued. Their children and dog were equally well behaved.

So their friends and neighbors would have been surprised if they knew the Browns had a vexing problem in
their marriage. Their sex life was poor. In fact, it was
almost non-existent. This problem bothered the Browns
for some time until they finally decided to do something
about it.

They consulted their family doctor. Unfortunately,
he had little to suggest. So they consulted another doctor.
The second doctor gave each a thorough medical examination and pronounced them healthy. He delivered himself of a set speech and dismissed them.

Since both doctors pronounced the Browns physically fit, the problem, they realized, lay in their heads. Up
until now, the notion of seeing a psychiatrist was repellant,
but the Browns realized that if they wanted a good sex life,
they would have no choice but to consult a "head doctor".

So they made an appointment with a psychiatrist. The psychiatrist listened to their complaint and prescribed a tranquilizer for Mrs. Brown. The Browns' sex life still did not improve.

Finally the Browns heard of a new doctor in Silo City who had a reputation for employing all the latest, up-to-the-minute scientific methods. The new doctor exhibited a considerable amount of scientific gadgetry in his physical examination of the Browns. He then asked the two to step into his office for consultation.

"Your problem is not unknown to medical science," he told the Browns, "But there are few doctors equipped to help you. In a far distant city, a famous research team has published amazing results and they have the answer for you."

Mr. and Mrs. Brown waited expectantly.

"Unfortunately," the doctor continued, "There is a long list of prospective patients waiting to be seen. The fees are considerable and the researchers expect you to stay at their hotel-clinic for two weeks. So we're talking about an expensive procedure."

But the Browns were undaunted and told the doctor they would spare neither trouble nor expense.

"In that case," the doctor replied, "I will get in touch with the Research Institute and have you put on the waiting list."

Finally the day came. The Browns were informed that the famous researchers were ready to receive them. Mrs. Brown packed their things and sent the children and the dog off to her mother's. Mr. Brown bought the airplane tickets and the two of them flew to the distant city of the renowned doctors.

The Browns at last were ushered into the presence of the white-coated specialists. They felt they had come to the sanctuary at the top of the mountain.

The doctors interviewed Mr. and Mrs. Brown both separately and together for the first day or two. And then the Browns were told: "You will now go back to your room. You will massage each other this way and that way, but do not try to have sex." It was implied that sex would come later.

The next day, more interviews followed and more instruction in massage and other sexual preliminaries was imparted. Successful sexual intercourse occurred towards the end of the Browns' stay at the clinic. And sex continued successfully back in the suburb of Silo City. So this story has a happy ending and everybody was satisfied—Mr. Brown, Mrs. Brown, Dr. Masters and Mrs. Johnson. Sex therapy for the Browns was an unqualified success. Or was it?

Mrs. Brown was very happy that at last she was a sexual person. The possibilities seemed limitless. The Browns held a cocktail party ostensibly in honor of Halloween, but actually in secret celebration of their new found powers. A friend of the family who had always found Mrs. Brown a fascinating person, now found her even more fascinating—in bed. Not too long after the Browns' return from St. Louis, Mrs. Brown had affairs with most of Mr. Brown's friends.

How did this sorry situation come to pass? It was not by accident that the task of packing belongings and packing children and dog off to mother, fell to Mrs. Brown. It was her job to take care of household work like cleaning, making beds, caring for children and all the boring trivia most wives and mothers in our society are expected to perform. And somewhere, in some secret part of her being, Mrs. Brown resented this role.

So Mrs. Brown found the life of a secret courtesan far more fascinating than the life of an acclaimed house-maid. She was most grateful to the good doctors in St. Louis for opening up an entire new world.

But unfortunately, resentment of her position as mis-tress of the mundane focussed on Mr. Brown as lord and master. Secret affairs were not enough to assuage Mrs. Brown's need to rebel against Lord Brown. So under the guise of honesty and openness, Mrs. Brown confessed all to her husband. Mr. Brown now bore the full brunt of his wife's vengeance. He believed he had no choice but to retaliate. And so the Browns bitterly regretted their St. Louis adventure.

Now what went wrong with the Browns' treatment? Why did sex therapy fail?

Dr. Masters and Mrs. Johnson are world renowned innovators backed by the full panoply of the medical es-tablishment—that same establishment that eradicated small pox and gave penicillin to the world. Could the Masters and Johnson research be seriously flawed?

No. The St. Louis research is not flawed. Masters and Johnson are careful scientific investigators and their work is valid and valuable. Unfortunately, a serious gap exists between their research versus the application of it to the Browns and to other patients: *Their technique for sex therapy has little to do with their scientific investigations.*

Investigation into the physiology of sex by Masters and Johnson, required a great deal of moral courage. The process of digestion has been thoroughly studied by medical science, as well as almost every other bodily process. But the sexual process in action: changes in pulse, breathing, blood pressure; changes in the sexual organs, themselves, during coitus, before the St. Louis research, had been as unknown as America before Columbus.

Masters and Johnson boldly measured these processes and arrived at some interesting facts: They found that orgasm is more varied in women than in men. They classified the female orgasm into three types, delineated by varying time, intensity, and frequency. Many other vital facts were discovered. But how do these discoveries relate to Mr. and Mrs. Brown's treatment? The answer: peripherally, if at all!

If new knowledge of sexual physiology had little to do with the Browns' St. Louis adventure, what actually was the operating principle underlying the researchers' treatment of the Browns? The real theory behind the St. Louis procedure was none other than the Asch "Follow the Leader" theory. Few Americans could resist the powers of the mighty medical establishment compelling the Browns to have satisfactory sexual relations.

A second thought about sex therapy: Discovery of facts is a valuable preliminary to theory, not a substitute for it. The St. Louis research brought to light new facts about sexual physiology, but it was devoid of theory. Cataloguing birds in the bushes—facts—is only an introduction to discovery of migration patterns. A full understanding of sexual behavior requires not only facts, but a theory about the total functioning of the person.

Sex is not an appended toy for diversion during leisure hours. Sex is an integral part of human interests and activity. A theory encompassing the full range of behavior is necessary to understand human sexuality.

An understanding of the Browns' sexual problem must be achieved in the context of their total relationship; their hopes, fears, wishes, needs and resentments. Although the Browns may have labeled their problem as "sexual", the difficulty was not limited to sexual behavior. Effective therapy for the Brown family would properly focus on the Brown family *in toto,* not solely on how they behave in bed.

Had the Browns undergone a therapy employing clear theoretical focus, their entire life functioning would be open to examination. Change in the Browns' sexual patterns would come about as a result of a change in their entire relationship. Mrs. Brown's resentment would have come to the fore and her anger at Mr. Brown resolved by a redefinition of their respective roles in the family. Wholesome sex could result, rather than hostile sex.

This critique of the Browns' botched up therapy and the unfortunate events following it, suggests criteria for the evaluation of all techniques of psychotherapy, just as criteria for evaluating theories were deemed essential in the previous chapter.

Sex therapy for the Browns bore no clear relationship to the St. Louis research. Since the Masters and Johnson investigations resulted in the discovery of interesting facts but yielded little by way of theory, "sex therapy" could not follow logically as an application of a new and valid theory.

Lacking new theory, Masters and Johnson inadvertently and perforce had to make use of an old theory: the Asch "Follow the Leader" notion. Poverty of theory is a serious omission when dealing with people's lives. Improvisation and tricks are resorted to, with unpredictable and sometimes unfortunate results.

An example of the need for technique to follow theory, may be seen in the story of the window that wouldn't open: Ann called out to her husband, "Marty, would you come here, please? I can't open the window."

Martin went to the window and tugged on it. Then he took a hammer and banged on it. The glass shattered but the window didn't budge.

Martin then called a glazier to replace the glass and asked him to get the window to slide open. The glazier fussed with the sash unsuccessfully until he finally noticed that the window frame, itself, was distorted. He told Martin "I think you may have some serious trouble here. You better call a contractor."

When the contractor was summoned, he brought with him an architect. The two of them discovered the original cause of the bent window frame: The earth on one side of the house had been washed away and the foundation of that side of the house rested on nothing but thin air. Thus, not just the window, but the entire house was distorted and its occupants endangered.

Techniques to remedy Ann and Martin's stuck window had to be based on knowledge of the inadequate foundation supporting the house: The sagging side of the house was jacked up and placed on a firm foundation. Merely fixing the window or its frame was thus irrelevant. Once the foundation was fixed, the window slid easily.

So window fixing or techniques of psychotherapy must follow logically from an examination of the founda-

178

tions of the house, or an adequate theory. *Techniques must bear an intrinsic relationship to the theory.* Lacking adequate theory, "sex therapy" resulted in disaster.

The second criterion for an effective technique is suggested by the Masters and Johnson inadvertent use of authority. The St. Louis healers report an astounding rate of success: Almost 100% of their patients are "cured". Such a high rate of remedy is due primarily to their "screening" process. Although the sex researchers may not have been aware of it, they chose their patients from that group of people, most likely to respond to the pressure of medical authority.

Only crutches belonging to devout Catholics of a different era were discarded at Lourdes. Only the impoverished of Haiti and others raised in a similar milieu are affected by voodoo. And only people who regard themselves as "hip" and educated undertake sitting on the hard chairs provided by "est" for an entire week-end, and are influenced by its "trainers".

So sex therapy is directed towards another special group, the carefully culled Browns of the American middle class—those most likely to be persuaded by the white garb of "scientific medical research". If the Browns viewed the doctors without their white coats would sex therapy still work? Probably not.

In sum, evaluation of the different techiques of psychotherapy will be guided by these two criteria:

1. Does this technique follow logically from an adequate theory? Is the technique intrinsically related to a fundamental understanding of human nature?

2. Is the technique contaminated by the use of unplanned or disguised authority?

Before beginning an evaluation of the different methods of psychotherapy, it is important to stress again the distinction between theory and technique. At the beginning of the previous chapter, the word, psychoanalysis, was used to illustrate the confusion of method and theory. Psychoanalysis, you will recall, has two very different meanings: 1. A theory of human nature, and 2. A technique of psychotherapy.

Do you know anyone who has been "in analysis"? Because of the double definition of "analysis" that phrase is misleading. Its imprecision results in confusion. Let us try, rather, to separate "psychoanalysis" into its component parts, theory and technique, by sketching the course of two people "in analysis":

Joseph visited an "analyst" five times a week. He lay on a couch and blurted out whatever came to mind. His therapist's comments had all the force, relevance and validity of "Dianetics".

Carl visited a therapist once a week. Because Carl suffered from claustrophobia, instead of sitting in the office, Carl and his therapist walked about in the park during sessions. Carl's therapist concentrated on Carl's feelings towards the therapist. One day Carl didn't show up and didn't telephone.

When the hour was almost up, the therapist decided to telephone his client. Carl told him he couldn't manage to come because he was too anxious. The therapist then suggested that next time Carl feels too anxious, a session could be tried on the telephone to find out what might be keeping him away from the session.

Was Joseph "in analysis" or was Carl "in analysis"? Or were they both "in analysis"?

Joseph was treated with the conventional and superficial form of psychoanalysis, an inexpert attempt at psychoanalytic technique. Carl's therapist, ignoring psychoanalytic technique, made use of transference and resistance, the two basic tools of psychoanalytic theory. Carl's therapist would have been quite willing to swing from the chandelier in complete disregard for psychoanalytic technique, if such a perch would have resulted in the dissolution of resistance.

Thus psychoanalytic theory and psychoanalytic technique differ widely. Just as Carl's therapist used a variety of methods to analyze transference and resistance, so almost any technique can be used with any theory, *as long as the method follows logically from the theory, itself.* For example, Dr. Alexander Wolf, mentioned in the previous chapter, used a group technique to analyze transference. Psychoanalytic theory, thus, is not inexorably tied to the couch.

Similarly, Interaction Theory is a valid basis for any therapy when two or more clients are seen together. Understanding the effect people have on each other—the two way street—may underlie the use of various techniques: group therapy, family therapy, couple therapy, or even "therapy" for a work situation like a business, factory, or hospital when workers find it hard to get along.

We shall now proceed to evaluate different techniques of therapy. We must be aware that many methods can be used with varying theories, as long as the techniques follow reasonably from the theories and are not contaminated by the use of unplanned or disguised authority. Individual methods will be discussed first; group techniques will be considered next.

Psychoanalysis (the method) is the original technique of psychotherapy. First used by Freud, the client lies on a couch with the therapist behind and a bit to one side. The client arrives five times a week and is expected to "free associate", i.e. to say out loud whatever comes to mind no matter how loose, disjointed, or irrelevant it may seem. The therapist tends to be silent except for sparing use of interpretation.

On the positive side:

> Five times a week provides a more intense experience for the client.
>
> Free association brings the client closer to his unconscious—a direct application of psychoanalytic theory.
>
> Not being able to see the therapist promotes projection of the client's needs. In Chapter 3 we discussed how people ascribe to the unknown or to the vaguely structured, their deeper fears and wishes as in the ink-blots, the dark, or the unknown boss. Thus an unseen therapist promotes options for transference—another logical application of the theory.
>
> The therapist's comments are sparse since a few words are heard more clearly than a torrent; jewels of wisdom are more prized than heaps of scrap.

On the negative side:

> Five visits a week are too expensive for most.
>
> Therapy outcome research has yet to prove the value of frequent sessions.
>
> Free association and the unseen therapist may bring the client in closer touch with the unconscious, but may

also remove the experience from the rest of life. What is learned on the couch may not be applied at work or at home. This is especially true for Harry in Chapter 3, prone to the defense of isolation, who delivers a 45 minute paragraph labeled, "therapy".

Few can tolerate a silent therapist. The resulting anxiety may be counter-productive.

The client may insist, with some justification, that transference came about only as a result of his prone position; that placing him on the couch is an exercise of authority by the therapist.

Is psychoanalysis a useful technique? It is, for the very few. If one is wealthy and articulate, he or she may decide to take two or three years out of life and do little else but concentrate on therapy by limiting other interests. Such an experience can promote a complete change. But most are not prepared to undertake this task.

Face-to-face psychotherapy is now the more common technique. It has been described in Chapter 3 with but one aspect missing—the exact wording of an interpretation. Analytic therapists differ in the way they phrase an explanation of the client's behavior. One passage in the course of Mr. Bender's therapy will be presented as an example of the different ways in which a therapist may present an interpretation.

Mr. Bender fills his sessions with complaints about his wife. He regales the therapist with tales of her selfishness, lack of kindness, and downright nastiness. She is a horrible person who makes life miserable for the client. Attempts by the therapist to deflect Mr. Bender and get him on to another topic prove useless. There is only one note in Mr. Bender's horn. Such single minded pursuit of a single topic is clearly a form of resistance. How may the therapist resolve this blockage?

Here are four of many possible interventions. You will note that all four therapists will find guilt a major concern, guilt being a prime component of the Super-ego. Thus the therapists apply psychoanalytic theory to their techniques.

> THERAPIST A: You keep talking about how nasty your wife is, so *you* won't feel guilty. This is why you blame *her*.

Although this comment may be true, it is clumsy and heavy-handed. No one wants to be told he or she is guilty, nor will Bender accept such an accusation.

> THERAPIST B: Pointing the finger at Sally, holding her to blame, draws attention from your own activites.

This explanation—virtually the same as the first—nevertheless avoids pointing the finger at Bender and holding *him* to blame. The question of guilt is alluded to, but not clearly stated, by the phrase, ". . . your own activities." So Bender would be more likely to accept Therapist B's comments.

> THERAPIST C: You keep insisting that I must agree with you, that Sally is a pretty awful person. This way both of us are certain that *you're* an Okay person.

Again Bender's guilt was implied, rather than told to him directly. C. suggested that the client was too vociferous in his accusations of his wife to be believed ("You keep insisting . . ."). By implication, one might imagine that Bender must be hiding something—could it be his own guilt? Could Bender, at the same time, be proclaiming his own innocence for a defensive purpose (". . . that *you're* an Okay person.")?

Therapist C also exposed Bender's perception of the therapist as a parental figure: Bender was trying to make C. into a judge, forcing him to declare Sally's guilt and the client's innocence (". . . that I must agree with you . . ."). Therapist C's comment is classical in that it was complete, referred to the transference obliquely, and implied projection (see Chapter 3) of guilt as Bender's defense. Therapist D, however, used a different strategy:

THERAPIST D: I'm sure that what you say is so. But Sally isn't here now, so whatever you tell me about her isn't going to help matters. Let's leave her out of this for the time being and see what you're about, since you're the one who is here.

Therapist D avoided the full interpretation given by Therapist C. D. wisely directed his comment towards one goal only—the resolution of Bender's resistance. The client's resistance was blocking the entire course of therapy and it was resistance alone that was properly the object of Therapist D's attention.

Therapist D *sidestepped* the resistance by agreeing with the client. Any further attempt by Bender to insist on Sally's guilt would be redundant, since he has already "scored" with his therapist ("I'm sure what you say is so."). Realizing that Bender was too caught up in reacting

185

to guilt for any insight to take place, Therapist D went so far as to absolve the client from guilt: he even implied that Bender was the "good guy" since he, and not Sally, was in therapy. Thus D. delivered the comment most likely to get Bender moving forward by providing a future occasion to explore guilt.

You have just witnessed a "first". This is the first time, to the author's knowledge, that a full and detailed explanation of the exact words of a therapist have been presented to the layperson—why a therapist phrases a comment this way and not that way. Such instruction in the specific skills of the psychotherapist has previously been confined to books carefully restricted to professionals.

The title of this book contains an implied promise, made explicit in the first chapter: to inform you as fully as possible what psychotherapy is all about. How and why a therapist phrases an interpretation is a key, a touchstone to the process of therapy.

If you think you may have missed some of the nuances of the four interpretations presented, you are at liberty to review them. Once understood, you will have a knowledge of psychotherapy in considerable depth.

The subtleties of interpretation, the art of attempting to understand what was bothering Mr. Bender, why he was illogically compelled to fill his own private sessions with his wife's doings, are a far cry from authoritarian "therapy".

Even Therapist A, whose comment, doubtless, would be unacceptable to Bender, did not try to tell the client what he ought to do. Therapist A may have lacked finesse, but his goal was to promote understanding, insight into

Bender's guilt. Conversely, a wholly different perspective was taken by Therapist X.

Therapist X is a disciple of a thinly disguised authoritarian school of therapy called, Rational-Emotive Therapy. The name, embellished with a hyphen, is designed to impart an air of scientific and philosophical distinction. Regardless of its brand name, authority is the active ingredient of that mode of therapy.

As this hyphenated "therapy" has no theory, only the founder's personal values, Therapist X lectures Mr. Bender, waving the banner of a down-to-earth, no-nonsense approach:

"You've spent almost an entire session complaining about your wife. If I didn't stop you now, you'd spend another ten sessions repeating yourself. Now will you please tell me what you are getting out of this marriage? Not much? I'd say nothing. You aren't even getting laid. The only reason you keep on with this marriage is because you think you're so unattractive that no other woman would have you.

"Now that is a very wrong idea and I want you to get it out of your head. And there is only one way to do it. I'm going to give you a homework assignment for next week. I want you to go out and get laid. Don't tell me you can't do it. You can, if you approach at least ten women. Now go to it and I'll see you next week."

Three possibilities now lie before Mr. Bender: 1. He could try to do his "homework" and would fail because his marriage is deeply rooted—the relationship with his wife, Sally, satisfies many powerful needs, unknown to Therapist X, 2. Bender may succeed in having an affair, leaning on the authority of his therapist to still his conscience, or

187

3. He might have the good sense not to return to Therapist X next week, spending the time more fruitfully in the search for a competent therapist.

In contrast to the bungling attempts of authority minded therapists to influence human behavior, the very highest order of skill is required in approaching an area of human function embodying the person's deepest needs and wishes—the dream.

Techniques of dream interpretation are at least as old as Joseph, Pharaoh, and the seven lean years. But instead of regarding the dream as a portent of what *will* happen, psychotherapy regards the dream as an expression of what the dreamer *would like* to happen, an outward product of the life force (libido) crucial to psychoanalytic theory.

Open expression in a dream of frankly taboo desires is limited to people with a shattered Ego, inhabitants of mental hospitals. People with a functioning Ego, disguise the wish underlying the dream. The skilled therapist interprets the dream in accord with the client's known defenses and his current life-style.

The therapist waited for Larry to begin. Larry had arrived a few minutes late and was facing the therapist silently. Finally he spoke, "I had one of those hateful dreams again."

"You had sex with your mother?"

"*And* my sister. I was making it with my sister when my mother started to disrobe, trying to entice me."

"Oh?"

"I hate having these dreams. They're disgusting."

"It hardly sounds like you really want incestuous sex."

"Well, I don't." And then Larry added in resignation, "But if that's what I dream, it must be what I want." Larry was applying psychoanalytic theory in a superficial manner.

But the therapist insisted, "If you wanted that kind of sex, you wouldn't be sitting here now. You would belong in a mental hospital."

"So what's it all about? Suppose you tell me!"

Larry's belligerence stemmed from his embarrassment at having to recount the dream. His therapist understood and ignored his truculence. The therapist continued, "I think it has a lot to do with that supervisor you told me about last week. She makes all these demands on you for detailed reports. If you give her everything she wants, you won't be able to get any of your own work done."

Larry agreed, "She's a bitch."

"But it's also an inner struggle," the therapist went on. "You hate to give in to her requirements, yet part of you is tempted to say to her, 'Here's the goddamned stuff and leave me alone.' "

"I don't like it when I do that. Give 'em a finger and they take an arm. You can't satisfy them ever."

"But I think this is what you're doing in the dream. Even to such a disgusting and unreasonable demand as sex with your mother and older sister, you eventually give in and say, 'Okay, Okay, I'll do it.' "

Larry nodded, "I've been doing that kind of thing all my life, being a nice guy. It's about time I stopped and just said no."

In order to make the interpretation, the therapist kept in mind Larry's one sided view of women and his compulsion to pacify them. Only recently had he begun to put his foot down when necessary.

Another element helping the therapist with the dream interpretation, was the "silent movie" analogy. The therapist imagined a silent film with no narration. A dream, like a silent movie, cannot utilize words like "and", "but", "although". These must be supplied from the rest of the client's life. In Larry's case, the needed word was "*Even* (such an act)". Larry's embarrassment and disgust when he related the dream, gave the necessary clue. His present struggle to avoid pacifying women, fitted the rest of the puzzle.

Larry's dream and the therapist's understanding of it was presented to remove the veil of mystery from dream interpretation. The province of dreams need not be limited to soothsayers and prophets of the occult. Seen in the light of the client's present conflicts and wishes, his current fears and hopes, and the style of his everyday life, interpreting Larry's dream was not an arcane art, but a skill acquired by proper training.

Yet sometimes different therapists compete in virtuoso display of dramatic dream dredging. Refuting a dream interpretation by presenting an alternative notion, perhaps more penetrating than the original, is a favorite game played by therapists among themselves. Yet for the layperson, such competition is confusing. How do you know whose interpretation is right?

Psychoanalytic theory states that no one bit of human behavior has a single cause. Animals, too, can be conditioned to make an identical response to different stimuli, according to stimulus-response theory. So both theories suggest that all human acts, including dreams are multi-determined, have many causes. Thus almost any interpretation of a dream may be "correct". Few understandings of dreams can be "wrong".

Hence our emphasis on the relevance of an interpretation to the poignant present of the client's life, rather than on its "correctness". Almost any notion can be "right", but what comment about the dream can the therapist make which will be most useful and significant for the client sitting before him?

Our uneasy client, Larry, had no use at the moment for an abstruse Oedipal interpretation. He saw women as demanding shrews whom he felt called upon to pacify. Even though other interpretations of Larry's highly Oedipal dream may be "correct", the one given, was of greatest use to Larry in the light of his present problem.

Dream interpretation can be one of the most effective tools in the therapist's kit. As long as the understanding of a dream is not reduced to an intellectual exercise, but is made relevant to the client's life, the dream can be used as a powerful instrument for change. The therapist did not have to use authority and urge Larry to stop pacifying women. Larry was so disgusted at his behavior in the dream, he became conditioned to change it, as stimulus-response theory suggests.

The very opposite of insight and understanding is provided by an emergency technique of psychotherapy called, TM (transcendental meditation). Like bio-feedback, TM can spread a soothing ointment over anxiety and worries, serving as a psychic tranquilizer.

The TM novitiate is given a "mantra", a "word" especially concoted for the individual trainee. He or she is never to reveal this word—ever. The initiate is then taught to eliminate the world! translated: go into a light trance.

Stripped of its Far Eastern, far-out format and its theoretical misconceptions, TM is a method for conscious control of denial and repression. The secrecy of the "mantra" teaches repression; "eliminating the world" teaches denial. Unconscious conflicts are thus driven underground by training in the conscious use of these two defenses.

Do you remember Charley, driver of the car with defective steering at the end of Chapter 3? His control of the defense of isolation enabled him to bring the car to a safe halt and perform needed functions while under severe stress. *Control of our defenses and their conscious use at appropriate times, can be a prized gift.* Although the approach of TM leaders is frankly authoritarian, the knowledgeable person can turn their training to his own purpose.

Distinguishing the authoritarian approach from the attempt to understand the client, is not difficult. But the conventional professional-to-client relationship in our society may prevent you from becoming aware of the exercise of authority. When you consult any professional—doctor, lawyer, or accountant—you expect to lay the problem before him and then be told what to do.

Naturally you will expect the same relationship consulting a therapist. And it is easy enough for the therapist to give you what you are led to expect by the professional-to-client format.

But the more you know about psychotherapy, its

aims and techniques, the less likely it becomes that you will be misled when consulting a psychotherapist. The authoritarian therapist will fulfill your professional-to-client expectation—he'll tell you what to do—but the competent therapist will not.

This same test of valid psychotherapy versus unknowledgable efforts at therapy, holds not only with individual therapy but also with group methods. In the previous chapter a distinction was made between a group method employing the Asch theory of "Follow the Leader" versus the Interaction theory of understanding the effect of group members upon each other.

So understanding the difference between Asch and Interaction, it will not be hard for you to make the distinction in a practical fashion between these two types of groups. Sitting in a group, it will take you only ten or fifteen minutes to note the difference. Do the group members speak to one another? Are they encouraged to "interact"? If so, the group operates with the Interaction Theory.

Conversely: is one member singled out for "instruction"? Is interest focussed on him for more than a few minutes? Are the group comments and the attention of the leader directed only towards that one person? If that is the case, the group follows the Asch "Follow the Leader" Theory. Unless you are an addict and the group's purpose is to stop your addiction, you are advised to pick yourself up and leave. Such a group is not for you.

On the other hand, if you find yourself in the first kind of group, the Interactive type, you have found a useful group. Even if you don't like the people in it, give it a solid chance and stay for at least ten sessions.

But suppose you genuinely dislike the other members? Please remember that a therapy group is not a social event; it was formed to help you change. A professor of philosophy once confided to the author when he was in group as a client, the person he disliked the most, he realized much later, effected most improvement in his relationship to others. Effectiveness, not enjoyment, is the purpose of a therapy group.

The reason you may not like the people in a group has to do with its composition. A problem solving group, on the one hand, is homogenous. Its members are alike. For instance, the members may all be mothers. They are there to solve common problems facing mothers; or its members may all be homosexuals—the group was formed to try to solve problems facing homosexuals.

A therapy group, on the other hand, attempts deeper change than a problem solving group. That is why its composition is heterogenous—members differ from each other. The professor's pet hate, the man he couldn't get along with, was a carpenter's helper. But their mutual anatagonism resulted in useful comment by the therapist. If you have few interests in common with the other group members, you won't be sidetracked by a common interest in baseball or the latest recipe for rhubarb pie. Instead, you will get down to fundamentals quickly, such as love and hate and friendship.

Not only will the fundamentals of human interaction be examined in group, but, should the therapist use psychoanalytic theory, ideas like resistance, will play a role. Here is an example of a somewhat different group technique used to deal with resistance:

The two men walked into the group meeting twenty minutes late.

"What happened to you?" the other members inquired.

"We had a wonderful experience with a waitress. She was terribly goodlooking and she was really interested in us. It was a very positive experience."

"Don't you think you could have put it off for another time?" one of the women in the group asked.

"Oh no. This was a growth experience for us. You know we have a problem with women. It was more important for us to interact with that woman than to be here."

The therapist wondered out loud if they hadn't used the waitress as a pretext. Other group members also demurred. But nothing could shake the two men from their conviction that they had a "growth experience" more vital to their development than coming to the group on time.

Finally the therapist stood up and began distributing the monthly bills to the clients. The group members became indignant. "Why are you wasting valuable time and exerting authority by handing out the statements?"

"Why, indeed?" the therapist replied. The clients gazed at him blankly. "I am not wasting your time nor am I exercising authority beyond our agreements to pay for therapy." The therapist continued, "I am, in fact, making an interpretation."

As a long standing group, the members were aware that resistance could block not only individual therapy, but group therapy as well. The two men refused to recognize that their lateness was a form of resistance. And no attempt by other members or the therapist to label their lateness as such, succeeded. So the therapist resorted to an action rather than using words which had proved ineffective. What was he trying to tell the two men? The light dawned on one of the women. "I think he's tring to tell the two of you that if you want to waste time by your resistance, you have to pay for it anyhow."

Another man in the group joined her, "Come on, fellows . . . What don't you want to talk about?" And the secrets came pouring out. Thus resistance constituted the theory; distributing the monthly bills was the technique.

The therapist's use of an action, rather than words, introduces us to a new universe of techniques produced by "Gestalt," "primal scream", and the human potential therapists. Week-end institutes such as Arica and Esalen demonstrated the possibilities of varied methods in group therapy.

The knowledgeable therapist is not deterred by the fringe therapies' use of authority, or by the absurdity of some of their theories. He or she will learn, borrow, beg, or steal any method—as long as it is legal and can be used in the service of an adequate theory—to stimulate interaction and understand the clients better.

One such method has been inaccurately called, "guided fantasy". A more exact term might be, "fantasy stimulus". The therapist suggests to group members that each, in turn, write an oral letter to a person with whom they have unfinished business, someone important to whom they had never communicated a vital message. "You don't need pencil and paper," the therapist might say, "Just dictate it out loud and start with, 'Dear . . . blank' whoever it is."

As a stimulus for unspoken thoughts this method is superb. The letter is often addressed to a parent, a mate, a former spouse, or a child. The fears, the loves, the broken hopes brought out often lead to unusual interaction among the members. Properly understood and assimilated, the process and its results can lead to awareness and resolution of the unfinished business, whatever its source.

Further expansion of group technique resulted from the work of Eric Berne, founder of TA (transactional analysis) mentioned in the previous chapter. Berne successfully analyzed that bane of every therapist's practice, the client who returns again and again, never giving up—and never improving. Such a client has been called by some, "the help rejecting complainer".

This indefatigable, eternal client often begins a group session by posing a problem to the other members, "I love to dance but my husband can't. I haven't danced for years because of him."

MEMBER A: Why don't you get him to take lessons?

CLIENT: I've tried to get him to, but he refuses.

MEMBER B: Why don't you explain to him how much he's missing?

CLIENT: Oh, I did, but he doesn't care.

MEMBER C: Well then, why don't you go dancing by yourself?

CLIENT: I couldn't go alone!

MEMBER D: How about going with some of your girl friends?

CLIENT: I tried it once but when I returned, my

husband was up waiting for me and I
felt too guilty.

The interchange may continue for a few minutes or
for the entire session, but the outcome, whenever such a
point arrives, leaves the group members in total pained
silence. Berne suggests that the very helplessness and frustration felt by group members when their kindly words of
advice come to naught, is the goal of the advice seeking,
but help rejecting member.

This earnest help seeker is not unintelligent. If questioned, she will admit to having tried the various solutions
proposed by the group. If she hasn't tried them, she is at
least aware of these obvious answers. Her aim, rather, is to
reduce her peers to a state of enfeeblement.

This client is a champion of the game called, "Why
don't you . . ." "Yes, but . . ." (Yes, but I tried it; yes, but it
doesn't work; yes, but you don't understand). She sometimes preys on the fringe therapists who naively believe
they can help by issuing dicta. After she conquers them by
reducing them to an abject state of fury—"yes, butting"
them to death—she goes on to ply her stratagem on new
therapists foolish enough to instruct, rather than understand the client.

The therapist who is not taken in by such guile is
often given the epithet, "Orthodox Freudian". This ma-
ligned therapist is curious as to why the professional Yes-
But client must maintain such a posture. What does she
gain from reducing group members and even some therapists to a state of angry impotence?

With the aid of Berne, the knowledgeable therapist
tells her after group members have been effectively si-

lenced, "That's too bad. I guess you'll never get to go dancing."

Indignantly she replies, "But you're supposed to help me."

"No one can help you. Let's turn to another topic."

The therapist effectively called her bluff. When later in the session she might be forced to admit that she really didn't need advice, but was using her pseudo-problem as "a means of getting attention", only then will the underlying dynamics come to light.

How can a rebellious child prevail against an all-powerful parent? She has found an ideal solution enabling her to get revenge on all authorities—parents, teachers, and counselors.

They've told her in the past, "But Mary, I *only* want to *help* you!" Now she is saying to her "elders" be they group members or therapists, with hidden malice, "Fine, go ahead and help me—if you can."

Chronologically an adult, yet psychologically a child, this client transfers with rebellious guile to peers and therapist as if they were her parents. In order to understand this obscured transference, Berne had to show us her "game" first and to suggest how to force her to stop playing it, so her transference could be understood.

Group therapy can be extended. The "marathon" held over an entire week-end, has also been called, time extended therapy. This innovation, quite likely, was borrowed from the Christian "retreat". While some research suggests it has value, it has yet to prove itself. The same amount of time spent weekly, that is, broken up into one hour and a half sessions, may be just as effective, if not

199

more so. Indeed, stimulus-response theory suggests learning is more effective when "spaced"—broken up, instead of swallowed in one vast, indigestible lump.

The most revolutionary advance in psychotherapy technique is family therapy. Most Americans do not live by themselves; they make their homes with at least one other person. For years, psychotherapy has been of limited value because it focussed efforts on the single individual.

To what avail does a therapist see a child one hour a week when the other 167 hours are spent at home or at school? Since Mrs. Brown must return to Mr. Brown's enslavement, the best efforts of her individual therapist are in vain. The conspicuous failures of psychotherapy are most often caused by the false notion that the individual functions apart from the people he or she lives with.

Before the advent of family therapy, parents of a peculiar child would metaphorically dump the child on the "head Doctor's" doorstep and say, "Here is the kid, Doctor. You fix him and we'll pay for it."

Do you remember the "schizophrenogenic" mother held responsible for her child's difficulty, in the previous chapter? At the same time her child was being "therapized", the mother, who was regarded as the cause for the child's behavior, would be given "guidance"—that is, told how to handle the kid. "Child psychiatry" was the rage in psychotherapy circles, because such treatment confirmed the family's need to scapegoat someone, by labeling him or her as the "crazy one". Therapists naively accepted the parental diagnosis and agreed that the child was the "patient". All along the *family* was the true client.

And here are more labels: In some sophisticated, but uninformed circles, you might overhear an argument between Mr. Van der Smythe and his Vassar educated wife:

> *"You're an impossible person! Even my therapist says you are controlling, manipulating, into martyrdom, sadism and hypochondria."*
>
> *"Oh yeah? Well, my therapist is President of the World Congress of Psychoanalysts and he says you're a schizophrenic."*

In both cases, the "crazy" kid and the arguing couple, the unkind labels so liberally affixed by family members on the other person, serve only to show how ineffective individual therapy often is. The tradition bound therapists of the peculiar child and the therapists of the Van der Smythes are equipped with a technique for individual therapy only. They may nod their heads sagely in the presence of their client, but alone, and to themselves, must admit total inability to help such families.

Today we are fortunate to be able to solve these problems with family therapy. Family therapy is not "marriage counseling" or "social work", doling out advice in the attempt to keep a marriage together or to manage a disruptive child. Family therapy is the application of group technique, based on Interaction Theory, to the family unit—a special kind of group.

The general theory underlying family therapy may be credited to Kurt Lewin's two way street; the specific theory, serving as the ground work for understanding the family, was originated by Talcott Parsons (1902-1979) of Harvard University. Born in Colorado Springs, educated in New England and then in Europe, Dr. Parsons ranks first as America's most brilliant theoretician in the field of sociology.

Unfortunately, his dense prose makes Parson's work inaccessible to many family therapists. His ideas, however, such as the "systems" approach borrowed from engineering, have filtered down to the rank and file. Professor Parsons was the first, and perhaps only scientist in the field of human behavior, to unify Interaction Theory with psychoanalytic theory in his understanding of the family.

Talcott Parsons did not know Jean and Burt, or other recipients of his gift for theory, yet these clients were helped by the therapist who examined their conflicts and understood them in the light of Parson's theory. Indirectly the Harvard professor aided the therapist when the therapist refused to be drawn into the family problem by responding to Jean's covert flirting; instead, he examined it. No amount of individual therapy would have prevailed with Burt and Jean, unless they had a year of joint sessions, in addition to their individual therapy.

Of the many vital and indispensable ideas in family therapy, none may be more important than the concept of "role":

"My children make me very happy. Arthur is the brain in our family. When he grows up, he's sure to be a doctor or a lawyer. And Suzie, well, she's not very smart, but she is a beauty, always looking at herself in the mirror."

Sometimes these prophecies are totally self-fulfilling, but very often such assignment of roles results in rebellion and disaster. Arthur decides to use the "brain" assigned to him by mother in the service of writing pamphlets for the Red Panthers. Suzie, narrowly escaping prostitution, consigns herself to watching TV soap operas, imprisoned by the white picket fence around the house, because of her assigned stupidity.

The father in the family continues to bring home the pay-check and nod out at 9:30 in the evening because he is the "steady one" of all family members. And mother? Her role is never mentioned out loud. She just runs the family since the others have been labeled incompetent, each in his own way.

When the family therapist, instead of taking what he hears from family members at face value, explores with the family what is really happening, progress is made possible. Without the understanding of family dynamics, clients often work their individual therapies into the fabric of the family system, ensuring that no waves are made. And, incidentally ensuring that the original complaint bringing them to therapy in the first place, is never altered. Neither the individual therapist nor his client realizes that the complaint serves a vital purpose, as yet unknown, in preserving the family.

Arthur and Suzie, mother and father may be rescued from their preordained roles, by insight and understanding, opening the gate to unlabeled, and therefore useful and productive lives. Thus family therapy, a specialized technique of Interaction Theory, may be the ultimate combination, unlocking the vault to individual fulfillment.

"Dyadic group therapy" stands in sharp contrast to the wide applicability of family therapy. It is not unreasonable to think that every person who lives with another is a potential client in family therapy. However, dyadic therapy, a new technique originated by the author, is highly specialized. It is conceived as an auxilliary method, that is, in addition to individual therapy.

Clients in dyadic group therapy consist of a man and a woman with heterosexual orientations who did not know each other before. They are seen jointly by the therapist, much as couples in family therapy.

What is the purpose of such a group? Has the therapist turned into a matchmaker? Hardly. The mature people seen in this new type of therapy do not need to be told the purpose of the group. They are there to gain insight into their behavior with a person of the opposite sex, to learn new ways of relating; not to find a boyfriend or girlfriend.

Dyadic group therapy may be regarded as a method combining the best in both couple and group therapy, but sharing the drawbacks of neither. Often feelings between two people who have lived together for some time, can be so intense, that in spite of the therapist's best efforts to enlighten the couple, they are not able to listen. Their love and their hate may be too strong. So reason and understanding are suspended while they engage in a life or death struggle, deaf to the therapist's comments.

Conversely, in a group of six to eight people, two of the clients, a man and a woman, may begin to have some feelings between them, useful for insight. But interaction between the two is often interrupted by others in the group—as it should be. An entire group session devoted to two people would be unusual, to say the least, and not very helpful to others in the group. Thus a group tends to dilute the beginnings of possible strong transferences between a man and a woman.

But it is these very transferences, distortions of adult feelings, that are the root of so many difficulties. The intimate man-woman relationship lies at the very core of a person's psyche and it is this relationship which is most often askew.

But is not the same effect achieved by transference to the therapist of the single client, seen individually? Not quite. Feelings about a therapist hark back to childhood in a more direct fashion than man-woman feelings. True, feelings about a mate may be based on childhood experiences, but they possess a quality all their own. Transference to a therapist tends to short-cut the man-woman transference directly to childhood, but in so doing, vital intermediate feelings are omitted from the therapy situation.

The author tried this technique first, with his own clients; then, in the attempt to gather more information about the method, volunteers interested in therapy, were enlisted. The volunteers did not, however, perceive a strong need for therapy at the time. Results suggested that people who have had a great deal of previous therapy, benefitted; but for those who had not had previous therapy, the method was almost useless. Thus dyadic therapy is seen as a technique for the few.

But the greatest benefit appeared to accrue to clients who were simultaneously undergoing conventional methods of therapy and who clearly perceived their man-woman relationships as deficient. This was the reason they were in therapy to begin with. Thus the client's motivation has much to do with the effectiveness of the method.

Another result, obtained from limited evidence, suggests that positive results came when the two people were matched as closely as possible for their cultural background and unconscious dynamics.

A secondary advantage of dyadic therapy would seem to be the minimal amount of training necessary for the therapist who is already skilled in both family and group therapy. Such a therapist, combining both skills in his work with the dyads, would probably require only a short period of practice under supervision to be able to use this new form of therapy effectively.

However promising dyadic therapy may be, it is still in its infancy. Quantitative research (therapy outcome research) is needed to verify or disprove its effectiveness.

Has the reader noticed a difference in the style of this account of dyadic therapy compared to descriptions of other techniques? In contrast to the report on family therapy told enthusiastically, replete with examples, dyadic therapy is explained in dry, theoretical fashion, *sans* stories or any other embellishment. Well then, if the author is unenthusiastic, even skeptical, about the value of his new method, why does he bother mentioning it at all?

Why, indeed? It is tempting, of course, to run naked in the street shouting, "Eureka! I have invented a new therapy!" But the author has not done so because of the requirements of scientific caution and objectivity. The method is new and relatively untested. More experience in its use plus full experimental evaluation are required before presenting dyadic therapy enthusiastically.

Perhaps the dry fashion used to present this new

mode of therapy illustrates best of all the difference between the fringe therapies and genuine therapy. When reason and logic are trusted rather than indulgence in hysterical promotion and public relations efforts, you can be assured, you are getting better help.

Like dyadic therapy, psychodrama may be regarded as auxilliary therapy. Improbable as it may seem, psychodrama is not a stunt or exhibition. It is a unique method for eliciting hidden material. During more than a quarter of a century, its practitioners have developed unusual methods to bring out unconscious material through the use of dramatic improvisation.

After a "warm-up" period, a member of the client-audience is selected. He or she recalls a crucial incident from his early life. This incident is then acted out, impromptu fashion, by clients chosen to take the parts of mother, father, and other family figures. Still other clients, standing behind the protagonists, act as "alter egos", blurting out the truer, less censored thoughts of mother, father, client and sibs played on the stage.

Therapists instructed in this technique are highly responsible and well trained. If you are in therapy, you might discuss with your therapist the possibility of adding psychodrama to your regular sessions, if psychodrama is available in your locality.

Which Therapy Is Best For You?

A careful distinction was made between insight therapy based on psychoanalytic and interaction theories versus therapy based on authority. This dichotomy may have led you to believe that insight therapy is the only therapy that makes sense, the only therapy you should choose.

Quite the contrary: you may recall in Chapters 1 and 4 we suggested that Pressure Groups were regarded as the only effective therapy for the addictions. And in Chapter 4 we advocated the use of Behavior Mod and Bio-feedback in some situations. The purpose of the argument in this chapter and the one before it, has been to clarify what the different therapies were all about, to enable you to make an intelligent choice. No recommendation was made for any single therapy under all conditions.

Discussion of the therapies, rather, was designed to label the ingredients comprising a specific therapy, just as the ingredients of a cosmetic or can of pineapple, are listed on the package. Unmasking the use of authority—often disguised in some therapies—when authority constitutes the "active ingredient", has been our goal. But should therapy based on authority be best for your condition, you will be armed with knowledge and be aware of the contents inside the packaging. You have a right to know what you are buying.

Our exposition of the therapies, both theories and techniques, was designed to ensure you do not select a therapy falsely labeled. The arguments advanced here were planned to prevent you from choosing a trendy therapy, purporting to be the result of a brilliant new scientific advance, but essentially differing not one whit from the guidance you received from your second grade teacher.

Which therapies may you choose from? Here is one way of classifying all the varied theories with their many techniques:

1. Insight therapy,
2. Supportive therapy,
3. Conditioning therapy (Behavior Mod and Biofeedback),
4. Authority therapy.

Which therapy you choose depends on your perception of your problem and the perception of your therapist. Your therapist may even, at some point during your uncovering therapy, change his or her approach and use authority rather than insight. The skilled therapist will not hesitate to use the Asch Theory when necessary.

Martin experienced such a change in the mode of his therapy when his therapist, Paul, abruptly told him during the course of a session, "I think it best at this point, that you avoid seeing Gloria."

Martin was indignant, "Aren't you pulling the old authority bit on me?"

Paul calmly replied, "Yes, I am."

"Well, I don't like it at all. I came to you originally because I chose insight therapy and we both agreed on this at the outset. Now you're telling me what to do."

"I think," Paul suggested, "that we've both seen what happens when you go back to Gloria. One evening spent with her can undo a month of therapy. It puts you back on square one. It is my judgment that you are not going to progress here unless you decide not to see Gloria for a while."

"So I'm to tell her, 'My therapist said you're bad for me. He doesn't want me to see you.' "

"You know, Martin, she might see things more clearly than you. She may even go so far as to agree with me."

In later sessions, Martin's resentment at Paul's use of authority had to be understood and interpreted. Changes in Martin's perception of the transference had to be evaluated. But Paul's intervention brought about an additional dividend for Martin which he hardly expected:

Martin believed up to this point that his therapist treated him mechanically and cared not the slightest for him as a human being. Paul, by insisting that Martin avoid seeing Gloria for a time, conveyed a new idea—Paul was not a machine. He truly cared what happened to Martin and wanted him to progress in therapy and in his development.

Before deciding on his move, Paul had given the matter a great deal of thought. While the therapist could not accurately predict Martin's response, Paul decided to take the risk and issue a flat *fiat*. On his part, Martin was sufficiently well informed to be aware of his therapist's change in approach. Moreover, Paul minced no words and did not try to disguise his use of authority.

It is not the better part of wisdom to advocate the same method for all clients all the time. Informed judgment on the part of the therapist and awareness on the client's part, contribute to an effective use of different modes of therapy, even if it be authority. Progress up the ladder of psychotherapy results from a flexible selection from many techniques, not doctrinaire prescription. While a therapist's theoretical position remains constant, the theory, itself, may suggest the use of alternate techniques.

CHAPTER

6

Choosing a Therapist

You are now ready to choose a therapist. You pick up the Yellow Pages and look up "Psychotherapists". But that entry appears to be missing. So you try again:

Printers
Propellors
Psychologists
Public Libraries
Public Schools
Public Speaking Instruction

You expect to find "Psychotherapists" sandwiched between "Psychologists" and "Public Libraries". But if your phone book is like most in the United States, you will come up with a blank instead of a listing.

You begin to wonder whether you wasted your money when you bought this book. You now know a great deal about psychotherapy. But what use is all this knowledge if there are no psychotherapists available to help you?

According to the laws of most states, the profession of psychotherapy is not licensed or regulated. It therefore doesn't seem to exist, at least for the telephone company. However, you did note, when your finger "walked" the

Yellow Pages, that "Psychologists" were listed. Further research will reveal that psychiatrists are camouflaged under the heading of "Physicians". If your telephone directory lists medical doctors by specialty, you will be able to find the listing, "Psychiatrists" under "Physicians". A third allied profession will be found under "Social Workers".

But to what purpose was all your research about psychiatrists, psychologists, and social workers? You don't want to be given tranquilizers or shock treatment by a psychiatrist; you are not interested in having your IQ tested by a psychologist; and you are not impoverished, so you don't need the services of a social worker. You want psychotherapy, not help offered by these three professionals.

True, psychotherapy is not usually recognized by most states as a separate profession; instead, it is practiced by social workers, psychologists, and psychiatrists plus a sprinkling of mental hygiene nurses and clergymen. After the practitioners of the three major "helping" professions receive their initial training and certification, they sometimes go on to get further training in psychotherapy. This further training is crucial: it prepares the social worker, psychologist, and psychiatrist to practice psychotherapy.

When the practitioner of each of the three disciplines receives further training in psychotherapy, he or she may properly be called a psychotherapist, even if the state does not recognize this profession. Years ago, when psychotherapy was limited to one technique—psychoanalysis—this further training entitled the professional to be called, psychoanalyst, or "analyst" for short.

But in order for us to select a therapist in an informed fashion, we must know first, what each of these three professionals does, how he or she is trained, what each is prepared to offer you besides psychotherapy. And second, we must know about the post-graduate schools of psychotherapy—the schools that train psychologists, psychiatrists, and social workers to be psychotherapists.

The psychiatrist stands at the top of the prestige ladder among the three helping professions. His or her position is largely due to an effective public relations effort by the American Medical Association. But the aura of knowledgeability surrounding the psychiatrist holds true only in our country. In the Soviet Union, the psychologist stands at the top of *their* prestige ladder since he—it is almost always "he"—walks in the proud tradition of Russia's outstanding scientist, Pavlov.

Yet having read the previous chapter, you are aware you want skilled psychotherapy, not authority emanating from the prestige of the therapist. As an informed consumer of psychotherapy, you will regard considerations of prestige irrelevant to your therapy. You will choose a skilled therapist, not necessarily a glamorous one.

Such knowledge may even save you money. Less informed clients will demand the services of a psychiatrist, replete with M.D. They will have to pay extra for the "magic" of his or her degree. Your therapist who may have a degree in social work and who is not addressed as "Doctor", may be as well trained, or even better trained in psychotherapy than a given psychiatrist.

But the social worker will charge you a more moderate fee. Should you be convinced by this argument and

215

seek a therapist whose original discipline is social work, you will have saved yourself hundreds, perhaps thousands of dollars. Well worth the cost of this book.

On the other hand, in some of our smaller localities, it is the psychiatrist who sometimes has had the most training in psychotherapy. It is worth paying his fee to get the right help.

In sum, considerations of prestige are irrelevant to your needs. Let us then, continue to the more relevant consideration: What does the training of the three helping professions consist of? What are their fields of expertise and how may this affect your therapy?

The psychiatrist, after completing medical college and a year of internship, like all physicians, stands for the state examination licensing him/her to practice medicine. At this point he still knows little about psychiatry or psychotherapy. The doctor then becomes a "resident" in a psychiatric hospital or other recognized facility. After completing at least three years of residency, the doctor becomes eligible to stand for his board examination in psychiatry and neurology, a single specialty.

Please note that the state requires only that the doctor pass the general medical examination for physicians. The final medical board certification as a psychiatrist is awarded by the medical profession, not by the state. A doctor is entitled to call himself a psychiatrist even if he has not passed his medical board examination. If he has completed his residency in psychiatry, he becomes "board eligible" and may call himself a psychiatrist.

The psychiatrist, after the usual residency, still has not received much training in psychotherapy. But he is well equipped to understand aberrant behavior, to dispense drugs and other forms of medical treatment for problems of adjustment, and most important, to make a diagnosis distinguishing a psychogenic problem from organic illness. The psychiatrist, if he passed his boards, is also qualified to diagnose neurological problems.

What are the advantages of seeing a psychiatrist as your therapist? There are occasions during the course of therapy when a client could make good use of a psychotropic drug (a drug that affects behavior and feelings). If your therapist is a psychiatrist, he or she can prescribe the drug for you.

Indeed, psychotropic drugs in general, are best left to the psychiatrist even though any medical doctor is legally permitted to prescribe them. It is next to impossible for any human being to know the full effects of the thousands of legal drugs available. The general M.D. can scarcely be expected to know them all thoroughly. But the psychiatrist has wide experience with the few available—forty or fifty—psychotropic drugs since he prescribes them daily.

These mood affecting drugs are probably the trickiest in the entire pharmacopoeia and affect different people in different ways. Hence if you need such drugs, even if you are not in therapy, you would be well advised to see a psychiatrist for a prescription.

Yet, if your therapist is a psychiatrist and careful not to use authority, he or she may not want to complicate the relationship by giving you the "magic" of a pill. He will refer you to another psychiatrist if he believes you could use a drug or you believe you could use one. Should your therapist be a psychologist or a social worker, he or she will make the very same referral to a psychiatrist. So it may matter little if your therapist is a physician.

Another important function of the psychiatrist is his or her ability to distinguish between organic illness and a psychogenic problem. In difficult cases, a psychologist is often called in to help. The young woman, mentioned in Chapter 1, whose epilepsy was functional, was diagnosed only after a psychologist and a psychiatrist with special expertise on physical brain problems, put their heads together and arrived at the right diagnosis.

But please remember that your therapist, whatever his or her original discipline is, will suggest you see an appropriate specialist when needed. So there is no inherent advantage to having a psychiatrist as a therapist because of his or her medical expertise. A responsible therapist will know when to refer you to the right experts should you need them.

And now the psychologist: His or her training is essentially in *research* on human behavior. The kind of reasoning found in Chapter 4 on theory is typical of the psychologist's thinking. After finishing college, the psychologist undertakes three years of graduate classroom study plus a dissertation. The dissertation, an original contribution to scientific knowledge, may take one year to complete or *ten years*. The psychologist is then awarded the Ph.D.

Of the different varieties of psychologists, it is the *clinical* psychologist who most often goes on for further training in psychotherapy. How is a clinical psychologist trained? After the three years of classroom study, he or she undertakes an internship in a mental health facility.

There he learns how to use varied psychological tests to assess the client.

The tests fall into two categories: The first are tests with limited options for your answers, like IQ tests or personality tests with four or five possible choices. "Check *a, b, c* or *d.*"

The second type are projective tests with almost unlimited possibilities for your response. The Rorschach inkblot test is an example. We explained in Chapter 3 how such a test offers many channels to project your needs, because of the vagueness of the forms.

While the first kind of test, the limited response type, can be scored by a computer, interpreting a projective test is a matter for human skill and experience. A skilled clinical psychologist can even obtain a measure of creativity and other apparent intangibles from a projective test. The greater the skill of the psychologist, the more likely it is that he can make almost any test stand up and do tricks!

But as with the psychiatrist who may be your therapist and who may prefer not to prescribe for you, the psychologist you may be seeing, may not want to test you once therapy is under way. He or she may not wish to complicate the transference by performing on you the "magic" of a test. If the question of your IQ is of legitimate concern to you, the psychologist you are seeing as a therapist will refer you to another psychologist to be tested.

In a medical setting, the clinical psychologist functions much as a pathologist does with the doctor asking the pathologist to test the patient's blood and urine. The psychiatrist consults the psychologist on matters like possible brain damage, requesting psychological tests. But the final diagnosis is the responsibility of the psychiatrist.

After the psychologist receives his or her Ph.D. and sufficient clinical experience, he or she then stands for the state licensing examination. Upon passing it, he/she is permitted to offer professional services as a psychologist to the public. Like the psychiatrist, the psychologist may still not know very much about psychotherapy, but must continue schooling in a post-graduate institute for therapy.

The social worker, after college, attends a two year graduate school of social work. Two days of class work a week are alternated with three days of supervised practice. Upon graduation, the social worker is awarded the degree of M.S.W. (Master of Social Work). Some years after receiving the academic degree and acquiring enough practical experience in an institution, the social worker is licensed by many states to practice social work independently.

Social workers specialize in any one of three areas: Casework, group work, and community relations. The caseworker who functions in a psychiatric setting like a mental health clinic is called a psychiatric social worker. It is he or she who may continue schooling at a post-graduate school of psychotherapy.

The social worker's area of expertise lies in the client's relationship to the environment. The social worker often can be the best person to refer you to other experts and sources of help, although any therapist in private practice must develop these sources.

Is there an advantage in choosing either member of the three professions to be your therapist? If you want a social worker to guide you, a psychologist to test you, or a psychiatrist to diagnose you, the advantages of a particular discipline are obvious. But if you want *psychotherapy*, the answer is a clear, definite "No". Should you need to be guided, tested, or diagnosed, your therapist will refer you to the right professional.

Post-graduate schools of psychotherapy usually require their students to be bona fide members of one of the three helping professions before entering the institute; but paradoxically, the training in psychotherapy given to the prospective therapists then goes on to erase their previously acquired professional attitudes towards people: They have much to *un*learn.

The social worker must learn not to guide people but to understand them; the psychologist must learn to deal with a person, not a "subject" in a test or experiment; and the psychiatrist must drop his notions about the "patient" as a machine with a broken cog, acquired in his years at medical school, and see his client as a human being. Professionals of the three disciplines who cannot adjust their outlook, have tended to drop out of the psychotherapy training institutes, fortunately for you.

Thus even if the therapist you may select has learned little in a post-graduate institute for psychotherapy—an extremely unlikely possibility—he or she has been screened, willy-nilly. Such a therapist, more likely, will be the right therapist for you with the right approach, better than a professional who has not undertaken a course of study at a school of psychotherapy.

How did the post-graduate schools begin? Training in psychotherapy was an outgrowth of the way Freud trained his disciples in psychoanalysis. Dr. A.A. Brill,

221

Freud's disciple and a highly talented organizer, came to America shortly before the first World War. He translated much of Freud's work from German into English, founded the first American society for psychoanalysis, and helped to establish the first post-graduate training institute for psychoanalysis in this country.

Freud and Brill entered into a furious trans-Atlantic dispute about "Lay-Analysts", as non-medical psychoanalysts were called then. Brill insisted that only M.D.s were to be trained as psychoanalysts, while Freud, equally adamant, demanded that qualified non-physicians should also be trained and be permitted to practice as "analysts".

Freud's position in favor of non-medical analysts stemmed from his wish to have the public realize that psychoanalysis was a general theory about human behavior, not a tiny sub-specialty of medical technique. In 1938 he wrote in English, so that nothing would be lost by anyone's translation, "I have never repudiated these views and I insist on them even more intensely than before, in the face of the obvious American tendency to turn psychoanalysis into a mere housemaid of Psychiatry."

Brill has been made the butt of much criticism by historians of psychotherapy, as the organizer of any movement will be. His views were regarded as narrow and parochial, contrasted with Freud's liberal and wide ranging views. As a translator of Freud, some critics agreed that Brill did a wonderful job with only two exceptions—one, Brill didn't know English and two, he didn't know German.

But Brill has not been given the credit he deserves. Dr. Brill's practical decision to shelter psychoanalysis within the embrace of the medical establishment in the United States, turned out to be a wise move.

Our country, with its freedom of religion, tends to nurture all kinds of off-beat movements. Had psychoanalysis, at first, not been restricted to the medical profession—a highly organized discipline—analysis, no doubt, would have been distorted and diluted into another "scientology". Even those of us who are still regarded with mild condescension by the psychiatrist-therapists as "Lay-Analysts", are grateful to Brill and the early founders of psychoanalysis in America for keeping psychotherapy within the confines of a science-based discipline—medicine.

But with the advent of basic research in human behavior by psychologists as described in Chapter 4, and the high requirements for entrance by almost all present institutes of psychotherapy, such medical exclusivity no longer obtains, nor is it necessary. Looking back on eighty years of psychoanalysis as an institution, most would agree that Brill's decision was a required expedient for the short run. Yet Freud's objective, keeping psychoanalysis as a general theory and a non-medical educative technique, thus training all qualified people, has been attained in the long run.

But the first institutes of psychotherapy in America were open only to medical doctors and taught only one therapy technique—psychoanalysis.

These institutes still exist, usually attached to a medical school. Should you choose a therapist trained at such a school, you can be assured that your therapist will be a highly skilled psychiatrist-therapist. He or she is called a

223

"psychoanalyst" or "analyst" for short and will be well trained but in only one method—psychoanalysis.

However, other post-graduate schools of psycho-therapy offer training now, not only to psychiatrists, but to psychologists and social workers as well. They sometimes teach a variety of techniques, but with an emphasis on individual therapy. Should you find a therapist with a certificate from one of these institutes, chances are you will have found a skilled therapist.

Still it may seem odd that a certified social worker, psychologist or psychiatrist should be required to sit in yet another classroom. Why? Couldn't a professional who must be an adult responsible person just sit him or herself down with Freud, Klein, Berne, Horney and other origi-nators, developers, and elaborators and learn from a book? Why must professionals be treated like college freshmen once again?

Very few skills can be learned from a book. Can you imagine learning how to drive a car by reading a book, or even ten books? "Impossible," you will argue. "You can learn traffic regulations from a book. You can learn *about* steering or gear shifting from a book, but you can't learn how to *do it* from a book." And you are right.

The same holds true for psychotherapy. A small part of the skill of therapy can—and must be—learned from a book or a classroom. But that is only a small part. So the psychotherapy institute may have only one or two class-rooms, but it will have many small offices, each one for a senior therapist and a therapist-in-training. Because the prime part of training in therapy is the student therapist's *own personal psychotherapy.*

The first psychoanalysts underwent six months of therapy or even less. Their therapy was called, a "didactic" or teaching analysis. Neophyte analysts were to be given a taste of therapy—just enough to give them some experience with their own unconscious. Later, therapists realized they needed more than just a smidgeon of therapy to do effective work. Nowadays, well trained therapists have been in therapy longer than almost all their clients.

Why must a therapist undergo therapy as a part of training? The best way to know a road is to travel on it yourself; a map is not good enough. Reading an account of therapy sessions, or even listening to a tape of a session is like flying over the road in a helicopter. Travelling the road of therapy with feet treading the ground, implies a personal experience in therapy.

"But you don't need to experience an appendectomy to be a good doctor." The medical analogy still does not hold: An appendectomy is performed when the patient is unconscious; observing the operation supplies more information to the trainee than undergoing it. Psychotherapy differs from medicine and so does training for it.

Secondly, personal therapy is the best way for the therapist to avoid getting entangled in his or her client's problems. Such intertwining is called, *counter-transference*, an emotional reaction to the client caused by the therapist's own childhood distortions.

Fortunately, the practicing therapist has clear cues to the presence of counter-transference: Dwelling on the client's problems outside of the office, wondering if the therapist should have said this or done that, imagining what the client is doing now, or dreaming about the client, all these indicate the therapist is becoming enmeshed in

his own childhood difficulties triggered by the client.
Should he be unable to trace the source of his irrational
response to the client, the therapist will return to his own
therapist for one or more sessions, in order to solve his
problem.

The second most important part of the education of a
psychotherapist is seeing clients under supervision. An
experienced therapist will listen to a neophyte therapist's
account of his session with a client and offer comments.
Sometimes the therapist may play a tape recording of the
session to the supervisor, or the therapist may be seen in
action through a one-way mirror. Of course the client's
permission is needed.

Here is a brief account of a therapy supervisory
session:

THERAPIST: I seem to have run into a real snag with
Joe Green. He claims his wife nags him
constantly, so I suggested that perhaps
she is trying to get close to him even if
he may not like the way she does it. But
Joe wouldn't accept this idea. He went
on to insist that she gives him no peace,
that she's trying to make life miserable
for him, and on and on. Finally I told
him to ask her what she really wants.
But Joe didn't like that suggestion at all.

SUPERVISOR: Perhaps the whole issue of his wife's
nagging is an avoidance of something
else.

226

THERAPIST: Well, that's just what I tried to indicate. But he wouldn't listen.

SUPERVISOR: How do you suppose you might get Joe to listen?

THERAPIST: I've tried just about everything and we seem to be completely stalemated.

SUPERVISOR: You might point this out.

THERAPIST: Well, of course I did. But that was no help at all.

SUPERVISOR: And you need help with this situation right now because otherwise, Joe is sure to quit therapy.

THERAPIST: That's for sure.

SUPERVISOR: How about the suggestions I made before?

THERAPIST: I've tried them and they didn't work.

SUPERVISOR: So what would you like me to do?

THERAPIST: I hoped that you could suggest something effective.

SUPERVISOR: And if I can't, then I'm not a very good supervisor.

THERAPIST: I didn't say that.

SUPERVISOR: But neither did your client say outright that you were not a very good therapist, yet he certainly applied a lot of pressure to try to make you feel at your wits end. Let's examine our own interaction: I made a number of suggestions and interpretations the same way you did with your client. But nothing I proposed seemed effective. I could end our session now feeling thoroughly frustrated with you since you refuse to accept anything from me. I could even end with an unpleasant feeling that there must be something wrong with me since I haven't been able to help you. I think you were playing the same game with me that your client was playing with you.

THERAPIST: Of course! Berne called it the "Why Don't You . . .?" "Yes, But . . ." game. And Joe was doing his best to frustrate me. This put him on top.

SUPERVISOR: Sometimes this kind of game can leave you feeling very helpless and ineffective.

THERAPIST: That's for sure.

The need for clarity in explaining supervision has, perhaps, made the process seem simpler and easier than it is, in fact. Just as some therapists have a talent for subtlety and others may be run of the mill, some few supervisors are unusually skilled and others are not.

A therapist enrolled in a post-graduate school of psychotherapy, will try to seek out the school's best supervisor and, of course, its best therapist. He certainly must find teachers and therapists with whom he can be *simpatico*.

Since good training in psychotherapy depends entirely on getting the right therapist and the right supervisor, some therapists will forgo formal institutes of therapy altogether. They will concentrate efforts on finding the right teachers either privately or in a clinic facility. Indeed, some clinics give intensive training to their therapists and are indistinguishable from the post-graduate schools.

With uncommon good sense, a perceptive educator suggested that education consists of a pupil sitting on one end of a log and a teacher sitting on the other end. He said nothing about buildings, credits, or diplomas. So you may find an expert therapist who never entered a psycho-therapy institute, but designed and executed his own training by sitting on the other end of the training log with a teacher whom he found himself.

Having, in effect, created his own institute and shaped his own schooling, such a therapist may be more adult and independent than a therapist who received all the right diplomas and certificates. Among the founders of group and family therapy are two highly able thera-pists, S.R. Slavson and Jay Haley. Their only diploma was in engineering!

But how are you to know? How will you know if a prospective therapist is well trained or if he is merely a self-appointed guru? The possession of a certificate is a helpful guide, but not an absolute prerequisite. Later in this chapter we will suggest five ways of finding a thera-pist. Using these five channels to find a therapist, is your best guide. Knowledge of your therapist's diplomas and certificates is simply helpful background information. Thus it is possible to find an expert therapist having no formal qualifications but with a background of years of serious education and training obtained on his own.

Formal qualifications, diplomas and certificates, are one aspect of the therapist's background. Informal qualifications—or disqualifications—may be equally important in the quest for effective therapy. One informal qualification, usually unsupported by a diploma, is the number of techniques your therapist can employ with proficiency. Has he or she had training and experience with group and family therapy? Are there any other techniques he is qualified to use? You might ask him.

You might also ask the therapist if there is a particular kind of client he prefers working with. Some therapists are especially skilled in working with children and adolescents. Obviously a family therapist must enjoy working with children.

Therapy with children offers great rewards since improvement may be rapid, even dramatic, as we explained in Chapter 2. Conversely, few therapists believe they are qualified to work with older people. If you are over fifty and have never experienced therapy before, you might ask your therapist if he believes he is qualified to work with you because of your age. If not, he may recommend a therapist specializing in the therapy of older people.

Most therapists prefer working with clients suffering from anxiety or depression. These problems are most amenable to therapy as we explained in Chapter 2. Therapists don't often succeed with people who obtain pleasure from their problem areas, so many therapists refuse to take them on as clients. But there are a few therapists who specialize in these impulse ridden clients.

One such therapist is Harold Greenwald. As the author of *The Call Girl*, his Ph.D. thesis, Dr. Greenwald, no doubt, had the distinction of writing the only dissertation in the history of science ever made into a movie. In the course of his research, Dr. Greenwald became well known to the underworld of commercial sex.

A most unlikely candidate for psychotherapy, a pimp, once consulted him. In an attempt to get the pimp interested in pursuing psychotherapy, Dr. Greenwald suggested, "There isn't much difference in the source of your livelihood and mine. We both live off the earnings of women. Yet I garner admiration, respect, and prestige from my work. But you must live on the fringe of the law, risking jail and earning the contempt of many. There must be something you're doing wrong and something I'm doing right. You could learn from me."

It is clear from Dr. Greenwald's experience that specialized approaches are required for these special clients and other clients with special needs.

At the other extreme of special needs, let us consider the handicapped. Suppose you are blind. Should you seek out a therapist for the blind? Another alternative might be to find a blind therapist.

Both these proposals are valid. But you may not find such a therapist. What are you to do? Try a non-specialized therapist. He or she may tell you that he knows nothing about blindness and wants you to explain everything to him.

You may well have found the right therapist. The specialized therapist on the one hand, may assume knowledge that both of you possess, so vital information will never be put into words. On the other hand, through his legitimate curiosity, an enquiring but unknowledgeable therapist, may insist that you articulate crucial material on the fringe of your awareness, relating to your blindness.

But a therapist for the blind may take such knowledge for granted. So you may be even better off with a therapist who knows nothing about your handicap.

We are discussing the therapist's informal qualifications. But can you trust a therapist to be honest about his special abilities or the lack of them? Generally, yes. A therapist spends a significant part of his life listening to people. It is not much of a life if he cannot feel *simpatico* with the people he sees. On their part, clients will desert him if they sense he cannot listen. So rarely will an expert therapist undertake therapy with a special category of client he senses he cannot help.

In a class all by himself, is the celebrity therapist. There seems little doubt at first, that he is qualified, but does it make sense to consult him as your therapist?

Let us distinguish between two types of celebrity therapists: First, is the therapist whose name is familiar to many of us. He or she authored a bestseller telling you how to improve your work, your marriage, or your personality. He or she appears on the television talk shows and tells women (and others) how to control their children, husbands, boy friends, and aged mothers. Soon, psychotherapy becomes a sideline; client fees are only a small part of their income, while most of their wealth is derived from public appearances as a TV "personality". At this point you might reconsider your original aim—are you considering a therapist or an entertainer?

In an entirely different category is the therapist who is highly regarded by his colleagues. He or she might even be considered something of a celebrity by other therapists. He has written innovative books and articles studied by

other therapists and holds office in the national psychotherapy organizations. Surely this therapist must be competent. But would he or she be a good choice as your
therapist?

In the attempt to find an answer to this question, the
author decided to take an informal poll of some fellow
therapists. The poll yielded some intriguing replies, even
though it was conducted with an unscientifically selected
sample of colleagues. A summary of the findings has been
condensed as a single interview with one therapist:

KADUSHIN: If you lived sixty years ago in Europe,
would you seek out Freud as your therapist? (Sixty years ago, Freud was a celebrity among therapists, but unknown to
most.)

THERAPIST: It might be an interesting experience.

KADUSHIN: But if you really needed therapy would
you . . .

THERAPIST: Oh, come on!

KADUSHIN: Well, would you?

THERAPIST: Hell, no. I'd find one of his disciples like
Theodore Reik (not Wilhelm Reich).

KADUSHIN: What's wrong with Freud? Wouldn't you
prefer the original?

THERAPIST: Never. He must have been a lousy therapist.

KADUSHIN: What do you think was wrong with him
as a therapist?

THERAPIST: As a therapist he was a great scientist! I
would want a therapist who would be interested in me as a person. Oh, don't get

me wrong. I'm sure Freud was a decent
enough human being, but I think he'd be
looking at me for some quirk he could
write about in support of a new extension
of his theory.

KADUSHIN: So you don't think you could get much
from Freud as a therapist?

THERAPIST: No, I don't. But I could ask him to refer
me to a competent therapist. I don't suppose Theodore Reik was well known,
even to other therapists, in the early
Twenties. So I'm sure Freud could have
referred me to Reik. Freud may even
have been supervising him at the time.

Neither the celebrity among therapists—like Freud—
nor the professional celebrity, once a therapist, must be
disqualified automatically and out of hand. But their services as your therapist are suspect.

More than suspect, is the therapist who doesn't listen.
Indeed, not giving the client full attention, is an out and
out disqualification. Oddly enough, it can happen. Such
behavior by a therapist is, in fact, a contradiction since, by
our definition, a therapist is one who listens.

While a therapist is also, by definition, a human being
and has "off days", these are rare. Unfortunately some few
therapists are more "off" than "on". Their concentration
on the client is thin, sometimes because of other duties
and responsibilities. This can be true of a therapist with a
large administrative load at a clinic or hospital. Another
such example is the celebrity among therapists. He is con-

stantly sought by colleagues and could well spend his entire time talking to them on the telephone.

That instrument causing the most disruption in the therapy session, the agent of distraction and faulty attention, is the telephone. Paying a full fee for a full session, you have a right to expect a therapist to keep his conversation brief. Conversations on the telephone—more than a minute or two, occurring habitually more than once or twice during a session—is sufficient reason to disqualify a therapist. Should the therapist himself, initiate a call during your session, it makes sense to pick yourself up and leave, never to return.

Some telephone calls are unavoidable. Your therapist may have to receive an emergency call from another client. But after a minute or so, the expert therapist will ask the caller where he can be reached and tell him he'll call back. A skilled therapist will then turn his attention back to you and summarize briefly the topic you were discussing before the interruption.

Failure to listen to a client suggests faulty technique. But a more fundamental disqualification is faulty theory, a danger sign for the client. Defective technique merely blocks progress in therapy, but erroneous theory, misconceived theory, or total lack of theory, can lead to serious mischief. We have seen an illustration of results ensuing from faulty application of theory, in the case of Mrs. Brown's misadventures after her St. Louis sojourn.

The chief offenders in the realm of theory are: The Crazy, The Know-nothing, and The Great Dictator.

The Crazy is literally just that—insane. His estrangement from the world about him is cloaked under an elabo-rate theory. At first glance, the theory appears to embody learned thought. But if you disregard the Crazy's diplo-mas and certificates earned earlier before his increasing alienation from his surroundings, you begin to suspect some peculiarity.

In form, the Crazy's theories are often prolix—"fat", fancy, and unnecessarily embroidered. The "facts" he presents are not always reliable, but even when they are, the theory is far more complicated than required to ex-plain these events. The voluptuousness of pure thought lures the Crazy from reality, thus seducing the less sophis-ticated client from whatever sanity he possessed at the outset.

In substance, the Crazy's theory often propounds forces emanating from outer space, voices from the past or future, a cosmic "eye", or a mystic "energy". The tech-niques he proposes to use on the client may involve body massage or exercises. These physical manipulations of one's anatomy are not regarded simply as healthy muscle activity like jogging or swimming, but supposedly have a mysterious connection with the forces of the Crazy's cos-mogeny.

Popular myth holds that all therapists are crazy. That's why they became therapists. Quite the contrary is true: If anything, most therapists err on the side of being too rigid and literal. They possess sanity at the expense of poetry. But unfortunately the field does attract a minority whose grasp on reality is tenuous.

At the opposite extreme from the Crazy is the Know-nothing. Instead of operating with too much theory, the

Know-nothing therapist operates with none. Trading on a strong trait in the American character stemming from the time of Populism and Andrew Jackson deriding European theory and the wisdom of Harvard and Yale, the Know-nothing therapist insists on conducting his operations with total lack of theory.

The Know-nothing thrives on ignorance—his own, and his clients'. Claiming to have discarded all theory and all technique, the Know-nothing proclaims, "I go to my office to enjoy myself." He must cure, then, by mere association with his clients; his magic presence must be responsible for whatever his clients derive from him.

Upon asking the Know-nothing what his orientation is, he will reply, "I work with Human Beings."

"I understand you do," you continue, "but do you have a theory as a basis for what you do?"

"Theories are fine in books," he explains, "but People need People, not Theories."

So much for the Know-nothing. The perilous journey of therapy had best be undertaken with a guide who can read a map, not an ignoramus who glories in his lack of wisdom.

The Great Dictator does not operate with too much theory, nor does he lack theory. He is strictly a pragmatist and uses the all-too-effective Asch theory.

Realizing that clients first come to him when they are at their wits end, when difficulties and vexations have made life intolerable, the Great Dictator proceeds to give such clients just what they secretly hoped from a therapist. In essence, the Dictator fulfills their unstated need for a demi-god who knows all the answers. He will tell the client, "I know exactly what is troubling you. Do as I say and all will be well."

This seductive approach, the laying on of hands, works wonders. It matters not what the Man tells them. As long as they fulfill the command of the Authority, the pressure from their Super-ego is relieved. And it is that pressure which is most often the cause of the pain— whether it be anxiety, depression, or psychogenic symptom. Thus the Great Dictator becomes the original parental figure and assumes the role of the client's mother or father, when he or she was a child. Psychoanalytic theory names this kind of treatment, "transference cure."

It is almost needless to say that the Great Dictator is careful never to point out what is happening between him and the client—the transference effect. The Authority must maintain his authority forever. Thus he continues his seductive operation as long as the client pays homage. In return for his obedience, the client remains free of symptoms while "under the influence of . . ."

But occasionally a knowledgeable client will appear in the Great Dictator's office. This client dares ask a question which may pull aside the drape concealing the true Wizard of Oz.

"What is your orientation?" asks the courageous client.

The Great Dictator replies in a deft parry, "Why do you ask?"

Should the brazen client then mention THIS IS PSYCHOTHERAPY and indicate interest in the therapist's theory, he will be told not to worry his li'l ol' head with such matters.

"I will do what's best for you." True, mother knows best, but a therapist's job is to interpret transference, not to re-enact it.

We have discussed the therapist's formal qualifications and suggested some informal qualifications. Disqualified therapists include the telephone addict, the Crazy, the Know-nothing, and the Great Dicatator. But at this point you may have a few considerations of your own about the therapist you want to see.

You may want a therapist who is older, rather than younger; a female, rather than a male; a married person, rather than unmarried; a Protestant, rather than a Jew or a Catholic; a non-hyphenated white, rather than an ethnic or a black; a conservative, rather than a liberal; and a non-smoker, to boot. Or just the opposite.

Should you, in fact, demand every last one of these attributes in a therapist, you will probably search forever, thus ensuring you never begin therapy. Being that finicky is simply resistance before entering therapy as we suggested in Chapter 3. Yet some of your considerations may be reasonable, not necessarily a sign of resistance.

A younger client may prefer a younger therapist, closer to his age, thus trying to avoid a generation gap. The older therapist, he believes, is remote from his concerns or his language. He may even associate the older therapist with his own parents, who were prone to condemn him.

Others may prefer an older therapist believing that sexual attraction towards a younger therapist would impede therapy. Neither of these considerations is valid: A competent therapist is not judgmental, whatever his or her age. He will insist on understanding the client's concerns however wide the generation gap may be at the outset. The younger client, wishing to avoid sexual attraction to the therapist, may be surprised at finding the older therapist attractive after all. Transference works in mysterious, albeit gradual fashion; but its presence, far from disrupting therapy, becomes vital to the process.

Yet, for other reasons, the therapist's age is not irrelevant. Age difference in therapists can make a difference: The younger therapist may be more alert and enthusiastic than an older therapist. But the older therapist has experience on his side and may be more skillful.

On those rare occasions when a therapist must give advice or intervene using authority as Paul did with Martin in our example at the end of the last chapter, the older therapist may have an edge over the younger therapist. Having lived more, he may have more savvy. The client can thus draw on the older therapist's greater life experience.

As a client, you will simply have to make up your mind which you prefer, enthusiasm or wisdom. But given the choice between a qualified therapist and one not so qualified, the question of age becomes almost trivial.

Of all the personal considerations you may have, the therapist's sex often is the most crucial. But again, not for reasons usually given by clients. You may recall that Jean feared entering therapy with a male therapist. Her ostensible reason was that a man would perform an act of psychological rape on her mind. Little did she realize at the time, that a part of her did, in fact, welcome such an act. But the therapist refused to enact the role of psychic rapist. By Jean's very expectation of psychological rape, she was enabled to understand her transference and thus become truly liberated.

Other clients, both men and women, may prefer a male therapist. They are imbued with our culture's notion of the man as the more powerful of the sexes, thus providing a more powerful "cure." Others may prefer a female therapist, believing that women are more compassionate and understanding. Such notions about therapists are largely incorrect. One bit of experimental evidence, found in the examination of therapists' responses, suggests that differences between the sexes of therapists have been totally erased by their training.

Yet the sex of the therapist can make a difference in your therapy. If you regard a major difficulty in your life as the male-female relationship, it makes sense, other things being equal, to choose a therapist of the *problem* sex. If you found Ellen's lonely, unloved character, sketched in Chapter 2, all too understandable, reminding you of aspects of yourself, it might make sense to choose a therapist of the opposite sex. You would thus promote, in therapy, a corrective experience for yourself.

But if you feel in your bones that it would be too hard for you to open up with a male therapist, if you are a woman; or some topics would be far too embarrassing for you ever to voice with a female therapist, if you are a man, then you must choose a therapist of your own sex. There is no point in piling up even more resistance, by choosing a therapist you just can't face. Later in your therapy, other techniques such as group or dyadic therapy, may be employed to help in your relationship to the opposite sex.

Some clients believe it to be far safer to choose a married therapist. The unmarried therapist, they fear, will make passes at his female clients. Indeed! Is not the reverse more likely? What better opportunity would a married therapist find for a clandestine affair than with a client? Conversely, the unmarried therapist is "safer." He has fifty percent of the entire population to choose from; why should he or she get involved with a client?

The competent therapist, married or single, does not have sex with clients. The incompetent therapist, whatever his or her status—married, single, divorced, or widowed—may.

But the never married therapist or the therapist who has never lived with anyone for an extended time in a sexual relationship, poses a problem. The prospective client will justly be concerned that such a person may, him or herself, be a half-person like Ellen, regarding others as cardboard cut-outs. It is best not to select a therapist who has never lived with anyone.

It is only natural to prefer a therapist with the same ethnic or religious background as yours. You can't help but assume that only a Catholic therapist can understand Catholic guilt; only a Jewish therapist can understand Jewish suffering; and only a Protestant therapist can truly fathom the moral strictures of fundamentalist parents.

Indeed, a black therapist once lectured a group of white therapists: "How can you people presume to do therapy with black clients? You people never lived in 'the street' and 'the projects.' Do any of you know what playing the 'dirty dozens' is all about?"

And so twenty white faces became suffused with guilt,

as the black therapist, no doubt, intended. But one in-
trepid white therapist replied, "No. I don't know what all
this means. Now will you please tell me? If you are not
willing to tell me, my black clients will be glad to."

The black therapist was assuming that only a black
can be effective with black clients. As we suggested before,
in the case of handicapped clients, the non-handicapped
therapist insists that matters taken for granted in the blind
experience, for instance, must all be carefully articulated,
redounding to the blind client's benefit. In the same way,
the black experience will be brought to full awareness, if it
has to be put into words for the benefit of a white outsider.

The white therapist will learn that "playing the dozens" means trading insults in a test of self control. The
one who bursts into physical violence first, loses. Thus
the white therapist will learn something he didn't know
before. But his black client may learn even more than
the therapist by examination of the latent content of the
insults.

WHITE THERAPIST: What *did* he say about your
mother?

BLACK CLIENT: Something disgusting.

WHITE THERAPIST: You denied it, of course.

BLACK CLIENT: Well, what would you do?

WHITE THERAPIST: But why bother denying it, if it's
ridiculous?

Had the black client mentioned playing the dozens
to a black therapist the matter could easily slide past, unnoticed by both therapist and client.

Preference for a therapist of your own ethnic or re-

ligious background is understandable. But should you select such a therapist, you may lose something by not being
forced to articulate matters to an outsider, a surprising
advantage in selecting a therapist outside your group.

But another matter entirely, are political considerations. Politics and therapy make a terrible mix, especially
when political organizations presume to screen therapists
for "correct" beliefs.

Rumor holds that security agencies of the government recommend specially selected therapists for their
personnel. These therapists have been carefully screened
for "security," that is, political reliability as defined by the
federal agency.

Sources of information slightly better than rumor,
reveal that within a few branches of the Catholic Church,
a list of therapists acceptable to the Church, has been
compiled. Like their "security" okayed colleagues, these
therapists have agreed not to lead their clients into paths
regarded as wayward by the Church authorities. Such
therapists then, are crowned with the Catholic equivalent
of "kosher."

But it is no rumor, indeed it is a matter of public
record, that the women's liberation movement has indulged in the granting of "imprimaturs." Branches of
feminist organizations have claimed that traditional psychotherapy, originated by a man, has been aimed at per-
petuating the inequality of the sexes; that male therapists
"mind rape" the unfortunate female client or worse. And
so the female authorities have set up a list of therapists
who promise not to do bad things to women.

These naive female activists must be sisters of the

woman who emerged furious from a psychologist's office. Upon being shown the Rorschach ink-blots, she became enraged at the psychologist for showing her "dirty pictures." In the eyes of the uninformed feminists, transference distortion such as aggression by a male therapist, has assumed the status of fact, rather than childhood fantasy.

We are not concerned here with the ethical issue: therapists submitting to political approval. Nor will the intrinsic worthiness of the causes represented by the Government, the Church, or Women's Lib be discussed here. Indeed, a clear bias in favor of women's rights is apparent throughout this book.

Our only concern here is the quality of therapy received by the prospective client: Will political considerations affect the quality of your therapy? The answer is, "Any constraint on the choice of topic in therapy or how the topic is treated will hinder, perhaps block entirely, the client's progress."

Therapy for a security officer may revolve largely on his possible defection to the Russians; therapy for a Catholic may balance on the problem of sin and guilt; therapy for a woman—Jean specifically—devolved on irrational worship of male "macho."

The very topics regarded as sensitive by a political organization will quite likely be crucial in the life of the client. The therapist must try to handle these topics with objectivity. Should the therapist approach such topics with prejudice, by having sworn allegiance to a third party, he has compromised his effectiveness.

A political constraint does not differ from any other constraint. A client may enter therapy with a demand that the therapist guarantee that his marriage not be disturbed. Such resistance is a sure indication that the marriage is the very source of the problem. Thus no therapist worth his salt will issue such an assurance.

When the client states, "Do what you will, Doc. But don't make waves in my marriage, my family, my friends, my hobbies, or my job," he is declaring that he agrees to go through the motions of therapy, but does not want anything changed.

A therapist who consents to stand on any pre-determined position is, in effect, agreeing to enhance resistance, not to understand it. Such a therapist has compromised himself. Taken to its logical extreme, the therapist will no longer engage in therapy, but becomes an agent of political indoctrination. You may regard any therapist whose name you find on a politically "approved" list as disqualified.

Knowing the kind of therapy and therapist you want—and the kind you don't want—you are ready to seek out a therapist. Even if you don't regard yourself presently as a candidate for psychotherapy, you may still find the suggestions we are about to make, of use to you. The five methods we shall outline for finding a therapist, can be helpful to an extent, in locating any needed expert, from accountant to zymologist. Here are five ways of finding a therapist:

The easiest way is through advertising. Do professionals advertise? Yes, indeed. A few years ago, the American Bar Association declared it no longer improper for lawyers to advertise. So attorneys were the first professionals to advertise and other professionals followed their lead. Physicians were the last hold-outs, but now even some doctors advertise.

You can learn from the advertisements inserted by psychotherapists. One "ad" states that the therapist is "warm and open-hearted." This therapist, most likely, is soliciting clients who want support, not insight. If you believe you need back stroking or T.L.C., such a therapist sounds just right. But if you want real change, forget about this fellow.

Another "ad" claims that "People are more important than theories." You need go no further. You have found a genuine, live Know-nothing.

A third advertisement: "Gestalt Bio-energetic Therapy." This therapist has not done his homework. "Bio-energetic" therapy begins with psychoanalytic theory and is firmly based on it. "Gestalt" therapy totally negates psychoanalytic theory. A therapist advertising this double hyphenated therapy, at best, is confused; at worst, he may be a Crazy.

An increasingly common subterfuge is the "Referral Service." Such a "Service," more often than not, is funded by a group of therapists. Upon dialing the number given in the "ad," an answering service purports to give you impartial information about different schools of therapy. Eventually you will be referred to one of the therapists who contributed to the expense of the advertisement and the answering machine. Why pay for this "Service" even indirectly, when the Yellow Pages will do as well?

The Yellow Pages are an improvement over the usual "ads" or the "Referral Service." Most states license social workers and psychologists; all states license physicians. And so only licensed members of the three helping professions will be found in most states under their appropriate headings in the Yellow Pages. You can be more or less assured that psychologists, social workers, and psychiatrists listed in the Yellow Pages are responsible professionals.

Unfortunately, as we stated earlier, you don't know how well trained in psychotherapy any single member of the three disciplines is. You have a reasonable assurance of correct guidance, testing, or diagnostics; but psychotherapy? At this point you don't know. In practice, the Yellow Pages can be helpful, but not a total solution. If you have found a therapist through other channels, you might look him/her up in the Yellow Pages. If the therapist is not listed, ask him why.

The next method seems, at first, like a good way of finding a therapist, but upon closer examination, turns out to be faulty: referral by your family doctor or by the clergyman at your house of worship. While your doctor knows a bit about diagnosing "mental illness," he knows little about psychotherapy. Chances are, your priest or minister knows even less than your physician. Unless the clergyman or doctor has made a special study of psychotherapy, you probably know more, at present, than he does.

Knowing little about psychotherapy, your doctor or clergyman cannot tell you how skilled a therapist is. But he may be able to tell you about the therapist's qualities as a human being. Using other means to find a therapist, it might be wise to check him out with your doctor or clergy-man. If you live in a smaller city, the therapist may be known to other professionals. It is important that your therapist be a decent person.

Here is a third way of finding a therapist: If you belong to a fraternal or charitable organization, a psycho-therapist may be invited to address your monthly meeting. This way, you have a chance to see what the therapist looks like and to hear him or her speak.

But please exercise caution: Remember, you are seeking a therapist, not an entertainer. If the therapist fascinates you, if you are persuaded that this fellow has the answer to all the world's ills, it is possible that you have found a Great Dictator.

Conversely, if the therapist presented new material, if you learned something, he or she may be a fine therapist, even if you found him a bit boring at times. Keep in mind, that you, not the therapist, will be doing most of the talk-ing. And it is unlikely that you will bore yourself.

Unfortunately, the usual format of a public meeting often proceeds this way: "And now I would like to intro-duce Dr. White, our local expert on child development, psychology, and marital happiness."

Even if Dr. White modestly disclaims his ability to know everything, he has, in fact, been "set up" by the person who presented him. Now labeled the Great Au-thority, Dr. White has become a target for the usual heck-ling "questions" following the presentation. Not a skilled professional politician, Dr. White can easily be made to look the fool, regardless of his qualifications as a therapist.

So please do not judge him on the basis of his ability as an entertainer or as a crowd pleaser.

A fourth means of finding a therapist is far better than the preceeding three: Recommendation by another therapist. You may be originally referred to a psychotherapist who has been in practice for a long time, well known by his colleagues. He or she may even be a celebrity among therapists. It is likely that he does not have a regular open hour at present to see you; or it is also possible that you cannot afford his fee on a regular basis. Ask him or her for a recommendation.

Like our condensed interview about Freud as a celebrity among therapists, such a therapist will know well the quality of work done by any therapist he refers you to. He may even have supervised the therapist he recommended. You will do well to follow such a referral.

The last method of finding a therapist is often the best: A good friend is in therapy and suggests you consult his or her therapist. Your friend may not be able to tell you much about the therapist as a person, but can tell you a lot about his own experience in therapy and how he perceives it. This can be more important in choosing a therapist than any other source.

Many therapists prefer recommendation by a friend because only their clients can give a full flavored orientation to others in the therapist's methods. So the new client more truly knows what to expect.

Of course you must keep in mind that your friend's experience in therapy with Dr. X may differ from yours. Dr. X will relate differently to his different clients, providing for their differing needs. Dr. X and your friend may also have goals in therapy different from your goals.

Another caution: You will be given a rosy account of the therapist as seen through the golden glow of your friend's transference. Still, therapists find that clients referred by a friend have a clearer, truer picture of the kind of help the therapist can offer, than clients referred through other channels.

But using the recommendation of a friend, do not ignore the other channels. The more information you can garner about a therapist, the better prepared you will be to select one.

We have reserved the question of money for the very last. "You get what you pay for" does not always hold, buying soap powder or buying psychotherapy. You can pay a fortune to a glittering gladhander or a modest fee to an unknown, but competent therapist.

Fees vary greatly and are constantly changing, but here is a rough guide:

1. **The fee of a non-physician therapist is half to two thirds that of the psychiatrist-therapist.**

2. **The clinic dependent on client fees, charges half to two thirds the fee of the psychologist or social worker in private practice.**

3. **A government funded clinic may charge as little as a dollar a session.**

A word about the clinic supported by city, county, state, or federal funds: Although there are exceptions, we find it hard to recommend the government funded clinic.

Any large organization, regardless of sponsor—government or private industry—is suited to some projects, but inexpedient for others. An automobile factory or a dam in construction, must be backed up by a large organization. But psychotherapy constructs neither cars nor a dam. It often attempts to reconstruct a person. So mass production will not work: the process is individual.

The administrator of a mental health program, sitting in his office in the state capitol or the nation's capitol, has little power, in fact, to promote high standards in the delivery of psychotherapy services. What can he really do to help the therapist at one end of the log and the client perched on the other end? Very little, if anything.

But since no one likes to feel powerless, the administrator must do something. So he orders his assistant to construct a paper form. The assistant to the assistant adds more questions to the form, justifying his job. By the time the form reaches the therapist, it has proliferated into a whirlwind of paper.

The therapist finds himself buried under this paper avalanche. No one in the state office can truly know how effective the therapist is with his client; the only information the administrators can be certain of, is the pen tracks on the form, filled out correctly or improperly. Thus paper becomes priority, people secondary.

The paper procession, while common, is not inevitable. You may find a state supported clinic devoted to a special research project. Or a government clinic may serve as a training institute for psychotherapists. Alternatively, you may find a clinic staffed by enthusiastic therapists who insist on climbing "Up the Down Staircase." Living in a small town, you are far better off trying a federally funded clinic rather than being "treated" privately by an incompetent. Should the clinic prove unsatisfactory, it is worth driving a hundred miles to a skilled therapist, even if the cost of gasoline amounts to half the therapist's fee.

Clinics supported by client fees are quite different. Since therapists in these clinics are paid only for actual sessions with clients, paper work is at a minimum. While the clinic must conform to certain state standards, it is directly operated by the therapist who may be supervising your therapist or by his close associate. Usually, the quality of supervision is high. If you live in one of our larger cities where these clinics function, you may receive very good therapy at half the cost of a private therapist.

Unfortunately, even the best of these clinics has drawbacks. Your chances of getting a good therapist are less than you might expect. Competent therapists tend to keep clients in therapy; less skilled therapists lose them to resistance. Thus clinic therapists of lesser skills often have open hours, while the expert therapists have none. So your chances of being assigned to a less skilled therapist within the clinic, are greater.

Secondly, you must keep in mind the limited commitment of a therapist to the clinic. Willy-nilly the therapist is less committed to his clinic clients than to his private clients. If you are fortunate in finding a therapist of promise at a clinic, he or she will not remain there forever, but will soon open a private office for financial reasons. The transition between a therapist's clinic practice and his or her private office can be difficult. So you may be better off starting therapy privately at the outset.

Your best bet, therefore, is to find a therapist in private practice. Should you be unable to afford the fee, you may have to resort to a clinic, preferably the kind supported by client fees. Remember, you are not inextricably bound to the first therapist assigned to you. If you feel you can't work with him or her, you may request another.

A great deal of information and many considerations have been presented here to help you find a therapist. Trying to keep everything in mind may be so frustrating, you may simply engage the first therapist listed in the Yellow Pages—or the one located nearest to your home. But think, more than money is involved. Choosing a therapist well, requires time and thought. The white pages you are looking at now must be used along with the telephone company's Yellow Pages.

CHAPTER

7

The Crucial First Session

The first session can be very difficult. If you are like many, you have resisted this appointment for a long time. But finally you realized you were resisting; and so you decided not to be like the super-finicky person mentioned in the last chapter, who copped out by insisting that the therapist conform to every last one of his specifications. Thus you made the appointment, even with lingering reluctance.

As the hour approaches, you find yourself becoming increasingly uncomfortable. This discomfort is not new to you. You've felt it before and identified it as anxiety.

But why should you be anxious? The therapist is not going to hurt you; he's not going to pull a tooth or give you a shot. So there is no reason to be anxious; indeed, you are not anxious at all.

But your attempt at denying anxiety doesn't succeed. Moreover, you realize there is little point in pretending. The discomfort is there so you might as well acknowledge it, perhaps even try to account for it.

Is there one event in your life you have never confided to anyone? Not even the person closest to you? In therapy you are expected to talk about it to a stranger. Even more, there may be events and feelings you are not fully aware of; these will come to light in your therapy. Increasingly, you realize that powerful, unknown forces will be brought to the fore. Psychotherapy is not going to be a pleasant indulgence.

Not every person will experience anxiety at his or her first psychotherapy appointment. But the conflict will be understandable to all. In fact, you may have recognized the attempt here, to begin your therapy on this page before the formal beginning in the therapist's office. We described the apprehension underlying the resistance, the attempt to deny it, then the acknowledgement of anxiety, and finally, one or two possible causes. So we tried giving you a taste of psychotherapy in the hope of making it less intimidating.

A superficial understanding of psychoanalytic theory suggests: once resistance to the first appointment has been overcome and the cause identified, the anxiety should vanish. It does not, of course.

Since your secrets are still secret and only the stage is set for transference, the anxiety will remain. But the apprehension has now been reduced to more manageable proportions. The vague, unpleasant feeling has been labeled as anxiety with a cause—a substantial cause even if not fully known.

On the other hand, suppose you had continued to deny anxiety: it is entirely possible that you then will have forgotten the time or the place of the appointment. Or for other reasons, you may well manage to engineer your absence. So it is better to acknowledge the anxiety and be enabled to keep the appointment.

Recognizing that you are still in conflict about seeing a therapist—even though you may now understand some of the problem—you will take special measures to ensure your presence. Making an appointment on the telephone, you make sure to write down the exact place and time, leaving nothing to chance. You also make sure of the correct spelling of the therapist's name.

Such advice may seem trivial, picayune. But if you are like many who have resisted therapy for a long time and then begin to suffer anxiety once an actual appointment is about to be made, you will make allowances for the tricks your unconscious may play on you.

So you will write down all the necessary information, leaving nothing to memory. While you may have a highly effective memory in other situations, getting to your first therapy appointment may be more chancy than you could predict: Repression and denial will be mustered by your Ego to avoid telling secrets to a stranger and to avoid transference and all that it entails.

If you are like Harry the Isolator—the one who delivers a 45 minute paragraph labeled "therapy"—you will arrive on the dot and march right in to the office. But if you are like most, having made full allowance for your anxiety, for repression and denial, you may well arrive half an hour early. Even if you must walk around the block first, then sit in the waiting room biting your nails, it is better to arrive early rather than late, since you and the therapist need every minute of the forty-five allotted to this crucial first session.

On the telephone, the therapist may have asked you upon your arrival to enter the waiting room and be seated without ringing the door bell. You do so and are surprised at the absence of a receptionist.

Again, your notion of a therapist may be colored by medical procedure. A doctor, by contrast, has a receptionist to oversee the many patients waiting. Since the physician cannot afford to waste time by waiting for people, he often is over-scheduled on purpose.

"The doctor is running late this afternoon." The doctor always "runs late" so that you will wait for him and not he for you.

On the other hand, a therapist must see you for 45 minutes at least, not for five or ten, so the therapist may not over-schedule. Only on rare occasions does he "run late". If you come late for your appointment or if you miss it altogether, he cannot substitute another client as can the doctor. The therapist, unlike the physician, must charge for his time. If your appointment is for 4:00 p.m. the therapist will be ready for you at 4:00 p.m. Your session ends at 4:45 p.m. when the therapist has another appointment.

So, to make sure every minute is used, you arrive a few minutes early. You sit down and look at your surroundings. What can you find out about the therapist from the appearance of the waiting room? What kind of person is the therapist? What are his/her tastes in art? What does he/she read by way of magazines?

If you are inclined to be charitable, you might characterize the pictures on the wall as "restful". Others, not so inclined, may call the pictures bland—if not boring. The rest of the room is similarly furnished in "Motel Modern".

Looking at the magazine rack, you expect no surprises there, either. Sure enough, you see *Time*, *Newsweek*, and *The Reader's Digest*.

"Good Heavens, doesn't this man have any opinion of his own? Is this fellow's brain homogenized and pureed into baby food pap? Where are *Ramparts* and *Mad Magazine*?" Later, when you enter the therapist's office itself, you are not surprised to find it, too, furnished in the same non-commital fashion as the waiting room.

Freud's office was not like this. Pictures of Freud's consultation room yield a totally different scene. Freud's hobby was archeology and his office was filled with primitive artifacts. Indeed, the famous office in Vienna, was crammed with books and papers, painting and sculpture. Freud had wisdom and character; this therapist and his office are non-descript. What's the matter with this fellow?

Nothing at all is wrong with this therapist, apparently so lacking in character and depth. Indeed, he or she is quite skilled and stands in strong contrast to Freud. Freud may have been a great scientist, but he had little skill or technique: He would give his clients little lectures on psychoanalysis and even threatened a client, once, to end his analysis by Christmas if he didn't get "cured". With good reason, some may regard Freud as having been a "lousy therapist".

In contrast to Freud, the American therapist of the Eighties, is far more skilled. And his office reflects his skill in therapy technique. Like the dark, the ink-blots, and the unknown boss, he or she offers you little by way of personal characteristics. The waiting room and office are furnished in such bland fashion to encourage you to project whatever your needs and fantasies may dictate, rather than provide you with a peg of reality on which to hang your appraisal of the therapist.

The therapist, in fact, may be a person with decided views and tastes, but he or she doesn't want to foist them on you. He wants you to project on to his person—including the office—anything useful for the purpose of therapy.

But there may be one distinguishing item in the waiting room—the therapist's diplomas and certificates hanging on its walls. The therapist has three possible areas to place them: The waiting room, the office itself, or hidden in a bottom drawer.

Diplomas mounted on the wall of the waiting room are there for your inspection. In addition to academic diplomas and state licensing certificates, you may note certificates from a post-graduate school of psychotherapy. The therapist may even have certificates attesting to knowledge of special techniques like group or family therapy. You may see evidence of membership in professional or scientific organizations.

This information can be helpful and save the time it takes to inquire about it in the session. But certificates from other organizations with fancy hyphenated names may, on the other hand, qualify the therapist as a Crazy or a minor Dictator. The previous three chapters gave you the needed clues to differentiate the scientific from the pretentious and preposterous.

Conversely, diplomas mounted and framed on the wall of the office itself are of little value to you. Once in the office, your attention is concentrated on your own problems. So it will be difficult, if not impossible for you to make out the writing on the certificates mounted behind the therapist.

Thus the diplomas are unlikely to have been affixed there for your benefit. More likely, they were hung there to fill the therapist's needs. He may not feel comfortable without them. Especially if placed behind the therapist's chair, the therapist may need the papers to back him up.

The third place, hidden in a bottom drawer, offers two possibilities: Either the therapist has no formal qualifications, or the therapist may feel so secure that his certificates mean little to him or her. In that case, you are welcome to ask the therapist for his qualifications. A full and frank answer is a plus. A "why-do-you-ask?" or other evasive or defensive answers suggest you look elsewhere for a therapist.

4:00 p.m. arrives and the door to the office is opened. The therapist stands there welcoming you, as the previous client steps out. Introducing himself, you can't help but notice the way the therapist is dressed. Is he wearing tie and jacket or turtle neck and jeans? Is she garbed formally in an afternoon dress, or is she too, wearing turtle neck and jeans?

Although the therapist would like to provide the opportunity for clients to project on to him or her what they will, in these days when many depart from the gray flannel suit and tie or corporation blue, the therapist cannot avoid making some statement by his or her attire.

Held true in the past, the following assumption is valid no longer: The psychoanalyst, member of the establishment, would feel naked without his tie; but the uniform of the fringe therapist is always jeans. Instead, the fringe therapist may now be trying for a more conventional image, while his conservative, psychoanalytically oriented colleague may simply have adopted the attire of the bookish college professor—corduroys or jeans plus sweater with no tie.

In practice, the therapist in suit and tie may be stating, "Most of my clients rush from a meeting with other IBM executives in formal attire. I don't want them to feel uncomfortable."

Conversely, the therapist in jeans might be saying, "Most of my clients are artists or teachers or contractors. They feel more comfortable when I wear what they wear." A suburban therapist will wear a sports jacket while a small town therapist will dress the way other professionals in his or her town dress. In short, if at all possible, the therapist will try to dress in an attempt not to be noticed, the better to melt into the background.

At the same time you take in what the therapist is wearing, you notice his or her personal appearance. Should the therapist be extremely obese or terribly emaciated or extremely unattractive for any other reason, there is little point in starting this relationship. Transference is going to pose many problems without the additional difficulty of trying to work with a therapist whom you find physically repulsive. But if the therapist's appearance is unobjectionable or even attractive, you may proceed.

You may find the therapist's manner appealing—too appealing. Who is responsible? Are the sexual hints the product of your needs or is the therapist evoking them? Is the therapist trying to seduce you or are you beginning to feel the tug of transference? Before spending much time and money, you may as well ask the therapist right now for his or her evaluation of what is happening between the two of you. You will then have to make up your own mind—and soon.

The therapist will ask you to be seated opposite him or her. And here the resemblance between a therapist and other professionals ends. Other professionals always keep a desk between the two of you. Even if only a corner of the desk obtrudes, it is still there.

The physician, attorney, or accountant is saying, in effect, "There is a client-professional structure between us. Please lay out before me exactly what your problem is. But you must structure it according to the kind of solution I am qualified to give you. Symbolic of the way you must outline your problem, is this corner of the desk I place between us."

The therapist, on the other hand, by removing the desk obstacle between the two of you, is saying, "Of course we have a client-professional relationship, but I would like to hear whatever is on your mind. Please don't recite your thoughts the way you believe I want to hear it. There is no need to structure what you say in terms of 'therapy'. Just tell it the way it comes to you."

Further removing obstacles, the therapist seated opposite you, will rarely cross his knees and fold his arms at the same time. With feet separated on the floor or crossed at the ankle, he or she is keeping himself open to whatever you say, however you say it.

Obviously, not all therapists will follow every detail of this model, our description of the therapist's first greeting to a client. But too many departures from it may legitimately be questioned.

Still concerned with the first few moments of the first session, a doubt may cross your mind. It may be too trivial to mention, so this imaginary conversation may take place:

CLIENT: Why do you reserve the bigger chair for yourself?

THERAPIST: When I chose it, I knew I'd be spending a lot of time in it, so I picked the most comfortable one I could find. Is your chair not comfortable?

CLIENT: It's Okay. But it's not as big as yours.

THERAPIST: I know. But I sit here for many hours, not just one. My chair is for comfort, not prestige.

Once you are both seated, the therapist may ask about your work. Why does he ask about your job? Chances are that work is not the factor impelling you to go into therapy. Precisely because work may not be the major item on your mind—it may be an easier subject to talk about than other, more pressing personal difficulties. Still, the therapist may glean valuable information about you, since your job does occupy a major share of your time.

Once you begin talking about work, it may then be easier to slip into the reasons bringing you to a therapist's office. The therapist will also want to know about your present life: whom you are living with and who your friends are. He will want to know about your past, your parents, brothers, sisters, schooling and so on.

You may be asked one or two odd questions: "If you had to be an animal, which animal would you choose? Which animal would you least like to be?" This question and others like it are designed to elicit indications about your unconscious. Together with a possible dream, your account of your past, and the way you came into the office and sat down, the therapist will form a tentative assessment of your personality.

In order to make this assessment more correct and valid, the therapist must ask a great many more questions trying to cover as much ground as possible. Forty-five minutes alloted to this task is a very short period of time.

It is possible that you had no one to listen to you up till now. Once the therapist asks about your current difficulty, the floodgates have been opened and everything dammed up must come pouring forth.

But the therapist may say, "I'd like to hear more about your wife, but for now, we must go on to another topic." Indeed, he expects to hear more in later sessions, but now a task must be completed.

If you have never been in therapy before, it must be disconcerting to be asked the kind of questions some therapists ask in the first interview. Questions about how you express sexuality, intimate details of your health and your use of drugs are pertinent to arriving at an estimate of your personality. How your Ego functions, its strengths, weaknesses, and flexibility, may be ascertained by using Harry Stack Sullivan's effective technique of intensive questioning. But you will find by their manner, most therapists are able to convey an impersonal, rather than a voyeuristic interest.

Keep in mind that a trained therapist may have spent years in learning how to structure this first interview, so please allow him or her to use the methods they learned. But since you do have important questions of your own, let the therapist know at the outset that you will need some information and suggest that time be set aside for your end of the interview.

Naturally, you are curious about what the therapist has learned about you. Many therapists will tell you one or two notions gleaned from the interview. But should you still be unable to shake off the medical model, you might yet ask for a diagnosis.

In asking for a diagnosis you are asking for a misconception. The very term, diagnosis, implies disease. And disease begins with a single cause like a virus; it shows up as a group of specified symptoms; and then proceeds along a known course to a more or less predictable end.

But the client with aberrant behavior caused by no single bacteriological agent, exhibits no inevitably consistent group of symptoms. His life proceeds along no single course. For some few, the only predictable end is the docility resulting from years of incarceration in a mental hospital.

Of the conditions affecting human behavior, the "disease" of schizophrenia is the label most often applied by the doctors. It is characterized by the supposed split (schizo) between emotion and thought.

Schizophrenia, commonly misused, does not refer to the classic abnormality—multiple personality—mentioned at the beginning of this book. Rather, the hypothesized "split" refers to a dulled, bland response to situations normally evoking feelings. In the "split personality"—the schizophrenic—feelings were thought to have been severed from ideas.

But our present knowledge yields a better understanding of the opaque, unfeeling demeanor of the
schizophrenic. Not a disease based sympton, this bland
quality is seen as a massive rampart erected against all
emotion because of an excess of feeling—a terrible
urgency disguised under an imperturbable exterior.

Thousands of experiments attempting to account for
schizophrenia as a result of physical defect or disease have
ended in failure. The most that can be credited to the best
of the experiments, is the discovery of differences in brain
chemistry *associated with* this condition, but not necessarily
the *root cause*. Animal studies, in fact, have demonstrated
gross under-development of the physical brain *as a result of*
environmental restriction, not vice versa.

Schizophrenia, a generation ago, was believed to stem
from heredity: Data showing greater incidence of schizophrenia among relatives, can now be understood as resulting, not from bad blood, but from family interaction.

Even the study of separated identical twins—studies
once believed definitive—upon closer examination have
proven invalid. The twins developing schizophrenia later
in life, had not been separated at birth, but were both
subjected to the identical unfortunate emotional climate
until the damage had been done. Even a few weeks will do
it. Later separation thus became irrelevant.

Ellen, whom the doctors would call *schizoid*, that is
afflicted with a touch of schizophrenia, led her lonely life,
not because of a bug or due to heredity, but because of the
way she was brought up.

A theoretical notion, the Ego, might be helpful in
understanding her better: A brittle Ego expending almost

its total effort in precariously balancing and shielding Id, Super-ego and the environment from each other, results from inadequate early care.

Confronted by infinite possibilities in the rearing of children, the attempt to label or diagnose people, must take into account the unfortunate results of all possible family environments.

Thus the number of sub-headings under the category of "schizophrenia" keeps proliferating. These futile attempts at disease labeling, keep bursting into front page headlines every ten or fiften years as the American Psychiatric Association tries yet again to cover all the many possible results of child misrearing under the irrelevant dialectic of disease entitities. A genuine disease like diphtheria, on the other hand, hardly needs reformulation every few years.

So there is little point in asking the doctor for your diagnosis—a judgment based on a misconception. The few comparatively rare difficulties with a physical, organic basis, serve only to highlight the fallacy of medical diagnosis for most aberrant behavior. Should such a disease be suspected, the competent therapist of any discipline will refer you to a psychiatrist for medical diagnosis.

Understanding, even assessment, can be helpful, but diagnosis of most problems of adjustment can best be seen as looking for a non-existent pew in the wrong church.

Demanding a diagnosis was not Robert's request. Dissatisfied with one or two notions the therapist suggested at his first session, Robert suspected there was more. And he kept after the therapist insisting that he be told.

Finally the therapist, against his better judgment, yielded, "You decided to seek therapy since you found yourself madly in love with a twelve year old girl. So of course you suspect something happening underneath that bears looking into."

"Quite right. And I want to know what it is."

"The problem is: no understanding at all of women. In fact, I think you fear them."

Upon hearing this, Robert thanked the therapist and left the office never to return. The therapist later learned from the client who referred him, that Robert thought the therapist's notion was exceedingly funny.

Robert told all his friends, "So this shrink says I'm afraid of women! Ho, ho, ho. But I didn't tell him about all my affairs. I know more about women than the shrink does—from direct experience."

After reporting his friend's reaction to the interview, the client added, "So that's what makes Robert tick! He's trying to show he's not afraid of women. You're absolutely right."

The therapist kept silent. If Robert chose to reveal a confidence about himself, that was his privilege. But right as the therapist was in his assessment of Robert, still he was wrong. The therapist erred in revealing material to Robert in the first session before Robert was prepared to hear it. The therapist should have held his tongue no matter how strong the client's insistence. Such an experience during a first interview, could well keep Robert from ever seeing another therapist again.

In addition to the demand for a diagnosis, and the

insistence that unconscious trends be revealed, a request for an immediate solution to a deep and long standing problem often is placed before a therapist in the first session. Sara presented just such a dilemma to the therapist during her first appointment.

Married for twenty years, Sara had acquired a lover and was now undecided whether to leave her husband for the lover or to get rid of the lover. And she wanted the therapist to tell her which choice was the wiser, in this very first session.

An immediate thought crossed the therapist's mind: Why had she limited the therapist to these two alternatives? Two other courses of action existed: to continue with both husband and lover or to leave both.

The most likely understanding of her insistence that the therapist tell her what to do was as follows: Sara needed to lean on the therapist and make him responsible for leaving her husband. Then she could enjoy the lover unfettered by both guilt and family responsibilities. Nor was Sara prepared at this early stage for just such an interpretation—that she really wanted to leave her husband while making the therapist responsible.

The therapist decided to choose this course: "You have been married for twenty years and have been seeing Roger for three. That is a long time. I understand that living betwixt and between is not a comfortable position to be in. So almost any choice seems better than none. And the sooner the better. But I do think this decision requires a great deal of thought. Perhaps right now is not yet the time to make it."

Dissatisfied, Sara sought another therapist. The second therapist, as astute as the first, realized too, what Sara wanted from him. But unlike the first therapist, he told her what she wanted to hear, "Leave your husband." Sara had the rest of her life to come to terms with a snap decision made at her behest by a Great Dictator.

But now the end of your first session is approaching. And you have a decision to make—should you enter therapy with this therapist or not? But unlike Sara, you would be well advised to realize that life does not necessarily consist of black and white decisions. Unfortunately it may take some time in therapy to learn that life rarely offers one choice only: climbing the ten foot wall; or even two choices: to enter therapy with this fellow or not, but three, four, and sometimes more. But for what it is worth, please consider this:

Towards the end of your first appointment, you have, in fact, four possible choices:

1. **You decide to work with this therapist. Having taken into account most of the information you've gleaned about psychotherapy up till now, you believe that this therapist fulfills most of what you have learned. So you decide this is the person you should see. You are careful not to be swayed by the many pitfalls along the way and rationally believe this therapist is for you.**

   Alternatively, you have seen three different therapists. You believe that of the three, this one fulfills more of the criteria outlined here than the other two. So you decide to "shop" no longer.

2. **You resolve to try one or two more sessions with**

this therapist. The therapist appears to fulfill the various criteria in this book, but perhaps something in his or her manner puts you off and you would like to deal with what bothers you about the therapist in another session.

Or else, this therapist fails to meet one or more of the attributes of the competent therapist. Yet, as a person, this therapist appeals to you. Perhaps he or she has a new slant or a special reason for using a method outside our criteria. You would like to explore this further.

3. You prefer to take a rain-check. Rather than make a second appointment, you would like to go home and think about it. Perhaps you are the kind of person who tends to make hasty decisions. Realizing this fact about yourself, you would rather not commit yourself. Instead you believe more time should be set aside for making this important decision, so you tell the therapist, "I'd like to go home and think about it."

Another reason for a rain-check might be, difficulty in meeting the time or fee of this therapist; you may want to explore other possibilities. Should you find other therapists unsatisfactory for more basic reasons—reasons other than time or fee—you would like to return to this therapist, even though his conditions are more difficult to meet.

4. You decide on the spot not to work with this therapist. Although you had reason to believe that he or she was qualified before you made the

appointment, you see now that the person is a telephone addict, a Crazy, a Know-nothing, a Great Dictator or physically repulsive.

You are not swayed by irrelevant disappointment: The therapist has not granted you a diagnosis, an immediate solution to your crisis, or more information about yourself than you are prepared to assimilate. You make your decision on the rational bases suggested by your present understanding of psychotherapy, not by saying, "I just *know* he's not right for me."

But the therapist also has a choice: He may or may not want to work with the client. Should the therapist decide it best that he not see this person, he may suggest the following: "I have had very little success in working with people who have a drinking problem. Generally psychotherapy is not helpful to people unless they have stopped drinking. I suggest you join AA, or get help from the National Council on Alcoholism, organizations with a strong track record. After you have managed to stop for a few months, please come back to see me."

"But if AA can cure me, why should I return to you?"

"AA honestly lets people know that although they may not have taken a drink for twenty years, they still remain alcoholics the rest of their lives. AA is an excellent way to stop the drinking, but does not remove the addiction, while therapy may. Please let me know as soon as you've got the alcohol under control."

Or else the therapist may say, "The way I see it, your problem requires carefully supervised medication. I would like to refer you to a highly competent psychiatrist who could see you for therapy as well as medication. Should your condition improve to the point where medication could be much reduced, then, if both you and the psychiatrist agree, I would be glad to see you. The same psychiatrist would continue to supervise medication.

"Meanwhile, if you agree to see Dr. Blank, I would like your written permission to communicate to him the results of our interview. I am certain he will find it helpful. This way you will not have wasted your time and money by seeing me now."

In the case of the latter client, the therapist probably believed that supportive, rather than insight therapy, plus medication was the preferred technique for this client. But since miracles can sometimes be accomplished with a combination of chemistry and psychology, the therapist foresaw the possibility of insight therapy for this client in the future. Hence, he left the door open for the client to return.

In addition to the assessment which the therapist would forward to the recommended psychiatrist, the interview had value even beyond an evaluation or a "second opinion": Such a therapist is aware of his professional limitations. By making the referral, he indicated a proper degree of responsibility. Thus the psychiatrist whom the therapist suggested, is equally likely to be a responsible, skilled person. So the interview, far from being wasted, had a double value—an additional assessment and a responsible referral.

You may walk out of the first session happy and relieved. You feel that finally, after so much doubt, confusion and pain, you have found someone who truly wants to help you. And who can. Besides, he has such nice eyes or she is so attractive yet "together" and confident. You can't help but fantasize about the therapist all the way home.

Obviously transference has begun. You are not fabricating anything about the therapist, but tend to see his positive aspects in glowing perspective.

But suppose you don't feel this way about the therapist. He or she is just a person like any other. While he is clearly interested in your problem and would like to improve matters, can he really do anything? You begin to have doubts about the whole process and wonder if it is not just a waste of time and money.

Your skepticism leads to further misgivings: If, in fact, you don't believe in psychotherapy, can it do you any good? In your skepticism you wonder what is the point in visiting a "shrink" if the whole process has about it an air of voodoo?

Voodoo, as we suggested in Chapter 5, works only with the poorly educated of Haiti; Lourdes was effective only with devout Catholics of a different day; "est" is fine for the "hip" and equally gullible; and sex therapy achieves its goals only for the middle class persuaded by the authority of the medical establishment.

But you are not entering authority therapy. Pyschotherapy, based on scientific principles, does not require belief. Indeed, your skepticism is to be welcomed.

All that is required is your presence and payment for the therapist's time. You need no faith. Psychotherapy works almost like sunrise and the tides.

Of course, in the human equation there are many unknown factors and uncertainties, so that unlike the sunrise, your therapy may fail. But like Gethel, who found that Contact with Air, not faith in Wodin, caused the water to evaporate, you will find that "faith" in psychotherapy has nothing to do with its outcome.

But surely, you must have heard some horror stories about psychotherapy. People have spent years and years and many thousands of dollars on the couch and got nothing for their efforts.

The purpose of this book has been to try to save you from a horror story. Knowing what you can legitimately expect from psychotherapy, knowing what it is and how it works, and knowing how to select a therapist, you have a far better chance than most for successful psychotherapy.

8

During the Course
of Therapy

What do you tell your family and friends?

At one time the very idea of visiting a "head doctor" was a terrible secret, a cause for shame. Just as one would not want to be seen entering an "X rated" movie, one did not want to be seen entering a therapist's office.

So many therapists had two doors in their offices. The first door opened to the waiting room, while the second led to a hall passageway fronting the street. Concluding your session, you would be ushered into this clandestine passageway so that the next client in the waiting room could not see you, nor could you see him.

The days of the two door office are fortunately drawing to a close. Most people are aware that visiting a therapist does not constitute confinement in a mental hospital. People don't have to be crazy to see a "shrink." They go to improve the quality of their lives. Archie Bunker may not know this, but Mr. Bunker is not generally regarded as in the vanguard of progressive ideas (although the actor, Carroll O'Connor is, and would cheer you on).

Of course attitudes towards psychotherapy vary in different circles. If your friends are still living in the past with outmoded ideas, it may not be wise to broadcast your efforts at self-improvement. On the other hand, some segments of our society look with favor at your wish to help yourself.

Some advertising agencies assuming *everyone* is in therapy, will question a new staff member routinely, "When is your therapy hour? We want to make sure not to schedule a meeting which may conflict with your therapist's appointment."

Differing groups have differing notions about therapy and only you can be the judge of the wisdom of mentioning that you are in therapy. Yet, believing that your therapy must be kept an awful dark secret, you may be surprised at your friends' comments upon revealing your status as a client in therapy. They may even say, "I think that's great! I should have gone years ago."

Letting your friends know you are in therapy, however, is very different from discussing with them the details of your sessions. "Talking out of school" is distinctly unhelpful. It constitutes a special form of resistance. Other unique methods of resistance will be discussed later.

But why should talking about your therapy be considered an obstacle? Here are three possibilities:

First, you may have a close friend to whom you confide everything. Knowing that you must tell all to your good friend, you may hesitate to bring up matters to your therapist, you may not want even your close friend to know. Your friend thus acts as a censor. You ensure that nothing comes up in the session that can't be told to your friend. Thus he or she stands over you, guarding your tongue in the therapist's office.

Second, if you must try everything out on your friend first, to see his or her reaction before bringing it up in the session, the material is no longer fresh. Ideas that just pop into your mind during the session are closer to the Unconscious. Old ideas worked over many times, may be so encrusted in defenses, they become of far less value to your therapy than brand new ones.

So please don't rehearse thoughts with your friend before the session. You do not need to present your therapist with a polished performance. He would prefer to hear your first raw reading.

Third, should you find yourself coming late to sessions, lingering over items that must be accomplished before your appointment, sensing a vague reluctance to be on time, most likely you are in a period of resistance for reasons unknown to you and your therapist. You begin to have a nagging sense that your therapist is doing you no good.

It is only natural, then, to complain about him or her to your friends. After all, if you cannot speak freely to your therapist, you need someone to talk to. Your friends will tell you, "I can see you've got the wrong therapist. Now *my* therapist is quite different. She will understand what you are going through."

Your friends will urge you to make an appointment with *their* therapist who may not be as qualified as yours, since they are unacquainted with many of the considerations presented here. It is even possible by complaining about your therapist you have unwittingly contrived your friends' referral, seeking to recommend you elsewhere.

But what of your spouse? Refusing to speak about your therapy can erect a wall of silence between the two of you, creating an unhappy situation.

It is only natural during the first few weeks of therapy to confide in your mate. But gradually, realizing that telling all thwarts therapy, both of you will be able to avoid excesses of "talking out of school."

But should either or both of you be totally unable to preserve a modicum of privacy after the novelty of therapy has worn off, perhaps regarding such privacy as betrayal of the other, it would be best for the two of you to be seen both jointly and individually by the same therapist. Let him handle the difficulty.

Another unique form of resistance arises from certain books dealing with psychological topics. *Passages* is just such an example. A popularization of the work of psychoanalyst and anthropologist, Erik Erikson, plus a premature and superficial account of a serious study by a Yale psychologist, *Passages* can do you no good if taken seriously.

Its main theme is the stages people go through in life. Proposing a kind of male psychological menopause, the author describes how some men survive this difficult stage and others are submerged by it. You gain an impression that your difficulties are simply "a stage you have to go through"; that psychotherapy can't help you because you are 35 years old, or 45; and thus problems are your destiny at a given age.

While people do go through stages, implacable biology is not the cause. You are not a larva destined to become a cocoon and then a butterfly. The environment plays the deciding role in human stages. The "terrible twos" are only terrible due to terribly permissive parents or other patterns of child rearing peculiar to Western culture. Even infants who, according to Shakespeare's seven stages of man, must "mewl and puke," do so only if they suffer from colic.

You are in therapy to overcome early environmental factors and you will succeed, if you do not permit yourself to get bogged down by the implied fatalism of books like *Passages*.

In another category are books that promise miraculous cures like *Primal Scream*. In Chapter 3 we noted that such therapy is neither new nor original. It is a repetition of Freud's "catharsis" which he eventually discarded. Like snake oil reputed to cure all ills beginning with ingrown toe nails and ending on top with balding, Primal Scream and other irresponsible therapies promise to "cure" all psychological ills from drug addiction to anxiety and schizophrenia. Even a "cure" for homosexuality is offered, a sexual preference whose status as a "disease" has been questioned and even ridiculed.

Should all psychology books be proscribed? Of course not. But you might discuss with your therapist your motives for such interests. Your curiosity about the field may be genuine or it may be motivated by resistance, or both.

Your reading matter is thus a legitimate topic of your therapy sessions.

Rather than a book, a word in common usage today, serves to build resistance and confuse the entire issue of anxiety. That word is "stress." Stress implies a force impinging upon us from the environment, much as a beam is stressed by the load of the building it supports.

Rationalizing that the trials of everyday living are far too much for anyone to endure, it places the onus on the environment. Your husband's inattention, the children's whinings, the broken dishwasher, are all too much for you. *They* are the cause of your headache or your anxiety. You are "stressed."

But you are in the womb no longer. Life as an adult takes you out of the cradle and offers responsibilities as well as rewards. If you find coping too difficult, there is little point in blaming others for your own emotional discomfort.

We had best reserve the word, stress, for Charley's predicament in Chapter 3 when he found his car dangerously out of control at 50 miles per hour. Charley, indeed, was "stressed" by the broken steering mechanism. But your headache, although triggered by your spouse, arose from your own unexpressed and quite irrational anger.

Your husband or wife cannot "give" you a headache. Only your Unconscious can.

In therapy you may find your mate's annoying little habits, merely annoying. But your unexpressed rage resulting in a headache stems from a far deeper resentment. Let your therapist help you.

The world cannot be reordered to ensure that nothing will rub you the wrong way, ever. Casting off the evasion caused by the word, stress, your therapy may now proceed to examine your internal reactions, rather than blaming those about you for life's expected tribulations.

In addition to well-meaning friends, popular but inaccurate books, and trendy notions like "stress," another source of resistance can arise from your need to defend against the process during the session, itself. Of concern may be the apprehension, "How am I going to fill up three quarters of an hour with talk about myself?"

So some people make lists during the week. Each time an event of interest or causing worry arises, the client jots it down in a little black note-book. Arriving at the office, he or she is now armed with a full agenda for the entire session.

Unwittingly, the little black book ensures that nothing untoward, nothing spontaneous can possibly arise during the session. Every event has been duly recorded, etched indelibly . . . leaving the therapist with nothing to say, except possibly to approve or disapprove (which she will refuse to do, of course). Structuring your session ahead of time may relieve you of anxiety arising out of the unexpected, but is an impediment to the process of therapy.

A final source of resistance, oddly enough, is engendered by the "help" a client appends to his or her therapy in the attempt to speed up the process. A friend in therapy may tell you, "I'm working hard on my therapy. I do a lot of thinking about my sessions. So valuable insights occur to me all the time."

At best, such "self-analysis" adds a fifth wheel to a car already in perfect working order. Often, however, this "help" offered the therapist is a conglomerate of rationalizations, pure and simple. A further obstruction to one's therapy, these "insights" must then be analyzed correctly by the therapist for therapy to proceed unhindered.

In Chapter 3 we noted Freud's psychogenic stomach problems arose because he lacked a therapist outside of himself to interpret Freud's own transference and resistance. You need someone outside of yourself to see you in correct perspective. Rarely, do you obtain useful insight on your own.

It is not pleasant to realize that only an outsider can see you as you are, in fact. Willy-nilly, your mind is subject to your own resistances, hardly gratifying, but a fact, nevertheless. A correct interpretation by your therapist, correctly timed and phrased, will do an effective job.

So leave the job to the therapist. Yours consists of arriving at the session and paying your fee on time. There are no "homework" assignments, so you need not invent any.

Is there nothing positive, then, that you can do to aid your therapy? Yes, there is. Knowing that dreams and fantasies are closer to the Unconscious than the minutiae of your job, it is helpful to do what you can to bring these products of your imagination into the session. This less focussed material is more you, more yours, than mundane details of your surroundings.

But many find it impossible to remember dreams. Even a vivid dream, clear as you were waking up in the morning, vaporizes into thin air and disappears beyond recall. Proof that such resistance is built in and not under your control, can be seen when you or your therapist go on vacation. After he's gone and dreams can no longer be understood or interpreted in therapy sessions, the "danger" is past and dreams suddenly reappear.

Your therapist may recommend that you keep pencil and paper at hand so you can jot down the dream before it disappears. Some clients use a small tape recorder. Alternatively, your therapist may decide that attempts to break such resistance would not be in your best interest and suggests you wait until you are able to remember a dream without taking special measures.

Fantasies of all kinds can be as useful as dreams. Yet, in this area too, some people are reality bound. They hardly ever muse on forthcoming vacations, adventures in strange lands, or a stranger of the opposite sex whose eyes happened to meet yours fleetingly in the super-market. Fantasies can be as "dangerous" as dreams if it is vital that you keep unconscious urges hidden.

Should you be a member of that considerable group of people who do not dream or fantasize, do not give up hope. Movies, indeed all works of fiction, are products of fantasy. Although such products of the imagination are not yours, but another's, perhaps one incident in the film, or the outcome, or a character may have made a strong impression on you. If so, by all means, bring it into the session.

Avoiding literary criticism, but telling the therapist with some heat and passion what struck you about the movie, is only one step removed from inventing your own fantasy.

Should your therapist have seen the same movie, he may be able to understand better why you chose a particular scene or a particular character for the session. If his memory of the passage in the film differs from yours, it is likely that his own fantasy did not dwell on the one bit you chose. Hence his version may be more faithful to the original. In this case, your "error" may have been no mere mistake, but inadvertently you have created your very own fantasy. So it will be helpful to welcome your misperception rather than argue with the therapist about who did what in the film.

But suppose your therapist did not see the movie. You may be reluctant to "spoil" it for him by giving away the plot and the ending. Please don't be so considerate of your therapist. Your therapy comes first, his personal enjoyment of the film trails, a losing second.

The most difficult matter to bring up in therapy is sexual fantasy. It is often regarded as "private" or, more bluntly, shameful, whereas dreams are sufficiently disguised and censored so there may be no hesitancy about bringing them up. One can always disagree with the therapist's interpretation.

Conversely, sexual fantasies may be direct products, hiding behind no mask, of your sadistic or passive motives. Disagreement with the therapist is not possible when such themes are out in the open. So it is very hard to expose them to another.

Too, the dreamer may declare innocence: "After all, I was sleeping when it all happened. It wasn't under my control." But sexual fantasies occur during waking life.

We concoct them consciously and hence feel responsible, guilty for having indulged.

Fortunately for all people in therapy, Nancy Friday rescued sexual fantasy from the pornography shops and published the fantasies of many in her books, *My Secret Garden, Forbidden Flowers,* and *Men in Love.* Many of us who believed at one time that we were secret perverts, unfit for decent people to associate with, are grateful to Ms. Friday for publishing her work, enlightening us, letting us know how widespread these fantasies are.

The days when people were thrown into dungeons for their thoughts are gone. You can think what you will, as long as you don't, in fact, enact anything illegal or hurtful.

Your thoughts are not omnipotent. They cannot harm the object of your fantasy. Realizing that you have, in fact, performed no crime, may make it easier for you to relate sexual fantasies to your therapist. He or she is very much aware of the full difference between thinking and doing.

Changing Therapists

When the novelty of therapy wears off, usually in three or four or five months, the client often reaches a plateau. Nothing much seems to be happening during the last few weeks. In fact, the client may be nearing the core of his or her problem. And so the plateau is a sign of resistance to a knotty, basic difficulty.

It is at this time, the client often breaks off therapy

with his first therapist and finds a second therapist. "Dr. A. simply didn't understand me," the client tells his second therapist, Dr. B. "But with you, I feel quite different. I know you are aware of just what I'm going through."

Dr. B. is not flattered. It is likely that another of his clients has walked out of Dr. B's office after four months of therapy and has begun again with a new therapist. Dr. B. may even fantasize that his former client, at this very moment, is telling a Ms. C., her new therapist, "Dr. B. simply didn't understand me. But with you, I feel quite different . . ."

It is well to expect a plateau of resistance after three to five months of therapy. Persisting with your therapist in spite of boredom and the feeling that nothing is happening in your therapy, will be rewarded by saving both time and money, wasted in a change of therapists.

But there are times when you simply must change therapists. Should months and months go by and both you and your therapist are agreed that you are in resistance, it is time to find another therapist.

One author proposed two lists of criteria, attempting to blame either the client or the therapist. Among other criteria blaming the therapist, was the notion that should you feel "down" or depressed after a session, the therapist is to be faulted.

Far from faulting the therapist for a post-session depression, it is possible that the therapist managed to remove a false hope, mentioned in Chapter 2. He or she made you realize that salvation will not arrive from "*this* one last man . . ." or "*this* business venture at last . . ."

Your unhappiness stemming from giving up false hopes may be depressing, but it is a sign of progress, not a flaw in your therapy, or your therapist's mistake.

Our lives are permeated with the notion of blaming ourselves or others. Permitting blame or guilt to determine the crucial issue of changing therapists, is a hinderance in your quest for therapy. It matters not who is to "blame." Without pointing a finger, changing therapists is a simple necessity after many months of lack of progress.

One example of the futility of assigning blame, is found in the therapy of a 24 year old woman. Transference appeared to be intense, movement was apparent, when the client suddenly stopped therapy. Her therapist was non-plussed until the young woman's husband explained, "It was all just too much for her. Her father was a dead ringer for you. He looked like you and talked like you. He was even a professor of classics as you once were a professor of psychology."

Thus, through no fault of either client or therapist, transference, with its "as if" quality, permitting both therapist and client to step aside and understand, instead, became the original and unfortunately all too genuine bind. So therapy could not proceed with the woman's first therapist, but had to continue with another who did not resemble the client's father so closely. Neither therapist nor client was to "blame." Changing therapists was a clear solution.

In changing therapists, all too few clients make use of an obvious procedure: Ask your therapist for a referral. It was not easy to find the right therapist at the outset, so why engage in the long, difficult procedure outlined in

Chapter 6, when all you need do is ask your present therapist for a referral?

Understandably you may feel you are deserting your therapist. This act of utter rejection on your part, may enrage your therapist or desolate him. How could you possibly ask him to find you a successor?

Alternatively, you may be angry at your present therapist, believing him to be a worthless, bungling fool. Any therapist he may recommend must be tainted with your therapist's incompetence. So he or she is the last person to ask for a referral.

If these feelings are strong and you must hold them tenaciously, a new therapist must be found on your own. But if you can manage to regard changing therapists as a rational procedure, made necessary by no one's fault, your best source of referral is your present therapist. He or she can save you much effort and time.

There will be times during your therapy when resistance ebbs and positive transference flows freely. At such times you cannot wait for your therapy session. It becomes the high point of your week.

At other times resistance will raise a barrier. You will wonder why you ever began psychotherapy; what use is it; why should you bother to continue?

These discouraging times will call upon your strength of will. There is much to be said for the old fashioned virtue of staying with a task until it is completed. It will be of great help to call upon your sense of workmanship, prompting you, once you undertake a job, to do it right and see it through to the end.

9

Up and Out of the
Ant Hill

Ensnared by a cult and a charismatic leader, devotees often develop a new language, understood only by co-worshippers. Chris was an enthusiast of the "est" cult. But his friend, Tom, refused conversion.

Finally Tom protested when he believed Chris was putting him off, refusing to see him. "I just can't believe you've been so busy, Chris. We've been friends for a long time and now, suddenly, you're unavailable."

"You're expressing your anger to me," Chris replied.

"Well, of course I'm annoyed. Wouldn't you be?"

"As long as you know you're angry, that's cool."

"But why did you keep putting me off?"

"Whatever is—is."

Tom couldn't contain himself, "For God's sake, will you stop giving me your cultist crap and tell me what was keeping you away?"

Far from being "honest-and-open," another cultist cliche, Chris was evasive under the guise of his "therapy" or "training." Had he been truly forthright, he would have told Tom what was keeping him away. Typical of converts to the fringe therapies, Chris had acquired a new vocabulary without a corresponding change in behavior.

Chris sincerely believed he was now a new person, having undergone an experience he thought reshaped his life. In fact, he was hypnotized into believing that his outlook had changed while he was merely using a new jargon.

Actually an illicit affair was keeping Chris busy so he had little time to keep in touch with his friend, Tom. He not only concealed the affair from Tom in an evasive fashion, but was using the cult's new language to rationalize old fashioned adultery. In the process, he also concealed from himself, his own marital problems.

Ten years ago, Chris probably would have been in conventional therapy, and would not have needed to play word games with Tom. A generation ago, Chris would have consulted his priest or minister. Traditional psychotherapy thus, would appear as a passing fad of the Fifties and Sixties. Therapy has now given way in our larger cities to the cults and strange new vocabularies.

How did this come about? Why was psychotherapy regarded by many as the answer to all problems ten or fifteen years ago, while new forms of self-improvement have now taken its place?

The answer lies partly in the political and social structure of our nation and partly in the goals of psychotherapy itself.

At its inception, America abdicated a role still played by many other governments. It was founded on the principle that only minimal needs were to be met by the State.

Unlike Communist Russia, Nazi Germany, and Islamic Iran, emotional security was to be supplied, not by the State, but by a separate religion of the citizen's own choice.

Such needs at one time were adequately met by the Sunday sermon, revival meetings, and the Christian life. Chris's father found these sources fulfilling. But some people, like Chris, became dissatisfied with traditional religion. They stopped going to church or synagogue or tent meetings, and turned to psychotherapy to meet these needs.

But Chris and his contemporaries made a grave error by turning to psychotherapy for their security needs. Therapy was never designed for such a task. Providing security in the form of faith was well beyond the ken of conventional psychotherapy. Why?

Psychotherapy is not a religion. It does not provide security or comfort beyond the temporary support given by therapist to client until his/her transference problems are resolved. By his interpretation of transference, the therapist aims to resolve the client's dependency needs and conclude therapy. The responsible therapist, unlike the therapist-Savior or cult leader, refuses to serve as a parental totem for the rest of the client's life.

But ten and fifteen years ago when conventional psychotherapy was in vogue, the distinction became blurred between needs that religion was designed to meet and needs that psychotherapy was to fulfill. And so deception was required on the part of both client and therapist.

Chris's contemporaries learned to phrase their complaints to the psychotherapists in acceptable fashion—in the language of psychotherapy. And the therapists acquiesced as willing accomplices. People applying for therapy told therapists they suffered from depression, not *ennui* or a sense of emptiness whose relief would arrive by a return to faith. Prospective clients' need for a Savior and a religion went unrecognized both by client and therapist, so neither could be faulted. The deception was perfect.

The result: Psychotherapy proved a disappointment. And rightly so. It offered a method for alleviating depression and anxiety when all along people like Chris really wanted salvation.

Just this need was fulfilled by the fringe therapies. Their enormous success in gaining adherents to their doctrines proved how huge a vacuum exists in people's lives when the State renounces responsibility for providing emotional security and the traditional religions, for Chris and his associates, become inadequate or ineffective.

And so Chris, who was a client for a brief time in conventional psychotherapy, found that his faith had been misplaced. He never should have believed in Freud. For Chris, Freud was the god that failed. Psychotherapy offered him no salvation. He dimly perceived that therapy is merely a technique, not a religion. Therapy was designed to help him in pursuit of his goals. But having no satisfying goals of his own, he turned to a quasi-religious movement that provided him with goals.

Chris went the entire route: From old time religion, which he found repressive; to conventional psychotherapy, which he found inadequate; to a brand new secular religion, all dressed up in the trappings and terminology of psychotherapy. The cult of the "est" provided him with Truth. And Chris found his pot of gold.

Why was Chris compelled to travel this route?

Chris grew up in a small town in the Silo State. He had a father who taught him how to catch a ball, a mother who taught him to wash his hands before eating, an older brother who taught him how to fib and get away with it, and a grandmother who taught him stories from her childhood.

Chris was a bright boy, the valedictorian of his High School graduating class. So he went to college in the capitol city, a hundred miles from his home town.

College was an eye opener. Majoring in English literature, Chris learned that bad girls are more fun than nice girls. He also learned how to smoke grass, play the guitar, and say "Man" before or after every phrase. Coming home for vacations, Chris refused to go to church on Sundays and found his parents didn't understand him.

Chris realized after his college graduation he would have to move more than one hundred miles from home. He decided to go to *the* Big City, the center of the communication industry, the Media. He would try to pit his communication skills in the Major League.

While Chris was setting his foot in the first niche of a famous word factory, he met Jane, a copy editor. They liked each other a lot and decided to get married. Life seemed great.

Chris thought he could do well without his father, mother, older brother, grandmother, high school chums, teachers and all others who told him what to do and what not. But he did not realize that this network of interlocking authorities lavished upon him vast amounts of sustenance and support. He needed these sources of reassurance for sheer survival even though he did not know it, at the time.

Although Jane was the first fountain of gratification for Chris, she was not enough. Chris came from an organized community of upholders and supporters. But Chris could only see their strictures, not their benefactions. Chris left the Silo State believing it to be a tomb, not realizing it was also a womb.

Feeling something lacking in his life, Chris began to make demands on his wife, Jane. Resenting these demands, Jane gave him less and less. So Chris demanded even more. Finally Jane had her fill and moved out.

Suddenly Chris found himself all alone in a strange city. He realized he had acquaintances rather than friends, people surrounding him at work, rather than a family. And all hell broke loose. He felt anxious and unhappy, taking too many pills, eating too much, drinking too much—treating his body badly.

Chris now had a gaping void in his life. He needed somebody to love and to worship. Since he rejected traditional religion, he became a ripe candidate for a Savior masquerading as a therapist. Chris was not "sick in the head." He simply was not getting his share of nurturance, needed for survival.

So Chris had to turn to religion. But as the old forms, based on a book, were no longer acceptable to him, he found a new secular religion, presenting him with a god he could see and hear. Thus preferring idolatry to contemporary religion, he was able to delude himself that he was still an atheist. But instead of God, he now worshipped the super-salesman of "est," an idol who knew just how to appeal to Chris and his needs. Chris was a sitting duck and didn't even know it.

Why wasn't Chris in therapy if he was so unhappy? You may recall that he was. But psychotherapy didn't work for Chris. His therapist regarded Chris's dependency on him as transference. The therapist wanted Chris to grow, but Chris resented this implied pressure to be independent. Chris needed a Great Man who would tell him what he wanted to hear.

And so he found Jack Rosenberg, alias Werner Erhard, the High Priest of "est". Chris could as well have been nabbed by the founder of "Dianetics" or by any one of a dozen other therapist-Messiah types who feed on Chris and all the other lonely and unhappy people inhabiting the big cities of our country.

Although the Rosenberg-Erhards, the leaders of the Moon cult, and the Dianetics demagogues may not be aware of it, they use Asch's group pressure theory to perfection. With their army of technicians and public relations experts and other assorted manipulators, they find waifs like Chris no match for their superior technology employing the group pressure theory. And Chris, himself, was a precariously balanced bowling pin trying to stand up before the onslaught of a ten pound Brunswick ball.

So even a highly intelligent and ambitious person like Chris, became a push-over for a dictator. His life was subordinated, like a neutered worker in an ant hill, to a queen ant, the therapist-Savior.

Chris's enslavement was paltry compared to Aldous Huxley's frightening vision of a *Brave New World*. Huxley's "epsilons" were in total bondage to the "alphas." But Huxley did not invent a new conception of society. Civilization has functioned for thousands of years like *Brave New World*, differing little from the ant hill.

Throughout the ages, false prophets, strong men, dictators, self-proclaimed Saviors have flourished. Pharaoh was the first human to be worshipped as a god and others learned his methods.

Napoleon faced his troops, far away from home, ragged and hungry, ready to revolt and run back to France. The stocky dictator confronted the men with two short words, "Mes enfants—my children". And the soldiers, these grown men, became his children once again.

So neither Rosenberg, the Rev. Moon, nor Jones of Guyana infamy, are new phenomena. Predictions of future enslavement like *Brave New World* and Orwell's *1984*—a date which now looms frighteningly near—do not tell us anything new. They belong to history and the Asch theory.

Unfortunately, the history of man's enslavement to a super-salesman promising eternal bliss in his loving embrace continues through time. Yet a minority exists: dissenters insisting, "No! I am my own person. I will pursue my own path to my own goal." Who are these rare people daring to stand above the ant hill?

In ancient Greece a man named Eratosthenes had no interest in the enslavement of other men by serving as a messiah to his fellow men. Nor did he agree to be in bondage himself. His interest, rather, lay in the stars and in the earth. Only a few miles short, he succeeded in the monumental task of measuring the diameter of the earth.

In Chapter 4 we invented a mythical caveman, an independent thinker by the name of Gethel. But Gethel is no fabrication. Fourth and Fifth Century Greece, B.C., gave rise to scores of Gethels and people like Eratosthenes—scientists, poets, and artists, the like of which the world would not experience again for two thousand years. To the Gethels, Pharaoh was irrelevant, Napoleon insignificant, along with the very much smaller Jack Rosenberg.

In spite of the dictators, independent thinkers and innovators persisted throughout history, even though at times, they had little support. Their path, the path of Eratosthenes and Gethel, differs fundamentally from the path of the Strong Man: The dictators are possessed with absolute certainty. They offer Eternal Truths and Lasting Verities. But the path of the innovators is uncertain. It is posted with signs reading, "Temporary."

The troglodyte scientist, Gethel, you may remember, merely *preferred* the Contact with Air Theory over the Wodin Theory for many reasons, the most convincing of which, was the results of his experiments. But Gethel was careful not to proclaim Contact with Air as an Ultimate Truth.

It is well that Gethel did not. His son, Ben, came to him one day and asked his father, "Why is it that we produce salt only during the summer?"

Gethel replied, "Because the water evaporates too slowly during the winter months."

"Why is that?" Ben persisted, "Does the water come into contact with more air in the summer?"

Gethel paused and thought, "No. There is no more

air in the summer than in the winter. Suppose you try to explain it, Ben."

Ben wondered if Heat is a factor in the evaporation of water. His father urged him to devise an experiment to test the Heat Hypothesis. Ben placed two pans, each with an Urd of water, one in the sun and the other in the shade. After some time had passed, he measured the remaining contents. Running to his father, he cried, "Eureka! Eureka! Your Contact with Air Theory is false. Heat is the correct cause!"

Gethel stood unmoved. "Your Heat Theory seems to have validity. Yet Contact with Air has stood the test of many experiments for many years. Do you suppose we are dealing with a two factor phenomenon?"

Ben, accustomed to the Absolute Truths of his tribe, could not grasp the notion of a two factor theory. Gethel had to explain to him again and again the possibility of two theories, both useful and fruitful. Finally Ben said, "Perhaps both theories, useful as they are, derive from one single theory encompassing both Heat and Contact with Air."

Gethel replied, "That is a distinct possibility. We have much thinking to do. Let us try to find that single theory." And so they tried.

Meanwhile, the chief engineer for the tribe's Salt Evaporation Works heard rumors of the new theory for the evaporation of water. He came to Gethel and asked him to explain. Gethel spoke to him for an hour until finally the engineer expostulated, "But Contact with Air works, doesn't it? So it must be Right! Why are you and your son wracking your brains for naught?"

"It may well be for naught, Chief. Perhaps you are right. But I fear we enjoy the pursuit and must follow our star."

But the High Priest of the tribe did not take the news as casually as the chief engineer. He summoned Gethel to appear before him. "Gethel," the High Priest intoned, "News has reached my ear that you have doubts about the Contact with Air Theory."

"It is but a theory, my lord," Gethel replied.

"No, Gethel. It is not a theory. Contact with Air is an Eternal Truth. It has been demonstrated by you and others again and again. I cannot believe that you and your son would question the very Basis of Existence."

Gethel, who valued his life, agreed with the High Priest that he would no longer indulge in idle speculation. Gethel was offered a face-saving compromise, but in effect he recanted and was allowed to return to his cave.

Meanwhile, the High Priest had his hands full with dissenters. Tomo, the Artist, had carved strange lines on the wall of his cave. People suspected these new designs to be a form of sorcery, a hex.

When brought before the High Priest, Tomo tried to answer the inquisition, "It is no strange design, my lord. It is merely a jar superimposed on a pan. There is also an attempt to simplify the lines of both by borrowing from each other. That is why they are superimposed."

After a long pause, the High Priest spoke, "There is no need to simplify lines, Tomo. Our fathers have been making jars and pans for many years and their fathers before them, according to the original design given by the Great God, Wodin. Now you will refrain from interfering with the potter's craft and go back to drawing scenes from our last epic battle. You will celebrate our great victory with another mural. Do not waste valuable time by doodling pictures of household goods."

Tomo agreed that doodling and play was for children, not for adults, and resumed his mural of the last epic battle of the tribe. His friend, Gethel, heard the account of Tomo's chastisement and went to visit Tomo.

"I understand, Tomo, that you are not to indulge in idle speculation. They don't want you fooling around with jars and pans."

"That is true, my friend, Gethel. I only wonder how you got away with it in making your first discovery?"

"I was lucky, Tomo. My experiments resulted in salt production."

"Indeed you were fortunate, Gethel. I can see no practical use for my work."

Gethel nodded sympathetically and added, "I am grateful, though, that you saw fit to commemorate my experiments."

"Because my subjects were a jar and a pan?"

"That was my notion. But perhaps I didn't understand your drawing," Gethel replied.

"You may be right about the jar and the pan," Tomo said. "But when I began the drawing, I wasn't quite sure what would come out. Even now I am not sure."

Gethel and Tomo sat quietly for a long time and then Gethel got up and walked back to his cave.

And so Tomo and Gethel walked the path of ambiguity, uncertainty, and experiment, while the High Priest trod the pre-paved highway of Eternal Truth, Principle, and Lasting Verity. The engineer did the bidding of the High Priest and his own belief in Contact with Air remained unshaken and unquestioned.

Neither queen ants nor workers, present day scientists and artists, when a theory is confirmed or a satisfying piece of art is completed, both cry out happily, "It works!"—not "This is the Ultimate!" But the engineer, chief of the worker ants, is wedded and welded to the Eternal Principles of Euclidean geometry; and the Saviors, queens of the ant hills, proclaim their knowledge of Ultimate Truth as certain and immutable as the axioms of Euclid were once thought to be.

No wonder Chris, rootless and uncertain, was ensnared by the High Priest of "est". This demi-god had Truth, Comfort, and Security in his hand. Chris had enough of ambiguity and experiment in his life in the big city. He needed certainty; and certainty was what he got.

The path of psychotherapy was not for him, a path of ambiguity and uncertainty.

But scientist and artist, both champions of the unknown and the provisional, may find the path of psychotherapy congenial, very much in accord with their own penchant for experiment. Based not on dogma or creed, but on scientific theory, the psychotherapist follows the path of the client wherever he or she may go. The role of the therapist is to hold a torch to illuminate the darkness, to seek out hidden byways.

Unlike the Savior or Dictator who violate the client's psyche with a bulldozer, forcing him to march on a superhighway mapped out in advance, the trained therapist

303

follows the narrow, winding trails of the client's own route.

Theory helps the therapist to find the way and theory suggests where the trail may lead. But the therapist does not know for sure. Like Gethel and Tomo, he tolerates experiment and uncertainty until the way becomes clear. Given a choice between torch or bulldozer, insight or dogma, artist and scientist happily choose the torch.

The curiosity of the scientist and the subtlety of the artist suggest a preference for an exploration of nooks and caves, not an earth levelling approach foisting on human beings the demands of dictators. The goal of thinking persons is freedom to pursue their own aims and interests wherever they may lead, regardless of accepted Truths.

We call upon artist and scientist to support freedom, to liberate the human mind and human abilities from security needs that cripple; cravings subjecting humanity to the Rosenberg-Erhards, the demagogues, the Rev. Moons, whose only interest is power over their fellow humans.

Now freedom is a noble sentiment. Fine words about its worth have been told to Chris again and again. But Chris is bored with such sermons. The small town in the Silo State was filled with preachers, both professional and lay. So Chris will listen neither to scientist nor to humanist, expounding the value of freedom.

Totally impervious to discourses on liberty, Chris's dependence on authority raises a massive barrier to thinking for himself, even to tolerate others who think for themselves. Struck by Chris's fear of the unknown and the provisional, his repugnance for the bold venture into the dark, his apprehensive insistence on the known Truths, the Gethels and the Tomos can do nothing but shrug their shoulders in resignation, burrowing deeper within their libraries and laboratories. Conveying to Chris their concern with the universe, the human condition, the tentative and the temporary, appears hopeless.

Yet a hair line crack can be distinguished in Chris's citadel, his fortress against uncertainty. Chris, at one time, tried the path of psychotherapy. Could he be induced to try it again, knowing that true satisfaction lies in self-knowledge rather than self-delusion in the quest for the right dictator?

Thus humanist and scientist may emerge from their learned lairs and burrows, lending Chris a hand, supporting Chris's efforts at self exploration. Speaking to the cause of liberation, artist and scientist need not immure themselves for all time in their specialties. They are urgently needed by Chris and his contemporaries. Indeed, the aid of all who stand beyond the ant hill is vital. Innovators are called upon to espouse the cause of psychotherapy.

Yet "Causes" nowadays are justly looked upon with suspicion, as preachments of the Saviors. There are naive souls on the left who have but to hear the word, nuclear, and immediately they are prepared to tear down fences and march through the barriers with placards. They care little that even the "anti-s" among nuclear engineers do not recommend that all nuclear power generation be stopped immediately.

The cause-addicts have been told by their prophets that Wall Street hates flowers and, to increase profits, the death dealing merchants intend to wipe out humanity with radiation. That article of faith is sufficient for the perennial protestors to practice their prowess in any province, knowledgeable or not.

Conversely, naive souls on the right, respond to their High Priests with the same unthinking reflex concerning the abortion issue; even to the point of throwing bombs at clinics. So any cause, no matter how worthy, has alienated many of us, who respond by trying to think an issue through first, instead of rallying to the ramparts before an idea connects with the cortex.

In contrast to many causes and the manner in which they are promoted, the cause of psychotherapy may well be a reasoned and reasonable task, an enterprise for both Tomo and Gethel, humanist and scientist; and for the rest of us who prefer to understand first and to act second.

We no longer must persuade people to enter therapy. Many millions in the United States are presently in therapy. Psychotherapy, whether conducted in clinics or in private offices from Alaska and Hawaii to Key West and Maine, is an established fact of American life, even though open discussion of one's personal therapy is limited.

Indeed, you may be surprised to learn that half the people on your block are, or have been in therapy—they just haven't discussed it with you. Psychotherapy is a hidden, but pervasive fact of life in our country.

So our concern no longer is to enlarge the number of people in therapy, but to inquire about the kind of therapy they are receiving. Government or personal funds may be insufficient to provide a thorough going analysis for every citizen. Therefore some "community mental health" authorities have urged brief authoritarian therapy for all who require help. Such therapy is disguised under the labels of "guidance" or "social work."

True, violent family arguments may be held in abeyance as long as its members know they must appear before a benevolent authority once a week. He will withhold approval upon learning that a vicious fight broke out the day before. But other than avoiding mayhem, what else would be accomplished? Would the clients be enabled to grow? Or would they merely be kept out of jail?

As an example, a family supported by "welfare" payments, consisted of a grandmother, aged 36, her son, 21, her daughter, 19, and the daughter's one year old baby. Violent fights centering about an apparent lack of food, threatened the existence of the family. Money for food was not, in fact, the issue since expensive lamb chops were one of the food items they fought over.

Careful inquiry by the therapist brought out a secret: After many years of household work in the homes of others, the thirty-six year old grandmother was now enjoying a fulfilling relationship with a boyfriend. Brother and sister were resentful of such behavior.

The therapist suggested, "Perhaps you really feel that mother should be standing over the stove preparing meals for everyone, instead of messing around with her boyfriend."

Brother and sister were shocked by this bald statement of their childish expectations. So an adult understanding dawned: Mother is also a woman. She has a right to her own life, not a life eternally tied up in apron strings, serving other family members. The arguments at home simply evaporated.

Alternatively, the use of authority to stop the arguments, as suggested by the public health experts, may have enforced family peace. But by the use of insight, rather than authority, brother and sister received an additional bonus:

The therapist carefully used the words, "messing around," to imply that mother's behavior, may, in the eyes of son and daughter, be seen as "immoral," that a love affair is unseemly behavior by a mother, and thus her proper role should be limited to the pot and the stove.

The bonus consisted of bringing to full awareness these childish "moral" strictures, which upon examination in the full daylight of consciousness, had little force or reason. Brother and sister both gained an inkling that motives on the fringe of awareness, drove them to continue repeating unreasonable and non-adaptive behavior, like screaming about food. Insight gained in therapy freed their energies for happier pursuits.

Therapy for this family, in accord with limited government funds, was restricted to only a few sessions. Thus the scope and objectives of the interviews were also held to a minimum. Yet, to a perceptible extent, the family's irrational drives were diminished, while control and Ego motives were expanded.

Few members of our society must be doomed forever to be driven by forces beyond their control, crippled by inner constriction and outer resignation. People need not function, impelled like ants, subject to the Rosenbergs and the Moons. Increasing areas of awareness may be opened for all.

Thus the dark of impulse, enslaving Chris, driving him into the arms of a therapist-Savior, limiting his opportunity and creativity, can be replaced by Ego—conscious, reasoning, placing Chris in control of his own fate.

We view psychotherapy not only as a device designed to remove aches and pains. Psychotherapy is a means to advance the cause of civilization. With its help, the dim side of humans, crowded with goblins and nightmares, inflicting war and suffering, may give way to light and reason.

Scientists, humanists, and other thinking persons together may have the power to bring Chris and the rest of the human race a bit further from the ant hill and a bit closer to the free market place of choice and opportunity.

Index

311

Psychoanalyst 214, 221–4, 261
Psychodrama 207
Psychogenic 26, 28, 66–7, 76, 99, 284
Psychologist 121, 221, 224
  animal 37, 45, 58
  training of 218–20
Psychosomatic 28–30
Psychotherapist 23, 213ff
  age of 239–40
  appearance 262
  celebrity 232–4
  clothes 261
  craziness of 236
  diplomas 120, 228–9, 260–1
  ethnicity of 242–4
  formal qualifications 213–29
  informal qualifications 229–46
  marital status 242
  office 258–60, 263–4
  other professionals 248–9, 263
  political orientation 244–6
  sex of 240–1
  silence 269
  telephone 235
  training 221–9
  untrained 117
Psychotherapy
  book about 12, 123
  clinics 251–4
  consumer 99–100
  definition 36, 123
  discipline 15
  discovery 13, 15
  fad 292
  number of clients 11, 306
  outcome research 45
  process 33, 50
  schools for 221ff
  supportive 41, 46, 209, 274
  uncovering 41, 46, 209
  under duress 56
Psychotropic drugs, see drugs

Rational-emotive therapy 187
Reaction formation 111, 113–4
Referral service 247
Reich, Wilhelm 156

Reik, Theodore 233–4
Reinforcement 138
Religion 293–4, 296
Repression 110–1, 152, 192
Resistance 97ff, 194–6, 239, 246, 278–84, 288–9
  first appointment 256–7
  talking out of school 278
Resolutions 73–5
Rogers, Carl 154
Role, see family therapy
Rosenberg, Jack 297
  also see "est"

Sachs, Hans 37, 45
Schizoid 14, 267
Schizophrenia, schizophrenic 201, 266–8
Schizophrenogenic 165, 200
Science 125
Scientology, see Dianetics
Sears, Robert 143, 145, 157
Seduction 90–1
Self-actualization 41, 154–5
Self-analysis 283–4
Self-improvement 12, 73–5, 141, 154
Session, time of 257–8
Sex therapy 172–9, 235
Sexual feelings 87, 96
Shakespeare, William 281
Skinner, B. Fredrick 145–8, 169–70
Slavson, S. R. 229
Social security 46
Social work 201, 307
Social worker 121, 214–6, 221
  training of 220
Socialization 87
Socrates 126
Spacek, Sissy 21
Stages of man 281
Stimulus-response 134–48, 169–70, 191, 200
Stomachache 25–6, 99
Stress 282–3
Sullivan, Harry Stack 109, 151–2, 162, 171, 265
Super-ego 140, 160–1, 268

314

For those readers given to ferreting out the hidden:

Two Latin words are found in the last sentence of a well known work by Freud. Much of Chapter 9 recasts this sentence in contemporary terms. What is the sentence?

Who is the physicist and what is the name of his theory regarded by the author as bridging psychotherapy and both worlds of C.P. Snow? If you would like a hint, turn the page.

Page 304, line 6, the third word

When you know something well, then you know the right words. In your business or your hobby, you can distinguish the informed person from the dilettante, by their correct or incorrect use of words. The same is true of psychotherapy.

Following are a few misused and misunderstood terms leading to fuzzy thinking when misapplied. You can check yourself on their meaning: